★ ★ ★ ★ ★ ★ ★ ★ ★ ★ ★ ★ ★ ★ ★ ★ ★ ★ ★ ★

EVERY FOUR YEARS

SMITHSONIAN EXPOSITION BOOKS

Distributed to the trade
by W.W. Norton & Company
New York, London

Second Printing

Contents

The Smithsonian Institution
Secretary, S. Dillon Ripley

SMITHSONIAN EXPOSITION BOOKS
Director: James K. Page, Jr.
Senior Editor: Russell Bourne
Editors: Alexis Doster III, Joe Goodwin
Business Manager: Thomas A. Hoffman
Administrative Assistant: Christine Nonnenmacher

Staff, EVERY FOUR YEARS
Editor: Robert C. Post
Picture Editor: Caren W. Keshishian
Assistant Editor: Amy Donovan
Picture Research: Nancy Strader, Frances Rowsell,
    Karin Kinney

Production Editor: Ann L. Beasley
Graphics Coordinator: Patricia Upchurch
Copy Editor and Index: Florence H. Blau
Assistants: June G. Armstrong, Francine Atwell,
    Therese M. Gates

Marketing Representative: William H. Kelty

Design Direction: Ron Wilcox, Wickham and
    Associates
Design: Tom Heffner, Wickham and Associates
Opening Illustrations: Bart Forbes

Separations: Lanman Lithoplate, Inc.
Mechanical Preparation: Pre-Press Studios, Inc.
Typography: Custom Composition Company
Printing: Rand McNally and Company

The editors wish to express appreciation for the
helpful guidance received from many sources within
the Smithsonian and beyond during the preparation
of *Every Four Years*. This includes primarily our
editorial consultants, Wilcomb E. Washburn, Margaret
B. Klapthor, and Marvin Sadik; also the directors
and staffs of museums and bureaus where scholarly
work on the Presidency is pursued, the National
Museum of History and Technology, the National
Portrait Gallery, and the Office of American Studies.
Special thanks is due to Herbert Collins, Kim
Nielsen, Beth Leary, and Eleanor Boyne.

Library of Congress Number: 80-80118
ISBN: 0-89599-005-9

Introduction

When putting this book together, we lined the walls of a fair-sized room with books on the American Presidency. That there is so much material on the subject attests to the crucial role of our Chief Executive in national and international affairs. It also attests to a traditional fascination with the Presidents—and thus raises a question: Why is the Smithsonian adding yet another book to that roomful?

There are good reasons. Congress initially set up the Institution as an "establishment" headed by the President, and that relationship still prevails. The White House is just a short walk from the Smithsonian Castle. The Institution's buildings have been favorite sites for Presidential inauguration balls. The most substantial reason, however, is suggested in a television commentator's remark at the close of a recent nominating convention. As the delegates streamed out of the hall, their task completed, the camera focused on a man sifting through the detritus of campaign hoopla on the floor. That man, the commentator explained, was a museum curator adding to the collections of the Smithsonian Institution.

Indeed, no place has so marvelous a collection of artifacts relating to the American Presidency. Some have actually been picked up off the floor, though most have come to us via more traditional channels—oftimes donated by Presidential heirs. Besides campaign memorabilia, there are also classic portraits, White House chinaware, and a dazzling array of gifts presented to Presidents by foreign potentates. There are everyday items such as the eyeglasses Presidents wore and the desks at which they worked. And there are the formal gowns of the First Ladies.

It seemed appropriate, therefore, for the Smithsonian to share its many riches with a wide audience. And it seemed timely to present a diversity of historical perspectives on the Presidency. Happily, the subject falls into discrete epochs, each of which is discussed herein by an authority on the period. Interspersed among the essays are pictorial features that look back and forth through time at one or another important (or merely winsome) aspect of the office.

As for the men who have occupied the office, it should be apparent that their talents have varied considerably, as have their ideas about the nature of their job—and so the variety in both the style and substance of the Presidency. The impression that will remain most vividly, we hope, is that here is a unique institution which has evolved rather like a biological organism in a changing environment.

While the Smithsonian is apolitical, it is simply not possible to deal with men who have been a focus of intense controversy without interjecting opinion. Once upon a time a naive notion gained some currency, a notion that history could be an "objective" enterprise, like, say, mathematics. We know it cannot. Indeed, even the most rudimentary aspects of recording history are subjective (choosing, for example, to treat one President at greater length than some other President), and commitment to an explicit point of view is central to the nature of historical scholarship.

The Constitution stipulates that every four years there will be a Presidential election in which the people decide among candidates. Just so, this book provides insights from Smithsonian and academic scholars, and offers them back to the people who will, as usual, make up their own minds.

—The Editors

PART 1

1789–1797

PRESIDENT

George Washington

★ ★ ★ ★ ★ ★ ★ ★ ★ ★ ★ ★ ★ ★

The Presidential Paradigm

Richard B. Morris

When, in May 1787, George Washington reached the outskirts of Philadelphia en route from Mount Vernon to the Constitutional Convention, he was met by three generals, escorted across the Schuylkill by a troop of cavalry, and greeted by cheering crowds and ringing bells as he proceeded to his lodgings. Washington's coming seemed a favorable omen indeed.

Although he seldom spoke at the Convention, Washington as presiding officer—a post to which he was elected unanimously—managed by his mere presence to influence the deliberations. That influence was especially felt when Article II was being drafted and debated, for issues pertaining to the executive power were of particular interest to Washington. Would there be a plural executive or single President? If the latter, would he be encumbered by an elective council? Would the President serve for life or for a set term? Would that term be three years, or four, or seven?

Washington voted with the Virginia delegation for a single President; he favored election by the people rather than by the state legislatures; and he would have preferred requiring a three-quarters majority to override a Presidential veto, rather than two-thirds. The only handwritten corrections that Washington made on the official account of the Convention concerned clarification of the role of an electoral college.

In view of the strong antimonarchical sentiment of the Founding Fathers—who had only recently waged a war against George III of England—and the attachment of the rank and file to a republican system, one can readily understand a reluctance to entrust broad powers to a single man. Yet the office defined in the Constitution made one man both Chief Executive and Commander-in-Chief of the armed forces, and made it impossible to remove him except for treason, bribery, "or other high crimes and misdemeanors." The power of the President had been made "full great"—so the aristocratic South Carolinian Pierce Butler wrote his son—because most of the delegates took it for granted that Washington would be the first incumbent. In a sardonic tone Butler concluded: "So that, the man, who by his patriotism and virtues, contributed largely to the emancipation of his country, may be the innocent means of its being, when he is laid low, oppressed."

Fortunately for the nation, the spectre raised by Butler did not materialize, not in Washington's time, nor afterward—perhaps because of the

In the earliest known portrait of George Washington, painted by Charles Willson Peale in 1772, he wears the Virginia militia uniform of the French and Indian War. In 1775 he arrived at the Continental Congress in this same uniform, ready to fight.

Thomas Pritchard Rossiter's Signing the Constitution *captures the historic moment, September 17, 1787. George Washington, convinced of the need to replace the Articles of Confederation, presided over the Constitutional Convention.*

character of the men the nation chose to succeed Washington in the Presidency, perhaps because of the checks and balances and the division of powers incorporated into the Constitution. Washington himself was discreet during the nine-month battle over ratification, declining to run for a seat in the Virginia ratifying convention. He expressed the view that the Constitution was the best obtainable, but left the door open to amendments if needed for ratification. Let it "stand or fall" on its "merits" or "demerits," was as much as he would say publicly.

Indubitably the likelihood of Washington's serving as first President was a significant factor in winning votes for ratification. Universally respected for his qualities of leadership, character, and judgment, Washington had already inspired a cult of hagiolatry. His image could be found everywhere and on virtually everything, from portraits and busts to household furnishings, from pitchers and bowls to needlework. Because the people had confidence that Washington as President could unite the country, they suppressed the fear of executive power so eloquently articulated by the Declaration of Independence, and they handed the helm of state to one man, along with great powers.

The very posture of disinterested nonpartisanship that Washington assumed, the self-imposed curb on ambition, served to reassure the nation. He was made President in 1789 by a unanimous vote of the electors. Only once more did any candidate secure a unanimous electoral vote—and that was Washington, again, for a second term in 1792. Projecting an image of a truly reluctant candidate, Washington showed no indications of that unquenchable thirst for office and power so common with modern Presidential candidates. Quite the contrary, he approached his initial term with dread. "My movements to the chair of government," he wrote, "will be accompanied by feelings not unlike those of a culprit who is going to the place of execution." The day he left for his inauguration in New York, he made this entry in his diary: "I bade adieu to Mount Vernon, to private life, and to domestic felicity, and with a mind oppressed with more anxious and painful sensations than I have words to express." Washington's anxieties were well founded. Yet, he would meet the challenge, shape the office, and, most important, set the nation on a steady course.

From the very moment Washington took the oath of office at Federal Hall on April 13, 1789, he seemed the paradigm of a constitutional Chief of State. He invested the office with a patrician style, grave, dignified, even austere. No, he would not be a monarch. He was too much a republican to assume that pose (and, even had he wished to, he knew that Congress was ready to pounce on any regal inclinations their President might betray). The matter of the President's title was quickly resolved. The Senate debated the merits of "His Elective Majesty," "His Elective Highness," and even "His Mightiness," but settled for the House's plain form of address, "Mr. President."

Still, monarchical precedents died hard—the tradition of the "Speech from the Throne," for instance. President Washington addressed Congress in person, while both Houses, as in England, made addresses in reply, to which the President formally responded. This practice persisted until 1801, when President Thomas Jefferson, never renowned as a public speaker, discarded "the rags of royalty," and sent his message to be read to Congress rather than delivering it in person. Jefferson's practice continued until President Woodrow Wilson reverted to Washington's—"not to revive a ritual," he said, but to demonstrate his "conception of a re-energized President."

For Washington there was to be no Buckingham Palace, merely comfortable private homes rented for him, first in New York, then Philadelphia, successively the capitals during his administration. True, Congress had already decided upon a permanent capital near Georgetown which, significantly, would bear the name of the nation's first President. Washington, delighted that the Federal City would be so close to his home grounds, was initially concerned with its general plan as well as with plans for the executive mansion. But he never lived there; his successor John Adams was the first occupant.

A high tone was the hallmark of Washington's personal style. His residential staff consisted of 14 liveried white servants and seven slaves (the latter in less conspicuous posts). When the President moved through the capital he rode in a cream-colored chariot, adorned with gilded and festooned cupids, bearing his coat of arms, and drawn by six horses. Critics called the President's social gatherings the "Republican Court." On Tuesday afternoons he held stiff, formal levees, invariably receiving guests while standing in front of the fireplace. Dressed in black velvet, clasping a pair of yellow gloves, holding a three-cornered hat decorated with a cockade, and carrying a long sword in a scabbard of white polished leather, Wash-

ington from his buckled shoes to his powdered hair stood every inch an imposing head of state.

A stiff bow rather than a handshake was accorded each visitor, and, as they formed a circle around the room, the President addressed them in turn by name. When Washington had completed his circuit, the visitors approached him in turn, bowed, and withdrew. The party was over. "Lady Washington" held weekly evening receptions, which served as a model for those of other ladies of Washington's "court" circle. (Having no wife, Jefferson, when he became President, would spare the country what he called "the burlesque of female levees.")

His critics notwithstanding, Washington's formality masked his basic shyness, his disdain of familiarity even by intimates. He disliked mixing in crowds or speaking extemporaneously to large gatherings. To compensate for these self-imposed restraints, Washington made a point of meeting people in the course of his extensive travels through the northeastern states in 1789 and the South two years later. He displayed energy and curiosity, yet, despite his deep concern with the people, Washington was distinctly not *of* the people. His own circle of friends was composed of elite sorts such as financiers, merchants, planters, and long-time political and military associates, along with

13

Interpreting literally his role as Commander-in-Chief, Washington rendezvoused with troops mobilized to quell the so-called Whiskey Rebellion of 1794.

GENERAL GEORGE WASHINGTON.
Reviewing the Western army at Fort Cumberland the 18th of Octobr 1794.

female confidantes like Eliza Powel of Philadelphia, a lady who combined charm with social position.

Washington's major contribution to the Presidency was to flesh out the bare bones of the office as set forth in Article II. As one scholar has remarked, he "invented tradition as he went along." "It was devoutly wished on my part," Washington said, "that these precedents may be fixed on true principles." Some proved ephemeral, though many endured to become a part of the "unwritten Constitution"—to be ignored by his successors only at their own peril.

It should be remembered that Washington brought to his office exceptional administrative skills, skills he had demonstrated both in the army and on his plantation. Before reaching a decision, he demanded all the facts and sought wise counsel. He solicited advice from his heads of departments, from the Chief Justice, and from Congress (this through his

friend James Madison, then in the House of Representatives). Toward the end of his first term Washington began convening his heads of departments for conferences. The word "cabinet" seems first to have been applied to such meetings in 1793. These Cabinet sessions reminded observers of the military councils of war that Washington had held in Revolutionary years.

The members of Washington's Cabinet could hardly be called "yes-men." There was habitual wrangling, as two formidable antagonists, Thomas Jefferson, Secretary of State, and Alexander Hamilton, Secretary of the Treasury, were (in Jefferson's words) "daily pitted . . . like two cocks." The elephantine erstwhile artilleryman, Henry Knox, the War Secretary, usually sided with Hamilton, and the Virginia aristocrat, Attorney General Edmund Randolph, would take a somewhat more independent stance. Although Washington did not feel bound by the vote of the Cabinet, occasionally he bowed to its advice against his own best judgment.

As chief diplomat, Washington was to make it painfully clear to the talented and prestigious Thomas

14

Jefferson that he was the master of his own foreign policy. At the start, he seems to have taken seriously the constitutional clause requiring the Senate's "advice and consent" for the ratification of treaties. The very first time a treaty was proposed, in August 1789, Washington appeared in person before the Senate, which insisted that it needed time to make up its mind. Though thoroughly irritated, Washington was a study in politeness. He withdrew to allow the Senators to debate privately. Yet he never repeated the procedure—thereby establishing the precedent that the Senate was to be engaged only *after* a treaty had been negotiated, not *during* the negotiations.

So far as the House of Representatives was concerned, Washington declined to concede it any role at all in treaty ratification. After the Senate had ratified the Jay Treaty in 1795, the House sought to hold it up by refusing to vote funds for enforcing its provisions. Washington deemed such action unconstitutional, and, with the unanimous approval of his Cabinet, he declined to obey a House resolution requesting delivery of executive documents relating to the negotiations. The House, he insisted, had no constitutional right to executive documents except in the case of "an impeachment which this resolution has not expressed." Here was an implied challenge which the House prudently declined.

Washington initially sought the advice of Chief Justice John Jay on constitutional questions. But Jay declined to render the executive department an advisory opinion in his official capacity, pointing out that "the lines of separation drawn by the Constitution" provided checks upon each branch of the government by the others. As the Supreme Court was a tribunal of last resort, he deemed it "improper to decide extrajudicially on such matters." Thus a precedent was established against the rendering of advisory opinions by the Court. At the same time Jay in his private capacity did not hesitate to give the President the benefit of his counsel when requested. He drew up a first draft of the Proclamation of Neutrality in 1793 and served as minister plenipotentiary to settle outstanding differences with Great Britain in 1794.

Regrettably from Washington's point of view, foreign affairs would become a preoccupation of the later years of his administration. As the French Revolution—first hailed in America as a harbinger of liberty in Europe—expanded into a general European war, it threatened to involve America. Should the United States stand by the terms of its old alliance and allow France access to American ports to refit ships of war and bring in prizes? Such an action, as Washington saw

it, would draw his country into a shooting war with England, one for which it was totally unprepared.

After consulting with Jay and with Attorney General Randolph, Washington issued a Proclamation of Neutrality, and thereby set another precedent. Although the Constitution invests Congress with the exclusive power to declare war, it is silent about the locus of authority to keep the country *out* of war. Critics might grumble at the President's unilateral declaration of neutrality, but neutrality was indeed enforced. Lacking any bureaucracy to implement his decision, Washington had the collectors of the customs, Hamilton's men, report violations to the federal district attorneys, who in turn would proceed under direction from Attorney General Randolph. In addition, Jay prodded his Supreme Court colleagues—required by law to sit in the federal circuit courts—to charge grand juries with enforcing the President's proclamation. By such means—and notwithstanding the rabid pro-French sentiments of a substantial segment of the population—neutrality became the law of the land.

The Constitution not only vests the executive power in the President, it also makes him Commander-in-Chief of the army and navy of the United States, and of the state militias when called to active service by the federal government. Whether or not the Founding Fathers contemplated an active military role for a President, Washington, the old soldier, actually took to the field with his troops—the only President ever to do so. The military operation in which he became involved is known as the "Whiskey Rebellion," though in reality it was nothing more than a strike by taxpayers. Today, resolution of such a dispute would probably be entrusted to a few young lawyers in the Internal Revenue Service. At issue was the refusal of the "Whiskey Boys" in western Pennsylvania to pay the excise tax imposed upon distillers in 1791 as an integral part of Hamilton's fiscal program. The tax was indeed a heavy one and it fell on interior parts of the country where whiskey had been traditionally accepted as a medium of exchange in the absence of hard money. Tax collectors were mauled and terrorized, and the operation of federal courts in the rebellious area was brought to a halt.

For Hamilton this was a true test of the authority of the federal government. At his prodding, Washington issued a proclamation calling on the insurgents to disperse, and, when they refused, he asked the states

to mobilize the sizable force of 12,900 men to suppress civil disorder. Commander-in-Chief Washington accompanied the army as far as Bedford, Pennsylvania, but he never got involved in the shooting because there was none. The Whiskey Boys vanished and only a meager bag of prisoners was prosecuted. Two were found guilty of high treason. Washington pardoned both, one as "insane" the other as a "simpleton."

Despite the lack of any actual confrontation, Washington had afforded a dramatic demonstration of the supremacy of the federal government. To his Chief Justice the President expressed satisfaction that the rebels had been brought to "a *perfect* sense of their misconduct without spilling a drop of blood." Others saw it differently, criticizing the government for magnifying the affair beyond its real danger to the republic. Nevertheless, by his crucial decision to use armed force to suppress a taxpayers' strike—one which took on the coloration of an armed insurrection— Washington established two key principles: that the law was supreme, and that the federal government was empowered to levy and collect taxes.

ing hands off the other two branches of the government, and he used the veto very sparingly—in fact, only twice in eight years. "From motives of respect to the legislature (and I might add, from my interpretation of the Constitution)," Washington remarked, "I give my signature to many bills for which my judgment is at variance." Washington set a precedent in executive restraint that was to be observed by the next five Presidents. Not until Andrew Jackson's time would there be a signal departure from this precedent.

The Constitution, while it empowers the President to nominate his chief officers with the advice and consent of the Senate, is silent on the President's power to dismiss appointees. This question was settled early in Washington's administration, when Congress sustained Presidential authority to remove the Secretary of Foreign Affairs (later called Secretary of State) without the consent of the Senate. The administrative system was thereby formally anchored to the Chief Executive. In Washington's eight years as President, dismissals were rare, however, perhaps owing to the high quality of the federal office holders. Three foreign ministers were removed, as well as two consuls, eight collectors, and four surveyors of internal revenue; six army officers were separated. An exceptional episode involved the Attorney General, Edmund Randolph. Presented with evidence that Randolph had been in the pay of the French government, and had sought to block ratification of the Jay Treaty—a charge that was never substantiated—an outraged President forced his long-time friend to resign.

Washington's successor, John Adams, pounced upon this precedent some years later to dismiss two Cabinet officers he suspected of conspiring against him. Adams had served as the first Vice President, an office for which the Constitution provided no active role but merely the passive one of presiding over the Senate. After some initial consultations with Adams, Washington ceased soliciting his advice. Nor did he include Adams in Cabinet meetings. This could have proven imprudent, since Washington suffered two potentially fatal illnesses, and during his second term he appeared to be in declining health. Excluded from the inner circle, the Vice President might have been at a disadvantage had he been forced to fill the President's chair. On the other hand, a John Adams could not conceivably have confessed to a lack of capacity to assume his constitutional role if the need had arisen.

Since Franklin D. Roosevelt, we have become accustomed to seeing important bills originate in the White House. In Washington's day Treasury Secretary Hamilton drafted major domestic legislation aimed at restoring public credit. It was, however, approved by the President before submission to Congress, and the general public as well as Congress regarded Washington as the sponsor of this program. Yet, despite the legislative initiatives from the executive branch, Washington was a staunch believer in the separation of powers. He was scrupulous about keep-

A distinguished expert on the Presidency has assigned Washington to the "passive-negative" category of chief executives—Presidents who consider themselves guardians of the right but "above the sordid politicking of lesser men." This may seem mistaken, since Washington was ever the man of action. Yet he did assume a judicious and high-minded posture, often under trying circumstances, and he remained aloof from the turbulence of factional strife. When he took office in 1789 the Antifederalists, opponents of the Constitution, were in rapid retreat. Everyone who accepted service in the government was considered a supporter of the Constitution. But, nonpartisan though Washington wished to be, he could not prevent the cleavages of interest and ideology which soon developed even within his own administration. Toward the latter part of his first term a Jeffersonian Republican party was emerging, based on a grass-roots organization of Democratic-Republican societies that proliferated as tensions mounted between the administration and the successive French revolutionary governments. The Federalists (or "monocrats," as Jefferson denominated them) regarded the opposing party as bordering on treason, and Hamilton's potent pen was incessantly deployed.

Washington had begun his administration without commitments to anyone. He appointed qualified persons to executive and judicial offices, just so long as they were "disposed to measure matters on a Continental scale." For the Supreme Court he sought "the fittest characters to expound the laws," while equally desirous of maintaining some semblance of geographic balance. In both regards the President was successful. Indeed, from Washington's day to the present, the maintenance of a regional balance on the Court has been a determinant for appointments.

Even after parties formed around the two rivals, Jefferson and Hamilton, the President insisted that he was "above politics." Because he held the balance between bitter opponents within his own Cabinet, his re-election was considered essential by both parties. During his second administration, however, Washington found it increasingly difficult to maintain a neutral posture. More and more he leaned toward the Hamiltonians, and his support of the Jay Treaty with England proved the last straw for the Jeffersonian Republicans. His opponents maligned him, as Washington himself put it, "in such exaggerated and indecent terms as could scarcely be applied to a Nero, a notorious defaulter, or even a common pickpocket."

In turn, Washington came to agree with his Federalist supporters that his opponents were a disloyal faction. No longer would he "bring a man into an office of consequence" whose political tenets were "adverse to the measures which the general government [was] pursuing"—to do so would constitute "political suicide." This partisanship provided another precedent: Save for national emergencies, Presidents have nearly always picked their appointees, major and minor, from their own party rolls.

The divisiveness pervading the country during his second term caused Washington regret at having stayed on. "By God," he expostulated, "I had rather be on my farm than be made *emperor of the world*, and yet they are charging me with wanting to be a king." The President had no press secretary and disdained countering the barrage of propaganda directly. On a few occasions his Federalist supporters rallied the public behind him, and Hamilton was always ready to raise his pen against the President's critics. In 1793, "Citizen" Edmond-Charles Genêt, France's newly-appointed minister to the United States, sought to mobilize public sentiment against the neutral course Washington had charted. He defiantly refitted an English brig, which a French frigate had captured and brought into the port of Philadelphia, and then arranged for it to slip away to do battle with the British. Jefferson sought through an intermediary to have Genêt stay his course, but the Frenchman threatened to "appeal from the President to the People." When his remarks were reported to the press in a joint letter from Chief Justice Jay and New York's Senator Rufus King, they evoked a wave of support for the President. Such support was again mobilized when it appeared that the House might refuse to appropriate funds to implement the Jay Treaty with England. Despite its deficiencies the treaty provided benefits nobody could question, such as the withdrawal of British troops from the frontiers. "A torrent of petitions," as Washington put it, helped turn the tide in favor of the appropriation and sustain the treaty.

Savage personal attacks saddened Washington's final days in office and inspired the warning embodied in his Farewell Address. The President implored his countrymen to discourage even "the first dawning of every attempt to alienate any portion of our country from the rest or to enfeeble the sacred ties which now link together the various parts." Stressing the need to guard the union from sectional divisiveness, Washington cautioned against "the baneful effects of the spirit of party generally." Parties might be useful in a monarchy, he conceded, but they were "not to be encouraged" in "purely elective" governments. To Washington, partisanship was "a fire not to be quenched. It demands a uniform vigilance to prevent its bursting into a flame, lest, instead of warming, it should consume." Alas from Washington's point of view, this was advice his countrymen did not follow. Although the Constitution nowhere recognizes a party system, Americans eventually regarded political parties as fulfilling not just a useful purpose, but an indispensable one.

It was against the background of maintaining America's perilous neutrality in a war-torn world that Washington drafted his Farewell Address. Long in formulation—a first draft had been prepared by James Madison back in February 1792, when Washington contemplated retiring at the end of his first term— the final address was based on drafts by Alexander Hamilton, and incorporated some oral suggestions from John Jay as well. Nevertheless, the final state paper was very much Washington's own. Hamilton's drafts faithfully followed Washington's scheme of organization and his main ideas, and were felicitously rephrased in Washington's own hand. The most durable of Washington's recommendations were those relating to foreign policy. While advocating the maintenance of commercial relations with foreign nations, he advised having with them "as little political connection as possible." Reminding his countrymen of the uniquely favorable geographic situation of the United States, he asked rhetorically: "Why forego the advantages of so peculiar a situation? Why quit our own ground to stand upon foreign ground?"

Though he did hedge a bit, pointing to the necessity of maintaining "a respectable defensive posture" and to the utility of trusting to "temporary alliances in extraordinary emergencies," Washington's "Great Rule" became the most cherished principle in the annals of American diplomacy. It remained unchallenged and unaltered until the perils of the 20th-century world—with its technology that has eliminated distance—dictated a refashioned and vastly enlarged role for America in world affairs.

Finally, Washington's decision to retire at the end of his second term, as expressed in his Farewell Address, ended any notion of an elective monarchy and laid the ground for the principle of succession based on the will of the electorate. The succession process is still one of the miracles of the American constitutional system, offering a standard that few nations have managed to emulate. Of President Washington it can truly be said that he established the fundamental legitimacy of the national government. By his astute, firm, and energetic administrative decisions he kept the initiative in the executive branch. By his staunch adherence to the principle of division of powers he kept a rein on executive usurpation. By keeping the nation out of war he assured its survival.

Crayon portrait of George Washington by C.B.J. Févret de Saint-Mémin is one of the last images of the President before his death on December 14, 1799, at the age of 67.

Washington's "Relics"

Amy Donovan

They did, after all, once belong to the Father of His Country. Their enduring attraction, therefore, is hardly surprising. In 1842, when a number of them were put in a display case in the Patent Office's Model Room, one writer deemed that case "the most interesting . . . in the whole collection." Indeed, these precious artifacts were the genesis of the Smithsonian's Presidential collections and ultimately the basis for some of the Institution's most vital and popular exhibits. Steeped in this country's history by virtue of association with their original owner, George Washington's "relics" (as they were then called) have an interesting subsequent history in their own right.

The Patent Office building (today the Smithsonian's National Collection of Fine Arts and National Portrait Gallery) was the first structure in the capital designed to be fireproof. Partly this was to avoid a repetition of the 1836 disaster in which the E Street building that housed the Patent Office burned with virtually all its contents, including thousands of inventors' models. Because it was thought safe, the new Patent Office quickly became the repository for diverse collections such as the natural history specimens gathered during Captain Charles Wilkes's expedition of 1838–1842; for works of art and "extraordinary curiosities" from a society called the National Institute for the

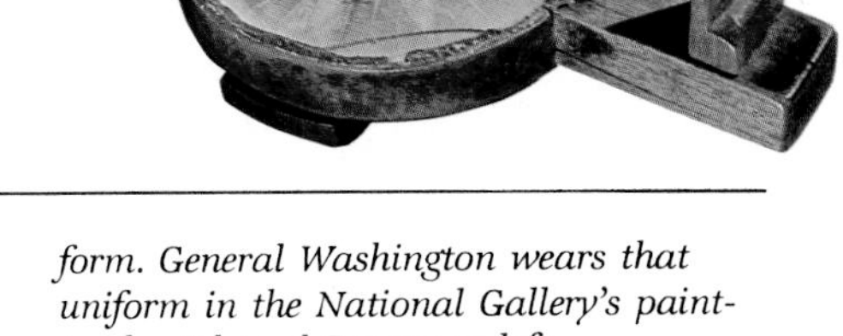

Artifacts from the Smithsonian's collection of Washingtoniana include a surveying compass and his Continental Army uniform. General Washington wears that uniform in the National Gallery's painting by Edward Savage at left.

Promotion of Science; and for the national historical treasures that had previously been scattered about the city.

National treasures they were indeed. Visitors could stroll down elegantly columned aisles and view such articles as the military coat worn by General Jackson at the Battle of New Orleans; Benjamin Franklin's printing press; and, in Case 23, the original Declaration of Independence. But the attraction "viewed by visitors with the utmost satisfaction," was Case 24—the relics of George Washington.

Mostly of "a personal kind," many of these articles had been given to the U.S. government by George Washington Parke Custis, one of the two grandchildren of Martha Washington (a widow when she married George Washington) whom Washington had adopted in 1781 after their father, John Custis, died at Yorktown. There were pieces of General Washington's camp equipage; the uniform he is thought to have worn when he resigned his commission at Annapolis in 1783; the surveyor's compass he used at Mount Vernon; and the "fine crab-tree walking-stick" that Ben Franklin bequeathed "my friend, and the friend of all mankind, George Washington."

The National Gallery, as the Model Room came to be called, was soon filled almost to overflowing. Some relief for the crowded hall came in 1858, when several exhibits were transferred to the recently completed Smithsonian "Castle." And yet the second half of the 19th century brought two additional col-

lections of George Washington memorabilia to the Patent Office, the first under the most exceptional circumstances in the most strained of times.

★   ★   ★

In 1831, Mary Ann Randolph Custis, the only child of George Washington Parke Custis, had married Robert E. Lee. They lived at her father's Arlington House just across the river from Washington. When the Civil War broke out and Lee became a Confederate general, the U.S.

government moved to occupy the estate, and Mrs. Lee and her family fled.

Early in January 1862 Brigadier General Irvin McDowell of the Army of the Potomac searched the mansion and discovered several pieces of "States" china, presented to Martha Washington by a friend of her husband's, and a set of china purchased by Washington through The Society of the Cincinnati, an order founded in 1783 by former Continental

Army officers. A subsequent search of the garret revealed important Washington papers.

McDowell's superior suggested to the Secretary of the Interior that George Washington's family heirlooms at Arlington House be placed in the Patent Office for "safe keeping." There they went and there they remained, on exhibit and undisturbed, until February 10, 1869, when Mary Custis Lee wrote President Andrew Johnson, imploring him to see to the return of "relics from Mount Vernon, bequeathed to me by my father." Johnson responded that they would be returned to her as soon as they had been properly identified. This turned out to be a promise he could not fulfill.

Many Washington "relics," displayed at the Centennial in Philadelphia, right, came to the Smithsonian in 1883. His field tent is shown outside Arts and Industries Building, above.

As President and general, Washington read by the light of a brass candelabrum, above right.

23

A notice in the Washington *Evening Express*, regarding the imminent return of the Mount Vernon memorabilia to the Lee family, raised Congressional hackles. The House Committee on Public Buildings and Grounds resolved that the Arlington collection was "of right the property of the United States" and that "any attempt to deliver the same to the rebel General, Robert E. Lee, is an insult to the loyal people of the United States, and they ought to be kept as relics in the Patent Office. . . ."

In the mid-1880s the Lee collection came to the Smithsonian, where the National Museum's curator suggested that the "articles be restored to their rightful owners." President Cleveland deferred to his Attorney General on the issue, who in turn deferred to Congress. And Congress still wouldn't budge.

Finally, on April 25, 1901, President William McKinley authorized the return ". . . to the present head of a historical family of these cherished heirlooms of the Father of His Country." The lingering passions of the Civil War at long last on the ebb, those "relics from Mount Vernon" originally bequeathed to George Washington's stepson departed the Smithsonian for their true heirs, the Lee family.

★ ★ ★

The second large collection of George Washington's possessions came to the government under far more auspicious circumstances and permanent terms. Eleanor Parke "Nellie" Custis, the second of the two grandchildren adopted by George Washington, married Major Lawrence Lewis, Washington's nephew. Upon the death of Martha Washington in 1802, in accordance with her husband's will, the Mount Vernon estate went to his nephew, Bushrod

Recent Smithsonian acquisitions include Washington's silver camp cup engraved with his family crest, and a folding camp stool that was listed on the same 1776 purchase order.

Washington; the estate's household accoutrements were divided up among Martha Washington's four grandchildren. Nellie Custis Lewis died in 1852. Some years later, in 1878, her children approached the U.S. government with an offer to sell their share of Washington heirlooms.

The government responded quickly. On June 20, 1878, it purchased for $12,000 the more than 90 items in the Lewis collection, and moved them into the last niches of the Patent Office. Fortuitously, given the Model Room's cramped quarters, a new U.S. National Museum was being planned by the Smithsonian. It would open in 1881 and soon prove the ideal repository for the Washington relics.

On April 18, 1883, Commissioner of Patents E. M. Marble wrote to Smithsonian Secretary Spencer Baird, asking him "to accept, to be placed in the National Museum the Washington relics and such other relics as are now in the custody of this office." Secretary Baird sent word on April 26 that "we have cases ready and shall put the collection on exhibition as soon as it has been examined and catalogued."

And so to the Smithsonian's National Museum (today its Arts and Industries Building) came all the Patent Office's Washingtoniana—the items which the government had owned for years before exhibiting them in the Model Room, the so-called Lee and Lewis collections, and gifts from other sources. It was the beginning of a long and beautiful association. Curators have sought constantly to expand the collection. Recent acquisitions include a portable camp stool and silver camp cup that Washington's personal friend and military secretary, Joseph Reed, is thought to have purchased for the general in Philadelphia in 1776, and a large china bowl purchased by Washington through The Society of the Cincinnati.

Housed since 1964 in the National Museum of History and Technology, numerous exhibits of this premier collection today honor our first President. In 1982, both as fitting testimony to the veneration still accorded the Father of His Country and to celebrate the 250th anniversary of his birth (as well as the centennial of the Smithsonian's Washingtoniana), the Museum will open a major exhibit on George Washington's life. He remains, as ever, "First in the Hearts of his Countrymen."

Pieces from Martha Washington's own "States" china service are decorated with an endless chain linking the states.

A bowl from Washington's service from The Society of the Cincinnati features his own motif—the "angel of fame" with an eagle.

The "Athenaeum Portrait" of George Washington, right, painted by Gilbert Stuart (1775–1828) in 1796, served as a basis for "Lansdowne Portrait," above. Compelling problems besetting the President may be reflected in his countenance.

★ ★ ★ ★ ★ ★ ★ ★ ★ ★ ★ ★ ★ ★

Portraying the Presidents

Marvin Sadik

Afusion of artistic skill and psychological insight is the foremost requirement for excellence in portraiture—and that was my principal criterion in selecting these Presidential portraits.

In making my choices, I discovered, rather to my surprise, that the task was more difficult than anticipated. This is not to say that every portrait of a President has merit; far from it. Yet, in surveying the field, I found a remarkably large number that were outstanding. There were, of course, a lot of plugs too, but in almost every instance these were as much the result of poor Presidential judgment as they were of artistic ineptitude.

I wanted to cover as many epochs of the Presidency as possible—from the 18th century to the present—showing, if I could, my subjects as incumbents, bearing the full burden of the office. Included are portraits by American artists whose styles were formed abroad, as well as examples by those whose artistry was

home-grown, one work by a non-American artist, and another by a native-born craftsman who is virtually unknown. Also considered from several points of view is the matter of photographic portraiture.

★ ★ ★

Because we have seen so much of the image of our nation's first President by Gilbert Stuart in so many forms—indeed if any American likeness can claim status as our national icon, it is this one—it has become increasingly difficult to see in the "Lansdowne Portrait" (opposite) the real person depicted.

George Washington agreed, in accordance with his letter to Senator William Bingham of Pennsylvania, to sit for Stuart "under promise to Mrs. Bingham." She intended to present the portrait to the Marquis of Lansdowne, who had been an outstanding supporter of the American cause. The image resulting from that session, unfinished save for the subject's head (now known as the "Athenaeum Portrait"), served as the basis for this monumental, full-length canvas. The entire Lansdowne was accomplished by late November of the same year, 1796, when it was dispatched to England. Now it hangs in the Smithsonian's National Portrait Gallery.

The format of this painting, both in terms of the type of its accoutrements and the pose of its subject, derives from contemporary and earlier European full-lengths with which the American-born Stuart surely would have become familiar during the period from 1775 to 1792, when he was first a student and subsequently a practicing artist in England and Ireland.

Having at the same time painted another version for the Binghams themselves—American patrons of the arts who were among the chief tastemakers of Federal society—Stuart also had to meet the standards of yet another audience. This demanded a special effort on the artist's part which would satisfy the unique purpose inherent in such an ambitious likeness: A portrait of the first President of the United States required a dignity as unassailably self-assured as that of the monarch of the country from which America had wrested independence by revolution.

A critic writing in the London *Oracle and Advertiser* proclaimed the Lansdowne portrait "one of the finest pictures we have seen since the death of Reynolds." Lord Lansdowne himself thought the painting "in every

Rembrandt Peale (1778–1860) painted Thomas Jefferson in 1800, the year before Jefferson became President.

way worthy of the original."

Most viewers, however, have remarked on the smallness of the subject's head in relation to his body. Any speculations as to who actually posed for the figure—which the President himself surely did not do—are nevertheless irrelevant in light of observations about Washington's anatomy made by several of his contemporaries. For example, David Ackerman of Alexandria, Virginia,

wrote to his son that Washington's "head was not large in contrast to every other part of his body, which seemed large and bony at all points. His finger-joints and wrists were so large as to be genuine curiosities."

No discussion of Washington's appearance would be complete without mention of his famous, ill-fitting false teeth. The set he was wearing in January 1797 was actually uncomfortable enough for him to have written his New York dentist, Dr. John Greenwood, to see if Greenwood might not come up with some suggestions as to how to put that painful situation aright. Still, before characterizing the set of Washington's jaw—and hence his expression—on this basis, one should know something of the subject's state of mind.

In fact, the time when Washington was sitting for Stuart, in April 1796, was one of the most unhappy of his entire Presidency. Republicans in the House were attempting to block the Jay Treaty—an agreement the administration had earnestly sought—by denying an appropriation to enforce it. In an open letter to the President, Tom Paine had wondered "whether you have abandoned good principles, or whether you ever had any."

Even after the House had finally voted the necessary funds on April 30 (though only by three votes, 51 to 48), the President wrote to the man who drafted the document, John Jay, "These things do . . . fill my mind with much concern and with serious anxiety. Indeed, the troubles and perplexities which they occasion, added to the weight of years which have passed over me, have worn away my mind more than my body." It is not difficult to believe, therefore, that this was a time in Washington's life when, as Jefferson had once observed, the President was prone to "one of those passions when he cannot command himself."

When the original owner of another version of the Lansdowne portrait first showed it to three

of his friends, he proclaimed: "Gentlemen, there is the man," to which they immediately responded, in unison, "The man himself!" A decade before this canvas was painted, a critic for the *London World* wrote of its artist: "In the most arduous and valuable achievements of portrait painting, *identity* and *duration*, Stuart takes the lead of every competitor. . . . Stuart dives deep into *mind*, and brings up with him a conspicuous draught of character and characteristic thought—all as sensible to feeling and to sight as the most palpable projections in any feature of a face."

Here, in the Lansdowne portrait of George Washington by Gilbert Stuart, is a national icon which transcends the myth to reveal "the man himself!"

★   ★   ★

Of all the portraits of Thomas Jefferson, the likeness by Rembrandt Peale was the most widely known during the subject's lifetime. This was due to the large number of prints made after it (the first having appeared in the very year the original canvas was executed), which were circulated in the United States as political propaganda both pro and con, and abroad, where the image personified what the Europeans admired so much in Jefferson.

The portrait was executed between December 1799 and mid-May 1800, when Jefferson was serving as John Adams's Vice President and the national government was located in Philadelphia. He turned 57 shortly before

it was completed and about a year before he became the Chief Executive. The artist, though only 22, had already been painting for some nine years, having been instructed by his father, Charles Willson Peale.

Five years earlier, alongside his father (who was painting the last of his many portraits of Washington), Rembrandt had been allowed to try his brush at a likeness of the first President. The result was a deeply moving, if utterly unidealized "warts and all" painting of the aged subject, far more expert in its execution than one might have expected from even so precocious a teenager. It is not altogether surprising, therefore, that the original canvas of this later Rembrandt Peale portrait of Thomas Jefferson escaped identification as the work of his hand until 1959. Rembrandt's Jefferson is light-years beyond his Washington. Few portraits of any President match it in the degree to which superb artistic skill and profound insight into character combine to reveal, with such perfection, both the appearance and the spirit of the subject.

★   ★   ★

Our life-size portrait of James Monroe was painted by John Vanderlyn during Monroe's second term as President. Vanderlyn had received his initial artistic instruction from the English-born Archibald Robertson, who had emigrated to America in 1791. A copy of Gilbert Stuart's portrait of Aaron Burr that Vanderlyn had been allowed to make brought him to the attention of the sitter, who made it possible for him to study with Stuart for a few months. After painting his own life-portrait of Burr, Vanderlyn was sent in 1796, as Burr's protégé, to study in France. There he resided for five years, during which time he was a pupil of François André Vincent. Vanderlyn returned to Europe in 1803 and remained working in Paris, Rome, and London for the next 12 years.

Despite its thinly veiled reference to the Lansdowne portrait (particularly in terms of pose and staffage), Vanderlyn's Monroe was as perfectly fitting a statement for its time as Stuart's Washington had been a quarter-century earlier. Monroe's presence is suffused with an immense gravity, serious and permanent, completely correct for the chief of a nation perceived to be solidly reset on course, after the vicissitudes of the War of 1812 and the negotiation of several diplomatic accords with Britain, against any future threats of foreign domination.

★ ★ ★

Asher B. Durand's likeness of Andrew Jackson came to be painted as a result of a patriotic impulse on the part of New York merchant and connoisseur Luman Reed, who commissioned the artist to provide him with portraits, in duplicate, of the seven men who thus far had been President of the United States—John Quincy Adams and Jackson from life, the others from Stuart's paintings. One set of these canvases Reed gave to the New York Gallery of Fine Arts and the other to the Brooklyn Naval Lyceum. The former is now in the New-York Historical Society and the latter in the United States Naval Academy Museum in Annapolis.

Durand's earliest artistic instruction had come from his father, who was, among other things, a watchmaker and a silversmith. After some success engraving designs on copper plates for the elder Durand, young Asher, at the age of 16, was apprenticed to the steel-plate engraver Peter Maverick for five years. Durand subsequently became Maverick's partner, an association that was dissolved in 1820 when John Trumbull chose the younger of the two men, on the basis of superior talent, to engrave his painting of the Declaration of Independence. While still an apprentice to Maverick, Durand had become acquainted with the portraitist Samuel Waldo, from whom he learned the rudiments of that art. Durand abandoned engraving for painting at just about the time he executed his portrait of Andrew Jackson in 1835. Later, he turned to the art of landscape painting, and he is best remembered today as one of the founders of the so-called Hudson River School.

The roots of the hard-edged, unblinkingly realistic style of Durand's Jackson are to be found in the work of such portraitists as Durand's teacher, Samuel Waldo, and in the ingrained finesse of his own earlier career as an engraver (often of other artists' portraits). In his late 60s, Jackson was no longer the dashing and romantic hero, but the battered politician two years away from retirement. Nor was the sitting itself conducive to an idealized image: "He smokes, reads, and writes, and attends to other business while I am painting, and the whole time of a sitting is short of one hour," the artist complained to his wife. Durand reported, after three similarly short sessions, that "all say I

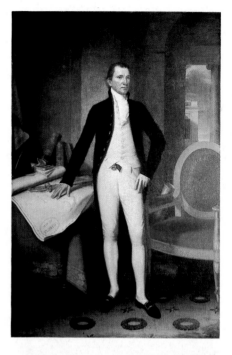

The neoclassical 1822 portrait of James Monroe by John Vanderlyn (1775–1852), top, stands in contrast to the stark realism of the 1835 portrait of Andrew Jackson by Asher B. Durand (1796–1886).

The finest portraits of Abraham Lincoln are photographs. Lincoln himself preferred this one, taken by Mathew Brady (circa 1823–1896) on January 8, 1864.

have an excellent likeness," but added, that "it is not good enough to satisfy me."

The artist's own opinion notwithstanding, we have considerable reason to be grateful for this finely crafted image of Andrew Jackson. The likeness not only tallies well with daguerreotypes made of the subject a few years later, but it has a veritable proto-photographic quality about it—a characteristic that it shared with many portraits, both European and American, painted during the two decades before the invention of the camera. Portraits such as these seem to respond to a desire for likenesses unfettered by stylistic convention or subjective sentiment, in which the only originality was that of the subject—a desire that, ironically, was to be extinguished by the camera itself.

★ ★ ★

Of all the paintings done of Abraham Lincoln while he was President, none was executed without the assistance of a photograph. Even Francis Carpenter, who actually moved into the executive mansion in pursuit of his project to paint his subsequently celebrated *First Reading of the Emancipation Proclamation,* used a photograph of Lincoln. This photograph had been taken especially for the purpose by Anthony Berger, the manager of Mathew Brady's Washington studio, on Tuesday, April 26, 1864.

It was not surprising that Lincoln would have lacked the leisure to pose for portrait painters. Also, artists' lives were subjected to the same dislocations that beset most other citizens during the Civil War. But neither of these factors was as important as the presence in Washington, at the same time, of two excellent photographers, Mathew Brady and Alexander Gardner, not to mention their able studio assistants who could stand in when Brady or Gardner were at their cameras on the battlefronts.

Although Brady began his artistic career as a painter and lithographer, he gradually turned to daguerreotypy, opening his first studio in New York in 1844 and a branch in Washington in 1847. He subsequently adopted a newer medium of photography, the wet-plate or collodion process. This yielded a glass-plate negative from which any number of paper prints could be made. Alexander Gardner, a former journalist who had come from Glasgow to join Brady, was particularly proficient at the wet-plate process. After Brady's apparently perpetual (and somehow inexplicable) improvidence left him unable to pay his associate's salary, Gardner opened his own studio in Washington. As an independent photographer, Gardner took his first subject on August 9, 1863: Abraham Lincoln.

The Brady-Gardner Presidential photographs of Lincoln are, almost without exception, so striking that it is difficult to choose from among them. Robert Todd Lincoln thought the photograph of his father made by Anthony Berger for the Brady studio on February 9, 1864, "to be the most satisfactory likeness of him." (This image is familiar to all, having served as the prototype for that on the five-dollar bill.) Others prefer Lincoln's last photograph, the profoundly affecting image on the cracked glass plate made by Gardner on Monday,

Rutherford B. Hayes was painted in 1877 by Thomas Eakins (1844–1916), the greatest American portraitist of the day.

April 10, 1865 (page 98). Lincoln himself selected the Brady image of Friday, January 8, 1864: "I don't know that I have any favorite portrait of myself, but I have thought that if I looked like any of the likenesses of me that have been taken, I look like that one."

John G. Nicolay, one of Lincoln's two principal secretaries and a man who saw him almost every day of his Presidency, believed that "graphic art was powerless before a face that

moved through a thousand delicate gradations of line and contour, light and shade, sparkle of the eye and curve of the lip." And Walt Whitman, who had seen Lincoln several times, felt that "none of the artists has caught the deep, though subtle and indirect expression of this man's face."

They have only caught the surface. There is something else there."

It is to the photographs of Lincoln that we must look for his finest portraits. Sometimes singly, but surely in the aggregate, they have preserved for all time the man through whose eyes, as one of his contemporaries observed, "his soul looked forth."

★   ★   ★

From 1870 to 1912, the period during which Thomas Eakins was a practicing artist, nine men held the Presidency of the United States, but only one of them was portrayed by Eakins, who is today recognized as the greatest American portraitist of his era. Eakins was born in Philadelphia and first studied there at the Pennsylvania Academy of the Fine Arts. Because life classes were rare at the Academy and Eakins loathed drawing from plaster casts, he enrolled in a class in anatomy at the Jefferson Medical College in Philadelphia. In 1866 he went to Paris to study at the École des Beaux-Arts, where the teacher he most admired was Gérôme. He also traveled in Spain, and there the art of Ribera and Velazquez made an enormous impression on him. Eakins became an instructor at the Pennsylvania Academy in 1876, but was forced to resign in 1886 as a result of his insistence on posing a nude male model before a mixed class. Although he later won awards and was elected to the National Academy in 1902, his realism was so uncompromising that most of his portraits were of family and friends.

It was the Union League of Philadelphia, a bastion of the Republican Party, that commissioned Thomas Eakins in 1877 to paint a portrait of the new President, Rutherford B. Hayes. Hayes, undeniably occupied with Presidential business, wished the work to be done from a photograph. Eakins gently insisted on painting from life, but the subject remained uncooperative. As Eakins described the situation: "The President once posed, I never saw him in the same pose again. He wrote, took notes, stood up, swung his chair around. In short I had to construct him as I would a little animal."

Reviews of Eakins's extraordinary work were generally favorable; but it was regarded as controversial. On June 15, 1878, the *Philadelphia Press* noted: "The Union League of Philadelphia has hung on its walls a portrait of President Hayes, which represents him with a rubicund countenance far removed from that supposed to characterize a temperant, not to say a temperance man."

Mrs. Hayes—"Lemonade Lucy"—had banned alcoholic beverages from the President's household and even the remotest implication to the contrary might have been regarded as potentially embarrassing to all concerned. In any case, Eakins's portrait of President Hayes disappeared from the Union League clubhouse and remains virtually unknown to this very day. Even so, this painting, executed under far less than ideal circumstances, is not without immense distinction. It altogether surpasses the work of William Garl Browne, whose artistry President Hayes had preferred, and whose canvas of him replaced the Eakins in the collection of the Union League of Philadelphia.

One clue as to why most of the portraits of Ohio Presidents of the late 19th century, like Browne's Hayes, constitute such a sorry lot artistically among the likenesses of our Chief Executives may be found in the acute observations of William Allen White. The editor of a Kansas newspaper, the *Emporia Gazette*, White was thoroughly conversant with the Presidential scene. In his brilliant *Autobiography*, published in 1946, White wrote in reference to one President from Ohio: "McKinley had been able to survive twenty years in Ohio politics, where survival values combined the virtues of the serpent, the shark, and the cooing dove. . . . He was destined for a statue in the park, and was practicing the pose for it."

It was just this mask, this pose, to which the art of Thomas Eakins was totally inimical; and therefore his portrait of President Hayes simply would not do.

★   ★   ★

After Thomas Eakins, Eastman Johnson was the most distinguished American portraitist of the latter 19th century. One might think that Johnson would have painted more post-Civil War Presidents, but he was called upon to do only two, Benjamin Harrison and Grover Cleveland. Although Johnson was primarily engaged in creating the genre pictures for which he is justly most celebrated, he had, since his earliest career as a painter, made portraits. In fact, it was as a remarkably expert portrait draughtsman that he began his life as an artist, having come to Washington in 1844, where for two years he drew likenesses of illustrious inhabitants. In 1846, Johnson went to Cambridge, Massachusetts, where he executed a brilliant series of drawings of great literary figures and their friends. His subsequent studies in the art of painting took place in Düsseldorf, in The Hague, and finally, for a brief period in 1855, in the studio of Thomas Couture in Paris—after which he returned to the United States to launch his career in earnest.

Grover Cleveland sat for Eastman Johnson twice: first, during the last year he was governor of New York, in 1884 (versions of this portrait are in the New York State Capitol and the New York City Hall); and second, in 1891, during the period between Cleveland's two terms as President, for his official White House portrait.

On January 16, 1897, Cleveland wrote to a friend who had inquired about a possible biography of the President: "I feel in this matter as I do in regard to my White House portrait. I am not anxious to have one on exhibition, but if it is insisted on I naturally would be glad to be represented in a way that would be recognizable. One of the last things I shall do [before leaving the White House] will be to put the Eastman Johnson portrait in the garret entirely out of sight."

Generally, people are very poor judges of their own portraits. What they behold is not the image that answers to their presence in the looking glass (particularly in view of the fact

Grover Cleveland's 1891 sitting for Eastman Johnson (1824–1906) resulted in this official White House portrait.

that a mirror image is smaller than the original it reflects) and, still less, what they see in their mind's eye. In these respects, Presidential vision is no different than anyone else's. Not having seen Cleveland at the time he was painted, we are at a disadvantage that cannot be surmounted even by examining a photograph taken at the same moment. The camera is monocular; it sees differently than a pair of human eyes.

One probably should take what Cleveland wrote about this portrait by Eastman Johnson with a grain of salt, or perhaps as an expression of modesty. Certainly, other Presidents have had similar feelings. John Quincy Adams, confiding to his diary, first wrote of his own portrait by George Peter Alexander Healy, in a pose similar to that of Cleveland by East-

man Johnson, that it was "such a picture of naked nature that I cannot look at it without shame." Later, however, Adams admitted to his diary, "Mr. Healy's picture is the strongest likeness of me that ever was painted."

Looking at this powerful portrait of Grover Cleveland, which is perhaps imbued with a touch of the grandiose in its mien, one cannot help wonder if the subject might not have thought it a bit too much "a picture of naked nature"—particularly when compared with the more benignly masked likenesses of other Presidents posing chastely for statues in the park.

★   ★   ★

Although American Presidents before and since William Howard Taft have sat for likenesses by European artists, never have they done so for what were to become their official White House portraits, as William Howard Taft did for Anders Zorn. The reason Taft did so is perhaps not difficult to explain.

Born in Sweden, Zorn first trained to be an artist at the Stockholm Academy. He studied and traveled widely in Europe and the Middle East, and lived and worked in Paris from 1886 to 1896. In 1893 he began a series of frequent visits to the United States. Zorn was certainly no more cosmopolitan, and scarcely less foreign, than the only other contemporary portraitist of comparable stature and style, John Singer Sargent. Though American by parentage, Sargent was born in Italy, studied in France, and lived mostly in England. But in President Taft's mind Anders Zorn had one deci-

Anders Zorn (1860–1920), born in Sweden, painted this portrait of William Howard Taft in 1911 in the Blue Room of the White House.

sive thing in his favor: Unlike Sargent, he hadn't painted the official White House portrait of Theodore Roosevelt.

Many Americans were making political comparisons between Roosevelt and Taft, ordinarily to the latter's detriment. And it may well have occurred to Taft that people would inevitably make personal comparisons— also to his detriment—if he, too, sat for Sargent. Though Roosevelt was far from slim, he carried his weight well; there was simply no way in which Taft's considerably greater girth could be heroically displayed. How much wiser, therefore, to turn to the artist who had stylishly portrayed a predecessor almost as wide as he (Grover Cleveland).

Zorn's portrait of Taft was painted in the Blue Room of the

White House, in the summer of 1911. Alice Roosevelt Longworth told the President that she thought the artist made him look pudgy, to which Taft could only respond, "But I am." Unwilling to have her opinion challenged even by the subject himself, but not dispensing any compliments either, Mrs. Longworth shot back: "Not as pudgy as that, Mr. President, and I would not have it." Yet it was not so much Taft's physique that weighed him down; much more significantly, it was Alice Longworth's father. "If I only knew what the President [he still called Roosevelt the President] wanted," Taft complained to an aide, "I would do it. . . . I

The 1921 inaugural medal of Warren G. Harding by Darrell C. Crain (1879–1969) was issued in gold, silver, and bronze.

am deeply wounded, and he gives me no chance to explain my attitude or learn his." All questions of political philosophy aside, what Theodore Roosevelt wanted was his old job back.

"The President is so weary that it shows in his face," Zorn told Taft's Secretary of Commerce and Labor, Charles Nagel. "Can't you come over and talk to him so I can paint him as he really is?" Nagel tried, but the President remained unchanged; and so the artist portrayed him, unerringly, as he was, imprisoned in mind and body by circumstances beyond his control.

★　　★　　★

The medallic portraits of our Presidents, which include commemorative and inaugural medals, and Indian peace medals, have had as uneven a history aesthetically as Presidential portraiture in all the other media.

The art got off to a brilliant beginning with the work of two great European-born medallists, John Reich and Moritz Fürst. In our own century, Presidential medallic art can perhaps be described most charitably as pedestrian, with but four notable exceptions. These were the inaugural medals done for Theodore Roosevelt in 1905 by Augustus Saint-Gaudens, for Warren G. Harding in 1921 by Darrell C. Crain, and for Franklin D. Roosevelt in 1941 and 1945 by Jo Davidson. Saint-Gaudens and Davidson achieved much greater

renown on the basis of more important sculptural works than these medals, and, furthermore, the most distinguished portraits of both Roosevelts are in other media. On the other hand, although Crain did inaugural medals of Wilson and Coolidge too, that of Harding is not only the best of the three but the finest portrait of this President ever done in any medium.

Darrell C. Crain was a Washington, D.C., artist and jeweler who, in addition to his three Presidential inaugural medals (a record number in this genre), designed insignia, cups, and awards for more than a hundred civic, educational, religious, and fraternal organizations. Although undoubtedly based on a photograph, Crain's medallic portrait of Harding superbly captures, in sculptural relief, not only the appearance but the character of its subject. Here is the face from central casting, in the lineaments of which Crain uncannily captured both the benign dignity (which so appealed to the politicians in the "smoke-filled room" where Harding is said to have received his Presidential nomination) and the pathetic anguish that destroyed him before the end of his term in office. Here is the Harding who had told the voters that "America's present need is . . . not nostrums but normalcy," and who had assured them that "there is more happiness in the American village today than in any other place on the face of the earth." And here is the Harding who, confronted by the disasters that were consuming his administration and his life, was to characterize his predicament thus: "My God, this is a hell of a job! I have no trouble with my enemies. I can take care of them. It is my friends that are giving me trouble!"

★ ★ ★

One does not think of portraiture as an important aspect of Andrew Wyeth's art, but the place it does occupy is far from insignificant, particularly if one considers the number of likenesses he has painted of his family and friends. To be sure, most of these works are generally considered more "character studies" than portraits. But portraiture—at its best—is as much the revelation of character as it is the depiction of likeness. Wyeth's portraits possess both qualities, and to a very high degree; they are not only carefully observed, they are deeply understood. Clearly, he knows as much about people as he does about nature.

At first sight, Wyeth's likeness of Dwight D. Eisenhower is a little unexpected. Most people close to the President didn't care for it. Those who are familiar with the irresistible charisma of the famous Eisenhower smile find its absence here somewhat unsettling. Even the fact that the subject himself said, "You know, I am one of the few people around here who liked that portrait," doesn't seem to help.

Only if one remembers the behind-the-scenes achievements of General and President Eisenhower—not Ike the military and

Likeness of Dwight D. Eisenhower by Andrew Wyeth (born 1917) portrays Ike in his seventh year as President.

political campaigner—can one begin to come to grips with the real person in the portrait. Eisenhower was chosen Supreme Commander of the Allied Expeditionary Force in Europe, over the heads of many higher ranking officers, because of his conciliatory talents, which ultimately assured that potentially discordant forces would unite against the enemy. The pattern of his Presidential leadership was not very different, and his style in office was far less dramatic than that of either his predecessor or his successor.

Painted during a period of

six hours, spread over four sittings, from August 15 to August 18, 1959, here is Dwight D. Eisenhower—the quiet man close to the conclusion of his public career, concerned about the future, and beset by the problems of uncertain health—summed up for us by Andrew Wyeth.

★ ★ ★

In reviewing these portraits, I am inclined to be optimistic about future portraits of our Chief Executives if only they will trust our best artists—and themselves—to portray them as they really are.

"Old Ironsides"

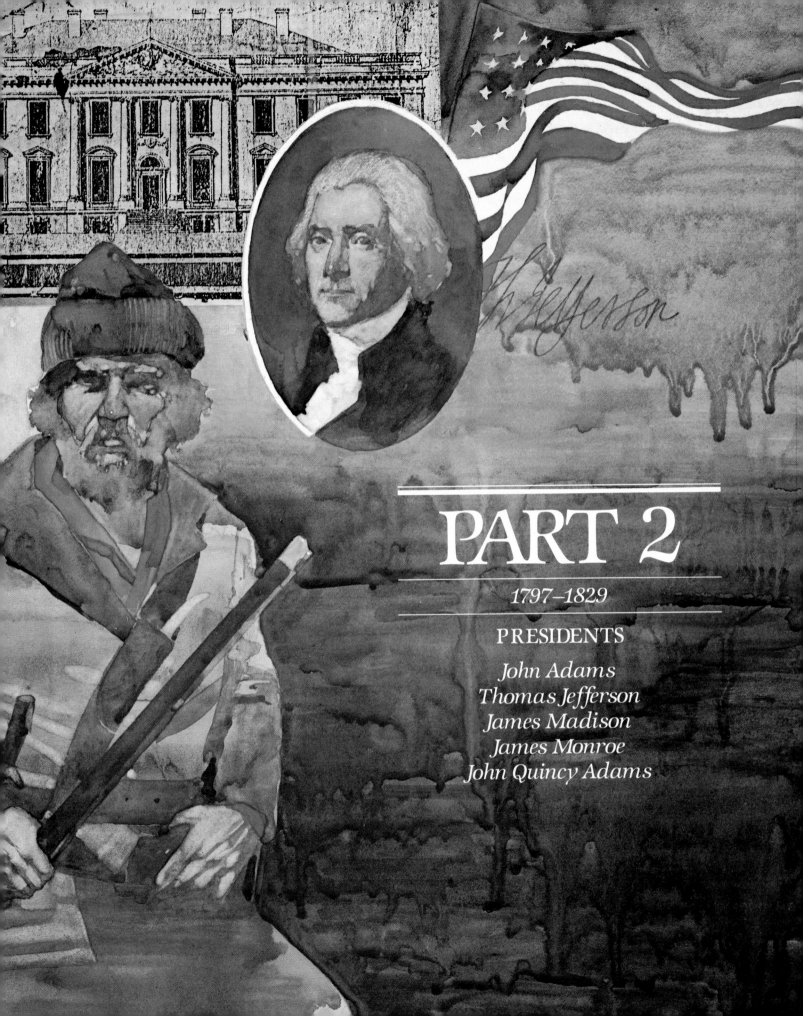

PART 2

1797–1829

PRESIDENTS

John Adams
Thomas Jefferson
James Madison
James Monroe
John Quincy Adams

★ ★ ★ ★ ★ ★ ★ ★ ★ ★ ★ ★ ★ ★

The President as Patrician

Noble E. Cunningham, Jr.

During all but eight of the years between George Washington's retirement to Mount Vernon in 1797 and the inauguration of Andrew Jackson in 1829, the Presidential office was occupied by the Virginia dynasty of Thomas Jefferson, James Madison, and James Monroe. Preceding and following this unique succession of Virginia Presidents, the Adamses—father and son—served single terms. John Adams, who succeeded Washington, belonged to the era of Federalist supremacy which came to an end at the turn of the 19th century, while his son John Quincy Adams was a transitional President between two eras. The election of the Adamses of Massachusetts and of three Virginia gentlemen who were close political friends gave the Presidency a patrician cast, but the ascendancy of these leaders was due more to talent than to birth, and all five came to office through the path of public service.

Each of them had enjoyed the advantages of economic security and good educational opportunities: The Adamses were graduates of Harvard; Madison graduated from the College of New Jersey (Princeton); Jefferson attended William and Mary before reading law with George Wythe (who also taught John Marshall); and Monroe left William and Mary to join the Continental Army in 1776, then studied law with Jefferson in 1780 and 1781. All of these future Presidents devoted most of their adult years to public service. John Adams was 35 when he took his seat in the Massachusetts General Court in 1770, but he had first gained prominence five years earlier when he attacked the Stamp Act. Jefferson was 25 when elected to the Virginia House of Burgesses. While in college, Madison was unsure of what he wanted to do in life but soon found his calling in public service. He was only 36 at the Constitutional Convention. Monroe was 24 when first elected to the Virginia House of Delegates at the end of the Revolution. John Quincy Adams was not quite 30 when his father became President. Already he had been minister to the Netherlands and in 1797 he would be transferred to Prussia by his father.

All five Presidents from 1797 to 1829 had previously gained substantial experience in diplomacy, where, as Chief Executives, they would exercise their greatest authority. All had served in major diplomatic posts abroad or been Secretary of State, and three of the five had done both. Only John Adams had never headed the State Department, but he had helped negotiate the treaty of peace with Great Britain in 1783 and after-

---

Thomas Jefferson sat twice for portraitist Gilbert Stuart. The second sitting, in 1805, produced the "Edgehill" portrait, preferred by both artist and subject. Stuart refused to give it to Jefferson until 1821, and even then not without a fight.

Entering politics in 1765 as an opponent of the Stamp Act, John Adams served in both Continental Congresses and held several diplomatic posts before being chosen Vice President in 1789.

wards had become the first American minister to the Court of St. James's. Jefferson had been minister to France, then Secretary of State in Washington's Cabinet for nearly four years. Madison, Monroe, and John Quincy Adams each served as Secretary of State under the President he would succeed. In addition, both Monroe and John Quincy Adams had had extensive diplomatic service in Europe. Monroe's major missions included negotiating the purchase of the Louisiana Territory in 1803. Adams spent 12 years in European diplomatic posts before heading the negotiations at Ghent to end the War of 1812.

Each of these five Presidents could also claim considerable prior experience in domestic politics. Both Adams and Jefferson had been members of provincial assemblies before serving together in the Continental Congress on the committee to draft the Declaration of Independence. While Adams and Jefferson were abroad in diplomatic posts at the time of the Constitutional Convention, Madison was in Philadelphia, and indeed was the single most important figure

in drafting the Constitution of the United States. Madison and Monroe served in the first Congress under the new government, one in the House of Representatives, the other in the Senate. John Adams was Washington's Vice President, and Jefferson held that office under Adams. During Jefferson's administration, John Quincy Adams served for five years as a hard-working Senator from Massachusetts. Both Jefferson and Monroe had been governor of Virginia before attaining high national office. Few, if any, periods in American history have brought to the Presidency a succession of leaders with such impressive backgrounds.

Once Washington retired from office, the political parties that had formed in Congress quickly took over the Presidential electoral process and transformed what had appeared about to become a formalized succession—when Adams followed Washington as President—into an effective mechanism by which control of the national government could be transferred from one party to another. This occurred for the first time in 1801 when Jefferson, a Republican, replaced Adams, a Federalist, and the Republicans replaced the Federalists as the majority party in both houses of Congress.

As has been characteristic of major parties throughout American history, the Federalists and the Republicans embraced within a common political allegiance diverse outlooks and interests. In general, however, the Republicans tended to regard the people as more trustworthy than did the Federalists, and they evidenced more concern about individual liberties and freedom of the press. Republicans also were suspicious of standing armies and navies, opposed to a national debt, and likelier than Federalists to insist on a strict interpretation of the Constitution. Jefferson himself proclaimed that he was "for a government rigorously frugal and simple." He believed that the Federalists were trying to steer the new republic on a course not sanctioned by the Constitution, and after his victory in the election of 1800 he spoke of returning the ship of state to its Republican tack.

The role of party was a significant determinant of the style of early American Presidents. John Adams, anxious to emphasize the continuity between his administration and that of the popular first President, kept all of Washington's Cabinet and sought to follow the precedents—political and social—that Washington had introduced. When Jefferson took office in 1801, he made the most dramatic changes in Presi-

Son of a President, John Quincy Adams sat for this portrait by Thomas Sully (1783–1872) shortly after the House of Representatives had decided the 1824 Presidential election in his favor. Sully recorded in his register: "Portrait begun Feb. 28, 1825, finished May 7, 1825."

dential style prior to the inauguration of Andrew Jackson in 1829. He named the first completely new Cabinet since the beginning of Washington's administration, and appointed only Republicans to office.

In addition, Jefferson greatly curtailed the formal ceremonies that Washington had initiated and Adams had adhered to. Instead of delivering his annual message to Congress in person, as Washington and Adams had done, he sent a written text to be read by a clerk, a procedure he regarded as more democratic, less imitative of the "Speech from the Throne" in Great Britain, and more convenient for Congress. Jefferson also dropped the levees, or formal receptions, of the Federalist era. Instead, he gave small dinners without pomp and ceremony, sitting with his guests at a round table that implied an absence of hierarchy.

Much to the discomfort of some foreign ministers to the United States, Jefferson abandoned formal rules of diplomatic etiquette. He offered no seats of honor at his dinner parties. At the same time, he made himself accessible to diplomats who wanted to call informally at the executive mansion and converse directly. President Madison continued this informality, though Mrs. Madison did revive the Presidential levee. Madison was never comfortable at the large, formal Wednesday drawing rooms, however, and Dolley Madison more and more dominated the gatherings.

When James Monroe became President in 1817, he instituted a formal diplomatic etiquette more in line with European customs, and no longer were envoys allowed to meet with the President casually. He also adhered to the accepted rules of ranking at state dinners. Elizabeth Monroe continued Dolley Madison's drawing rooms, the fortnightly receptions that were the major social occasions in Washington not only for members of Congress, diplomats, and public officials, but for private citizens as well (they were open to all who came suitably dressed). Fortnightly receptions continued under John Quincy Adams, but, since practically anyone could now attend, the Adamses also gave weekly dinners when Congress was in session for legislators, diplomats, and other selected guests.

Of all the Presidents before Jackson, Jefferson was the only one who was simultaneously the Chief of State and the head of a political party. Washington considered himself above parties and issued a ringing rebuke of partisanship in his Farewell Address, first published in September 1796. Although John Adams was elected as the Federalist candidate in 1796, he was either unwilling or unable to assume party leadership (a role that Alexander Hamilton, much to Adams's embarrassment, did not hesitate to fill). Still, the Adams administration was clearly partisan. Only Federalists were appointed to office, and a Federalist majority in Congress enacted the Federalist program over Republican opposition. Like Washington, Adams took a stance above parties. But, in reality, the Federalist party was crucial to his success, while his loss of party support undermined his administration and his chances for re-election.

In defeating Adams in 1800, Jefferson did so as the leader of the Republican opposition. His election was a party victory, and, as President, Jefferson remained the head of the party. He kept in touch with state and local party leaders and fostered the growth of Republican strength by means of the appointments he made and the policies he pursued, while at the same time remaining aloof from local party squabbles. With a strong Republican majority in Congress, Jefferson's administration was one in which party played a major role in the process of government.

As Jefferson's closest political confidant and the leading organizer of the early Republican party in Congress, it was only natural for James Madison to become a major figure in Jefferson's Cabinet, and he served for eight years as Secretary of State. With this background, he was Jefferson's logical successor. He might have been expected to act, like Jefferson, as a strong party leader. But Madison was a retiring man who lacked the very qualities that Jefferson possessed most strongly. Moreover, he took office under circumstances less favorable to assertive leadership than Jefferson had enjoyed. In 1800, Jefferson had become the candidate of the Republican party by popular consensus, without even a formal nomination. In 1808, had Madison not been endorsed by the Republican Congressional caucus, his election would have been uncertain. Madison's years in office coincided with a period of Congressional independence, and he never developed the close working relationships in Congress that Jefferson had cultivated and maintained.

C.B.J. Févret de Saint-Mémin's portrait of Thomas Jefferson was drawn with a physiognotrace, a graphic mechanism that provided an accurate profile of the subject's head and shoulders.

Prior to the Jacksonian era there was no general acceptance in the United States of the concept of a legitimate political opposition. Some statesmen such as Hamilton saw political parties as evils to be avoided or even suppressed. Others such as Madison conceded that parties were unavoidable in free governments but thought they should be kept in check. Few argued that parties were a positive good. Even the men who organized the parties tended to regard their own as legitimate and the opposition as subversive. When in power, the Federalist party simply equated itself with the government and viewed the Republicans as a conspiracy to subvert the government. The Republicans, on the other hand, saw themselves as striving to rescue the government from Federalist subversion of the Constitution. When Jefferson became President, he sought to reconcile parties, but soon came to regard Federalists he failed to convert to Republicanism as unworthy of consideration. Jefferson never recognized, while President, the legitimacy of the Federalist opposition.

None of the Jeffersonian leaders was more hostile to parties than Monroe. Assuming the Presidency in 1817, at a time when the Federalists had disappeared as a national party, he regarded himself as a harbinger of a new era freed from the divisive force of partisanship. Monroe sought to reconcile Federalists to his nonpartisan administration, though he stopped short of bringing Federalists into his Cabinet. When John Quincy Adams—a former Federalist who had joined the Republican ranks before the end of Jefferson's Presidency—succeeded Monroe in the White House, he too sought to be free of parties. The election of 1824, in which no candidate gained a majority of electoral votes and the decision had to be made by the House of Representatives, signaled the demise of the first American party system, but it also marked the birth of a second party system that would mature in the 1830s. As President, John Quincy Adams refused to assume a party role, and he went down to defeat in 1828 to a man who had no such qualms—Andrew Jackson—leader of the new Democratic party.

Among the many roles of the early Presidents, none was more important than that of chief diplomat. Washington had established Presidential dominance in the conduct of foreign affairs, and all of his immediate successors—men more experienced in diplomacy than Washington had been—kept control. John Adams defied his own Cabinet and his party in Congress by making decisions on foreign affairs, especially in deciding to send a second peace mission to France in 1799. Jefferson devoted more time to foreign policy than to anything else. Indeed, he regarded the conduct of the external affairs of the nation as the primary purpose of the government in Washington; domestic concerns were to be left as far as possible to the states. As President, Jefferson experienced his greatest success—the Louisiana Purchase—and his great failure—the Embargo of 1807—in the realm of foreign affairs.

Historians still argue over whether it was President Madison or the Congress that led the nation into war against Great Britain in 1812, but Madison's active role in the conduct of foreign relations is a matter of record. Indeed, at the beginning of his Presidency, after Congress blocked his plan to make Albert Gallatin Secretary of State, Madison was largely his own Secretary of State during the two years that the undistinguished Robert Smith held the post. Even after Monroe was brought into the Cabinet in 1811 as Secretary of State, Madison depended upon him more in other areas than in foreign policy.

When Monroe became President in 1817, he relied heavily on his Secretary of State, John Quincy Adams. Yet it was the President himself who announced in his 1823 message to Congress that "the American continents . . . are henceforth not to be considered as subjects for future colonization by any European powers" and stated the other principles that comprised the Monroe Doctrine. John Quincy Adams, who had spent most of his career as a diplomat, naturally retained firm control over the conduct of foreign affairs when he became President, yielding supremacy in that area to no one, including his Secretary of State, Henry Clay.

By rendezvousing with the troops sent to suppress the Whiskey Rebellion in 1793, Washington had clearly affirmed the role of the President as Commander-in-Chief. But Washington was a general, and not until Andrew Jackson would another general be elected President. Of the five Presidents in between, only Monroe had ever seen active military duty. Previous military command, however, did not determine Presidential willingness to exercise the powers of Commander-in-Chief. No President has been less militaristic than Jefferson, yet Jefferson did not hesitate to exert his authority as Commander-in-Chief soon after taking office, when he ordered a fleet to the Mediterranean to suppress the Barbary pirates. On the other hand, during the war scare with France in 1798 John Adams had nearly relinquished the role of Commander-in-Chief, by appointing Washington as the commanding general and permitting him to name Alexander Hamilton as second in command.

When the United States entered the War of 1812 militarily unprepared and with both the War Department and Navy Department headed by incompetents, Madison could hardly avoid assuming the role of Commander-in-Chief. Because of difficulties in finding capable administrators and military commanders, he remained directly involved in the conduct of the war and incidentally revealed the problems that could be entailed when a President actively pursued the role of Commander-in-Chief. Madison did not seek broad powers, as other Presidents did in subsequent wars.

The U.S. deployed only a small regular army made up of volunteers and raw militia, poorly equipped and supplied, and with few capable commanders. The Navy, though its manpower was efficient and well trained, had but 16 seagoing vessels.

The lack of a national bank deprived the government of any centralized machinery for financing the war effort. Still, Madison's faith in republicanism seemed vindicated when the nation survived the war in spite of its haphazard mobilization of military and economic resources.

President Monroe was presented with an embarrassing situation by General Andrew Jackson's unauthorized seizure of Spanish posts in Florida in 1818. The dismissal of Jackson would have forcefully affirmed Monroe's power as Commander-in-Chief. But, while he made it clear to Jackson that he had exceeded his authority, Monroe refrained from dismissing him because Jackson's actions did provide an opportunity to pressure Spain to cede Florida.

In their role as Chief Executive, the early Presidents were expected to administer the government directly. John Adams drew strong criticism when he left department heads in charge of the government while he returned home to Braintree, Massachusetts, for long periods of time. But Jefferson took personal charge of administrative matters, staying on the job continuously, except for a short spring vacation after Congress had adjourned and two summer months when he, in effect, moved the Presidential office to Monticello. Washington had initiated this summer recess, and Jefferson's successors continued the practice.

As for a White House staff, all of the Presidents had a private secretary, but they had to pay for his services out of their own pockets. Jefferson, who penned all of his letters and most of his speeches himself, employed his secretary primarily as an aide-de-camp to carry messages to the Congress, greet guests at the executive mansion, and conduct an occasional confidential mission. John Quincy Adams's son served his father as private secretary, though neither he nor any other copyist could read his father's shorthand. While no President before Jackson employed a speech writer, they all relied on members of their Cabinets to supply portions of their annual messages to Congress. With department offices in Washington located near the executive mansion, it was the Cabinet officers who worked most closely with the President. There were almost daily contacts among them; Cabinet meetings could be called on short notice, and the President himself could walk to department offices if necessary.

The early Presidents spent much time dealing personally with official appointments. Jefferson read every application and recommendation sent to him

Presidential medal depicts James Madison; the reverse image symbolizes goodwill. Such medals were often given to Indian chieftains as tokens of friendship. Madison, born in Virginia, and a graduate of the College of New Jersey (Princeton), earned the title "master builder of the Constitution" at the Constitutional Convention of 1787.

and compiled long lists of applicants with notes on their qualifications. He regarded making appointments as the most onerous task of the Presidency. John Quincy Adams found the supplications of office seekers even more oppressive. In Jefferson's day, they had generally applied by letter or through friends and Congressmen. By the time John Quincy Adams became President, more and more job seekers sought personal interviews. Adams's diary reveals his frequent weariness with their interruptions. Indeed, he tired of the steady stream of visitors in general. After one particularly busy day, he noted that he could "scarcely conceive a more harassing, wearying, teasing condition of existence. It literally renders life burdensome."

President Jefferson rose at five in the morning, devoted the hours before breakfast to writing, and after nine was ready to receive members of Congress, department heads, and other visitors. Cabinet meetings were commonly scheduled around noon. At one in the afternoon Jefferson usually went for a ride on horseback. At 3:30, he had dinner, frequently inviting individual dinner guests for private consultations a half-hour beforehand. Guests usually departed by six, and Jefferson, who never accepted evening invitations, spent another four hours with paperwork before retiring at 10. After six months in office he wrote that his routine had "now got to a steady and uniform course. It keeps me from 10 to 12 and 13 hours a day at my writing table, giving me an interval of 4 hours for riding, dining and a little unbending."

Twenty-four years later, at the beginning of his Presidency, John Quincy Adams described a daily routine that—except for Bible reading—was not greatly different from Jefferson's, though it did suggest increasing intrusions on the President's time. In his diary for April 30, 1825, Adams recorded:

Since my removal to the Presidental mansion I rise about five; read two chapters of Scott's Bible and Commentary, and the corresponding commentary of Hewlett; then the morning newspapers, and public papers from the several Departments; write seldom, and not enough; breakfast an hour, from nine to ten; then have a succession of visitors, upon business, in search of place, solicitors for donations, or for mere curiosity, from eleven till between four and five o'clock. The heads of Departments of course occupy much of this time. Between four and six I take a walk of three or four miles. Dine from about half-past

James Monroe sat twice for the French-schooled portraitist, John Vanderlyn. This painting was done in 1816, when he was President-elect; the other (see page 30) dates from 1822.

five till seven, and from dark till about eleven I generally pass the evening in my chamber, signing land-grants or blank patents, in the interval of which, for the last ten days, I have brought up three months of arrears in my diary index. About eleven I retire to bed. My evenings are not so free from interruption as I had hoped and expected they would be.

In warmer weather Adams substituted early morning swims in the Potomac River for evening walks. Later he switched his walks to the early morning also, explaining that "it is established by custom that the President of the United States does not go abroad into any private companies; and to this usage I conform. I am, therefore, compelled to take my exercise, if at all, in the morning before breakfast." A capital in which Thomas Jefferson could ride undisturbed on horseback and John Quincy Adams could swim unnoticed in the Potomac did much to set the tone for the Presidency. The Presidents continued to live remarkably private lives.

While a citizen who journeyed to Washington could expect to see or even meet the President, direct contacts between the President and the American people in the country at large were few. In a society that was still largely deferential, Presidential candidates did not openly campaign for office. At times, they engaged in letter writing, circulation of political literature, and behind-the-scenes organizing of campaign activities, but they gave no speeches and made no electioneering tours. Presidential traveling was largely restricted to trips back and forth between the capital and home. Washington had toured New England and the southern states, but nobody followed his example until Monroe, who also made tours to New England and to the South and West.

Washington's tours came at the beginning of the new government under the Constitution; Monroe made his in the period of renewed nationalism that followed the end of the War of 1812. Both Presidents were concerned with promoting national unity. Aside from these major exceptions, though, travel to promote contact with the American public was not part of the style of the early Presidents. When John Quincy Adams was invited by the Maryland Agricultural Society to attend its cattle show and exhibition of domestic manufactures near Baltimore, he declined—not only because this would take time from his duties but also because he disapproved of the whole idea. "From cattle-shows to other public meetings for the purposes of utility or exposures of public sentiment, the transition is natural and easy," he thought—and he wanted no part in encouraging such a trend. During his annual trips home to Massachusetts, he tried to avoid any public display.

No President in the young republic regarded himself as the chief legislator, although all made legislative proposals in their annual and special messages to Congress, and Thomas Jefferson went considerably beyond that. With the aim of getting his legislative program enacted, Jefferson employed various techniques that would become characteristic of strong Presidents. He kept in contact with key members of Congress. He personally drafted bills and sent them to friendly legislators to introduce.

Members of his Cabinet did likewise, and also worked directly with House and Senate committees to push legislation through Congress. Three days each week when Congress was in session, Jefferson invited legislators to dine with him at the executive mansion.

Jefferson's influence on Congress was enhanced by his immense popular support, and he was skillful at bargaining to advance administration policies. His three successors, however, exercised far less influence on Capitol Hill. Madison was repeatedly forced to yield to Congress, which even went so far as to keep him from forming his own Cabinet as he wanted it. Monroe's Cabinet was composed of leaders who were virtually independent and had personal followings in Congress; thus, all administration proposals for legislation had to be hammered out in the Cabinet before ever being sent to Congress.

The only truly strong executive between Washington and Jackson was Jefferson. During most of John Adams's Presidency, the Cabinet was dominated by men whose first loyalty was to Alexander Hamilton. The scholarly Madison—though he had been effective in the Constitutional Convention, the Congress, and the Cabinet—turned out to be an ineffective President. Monroe was more successful than Madison in asserting leadership, but his power was circumscribed by his Cabinet, whose support was essential to any Presidential initiative. Monroe enjoyed greater popular support than Madison, who had come close to being defeated when he stood for re-election in 1812— DeWitt Clinton of New York carried all of New England except Vermont and all the middle states except Pennsylvania. In contrast, Monroe won a second term by a nearly unanimous vote in the Electoral College (231 of 235), yet even this margin of victory did not increase his influence over Congress.

John Quincy Adams's leadership potential was irreparably weakened as a result of the election of 1824 having to be decided in the House of Representatives. His appointment of his erstwhile rival Henry Clay as Secretary of State gave rise to charges of a "corrupt bargain" by the partisans of Andrew Jackson, who actually garnered more popular votes and more electoral votes than either Adams or Clay (or a fourth candidate, William H. Crawford, who had been Monroe's Secretary of the Treasury), yet had to wait four more years to gain office.

None of the Presidents before Jackson acted upon or even articulated the theory that the President, elected by the people of the whole nation, was more representative of the national will than was the Congress. The constitutional principle of separation of powers prevailed, and no branch of government was supreme either in theory or practice. No President assumed that he could substitute his opinion for that of Congress, except where constitutional issues were at stake. Thus, the veto power was used sparingly. Neither John Adams, nor Jefferson, nor John Quincy Adams used it at all, and Monroe did so only once. In vetoing seven measures, Madison was the exception among the early Presidents.

American Presidents at the beginning of the 19th century were not world leaders. When Frances Wright returned to England after her visit to America in 1818 and 1819, she found that many of her countrymen who questioned her about the new nation confused the President of the United States with the president of the Senate (the Vice President). Jefferson, Monroe, and both the Adamses were known in Europe from their diplomatic service there, but the nation they represented did not command attention comparable to that of the great world powers.

The United States in fact was a minor power, newly emerging from colonial status; its leaders received little notice in the foreign press or among the ruling circles of Europe. Jefferson's election in 1800—which

After leaving the White House, John Quincy Adams served in Congress from 1831 to 1848, and became known as "Old Man Eloquent."

he regarded as a revolution nearly as important as that of 1776—was noticed only passingly in a Europe where Napoleon had come to power 16 months earlier. American grievances that led to the War of 1812 grew mainly out of the wars in Europe, exacerbated by England's concentration on the struggle against Napoleon. By contrast the American problem seemed secondary. In 1823 no one talked about the Monroe Doctrine, because the world knew that British naval power—not a mere pronouncement by the American President—had thwarted European intervention in Latin America. The early American Presidents were aware of their lack of influence over the affairs of Europe, and they were all the more conscious of the necessity of maintaining the strength of the Presidency in preserving the independence of the United States.

Both the country and the nation's capital grew and changed greatly between 1800, when John Adams moved the government from Philadelphia to Washington, and 1829, when John Quincy Adams left the White House. It was inevitable that the office of the President would also change. When John Quincy Adams turned the Presidency over to Andrew Jackson on the steps of the Capitol on March 4, 1829, before a crowd of thousands, the oath of office was administered to the new President by Chief Justice John Marshall, who had administered the same oath to Thomas Jefferson in the Senate chamber in 1801. Marshall was a symbol of continuity in a government which in four decades had established its permanence and stability. Yet the eyes of the people who had thronged to Washington for the ceremony were focused not upon Marshall but upon Jackson, and they seemed to sense an impending change in the tone and style of the American Presidency.

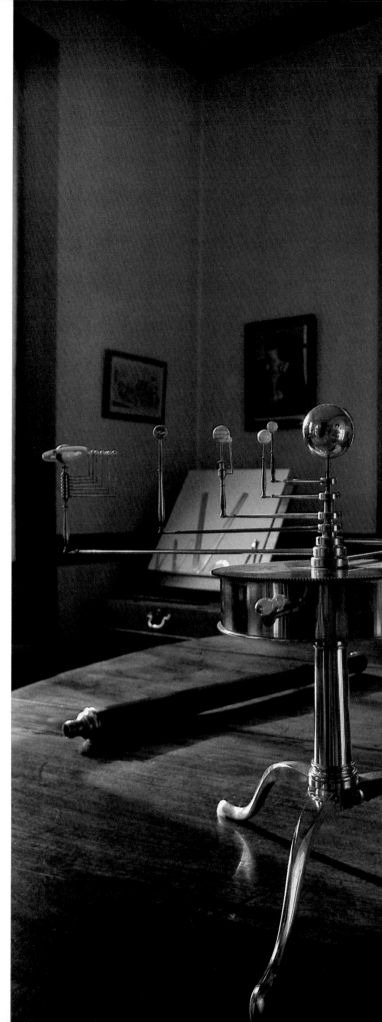

Thomas Jefferson was America's Renaissance man par excellence. Apparatus pictured is suggestive of his interest in science and invention. In foreground at right is a brass orrery—a model of the solar system—of the kind Jefferson was familiar with. Multiple-writing device, top, is one of eight such "polygraphs" that Jefferson owned. Above, aquatint, 1798, was done after a drawing by Polish patriot Tadeusz Kościuszko.

★ ★ ★ ★ ★ ★ ★ ★ ★ ★ ★ ★ ★

They Weren't All Lawyers

Michael L. Lawson

American mythology would have our Presidents spouting democratic maxims from their infant cribs and aspiring as adolescents to command the ship of state. Actually, few of the eventual occupants of the White House, even at middle age, ever considered themselves destined to lead the nation. Most arrived at the office only through a combination of circumstance, happenstance, and fortuity which has, often as not, had little to do with individual talent.

True, the majority of our Presidents spent their formative years in the political arena, with nearly half being elected to some sort of public office before they were 30. Over two-thirds graduated from college, and over half practiced law. Twenty-four served in the armed forces, 10 of whom were generals, and, though we have yet to elect an admiral, the most recent Presidents have all been former naval officers. Perhaps the biggest disparity among these 39 men has been in their affluence. A few have enjoyed a silver-spooned upbringing; many more have known poverty. It has only been during the present century, in fact, that we have consistently chosen men of substantial wealth.

In looking about for Presidents whose prior careers differ substantially from established norms, we find at least six who seem worthy of closer examination: Thomas Jefferson, who came the closest of any American to embodying the 18th-century ideal of a universal genius; Andrew Johnson, who never had a day of formal schooling; Ulysses S. Grant, an utter failure in civilian life; Woodrow Wilson, the only man ever to rise to the Presidency out of academia; Herbert Hoover, the multimillionaire mining engineer; and Harry S Truman, the ex-haberdasher who at 38 showed the least promise of any man who ever became President.

★ ★ ★

Addressing a group of Nobel laureates in 1962, John F. Kennedy described his guests as "the

Andrew Johnson used these shears in his tailor's craft. His shop in Tennessee became a political gathering place.

During eight years of civilian life, Ulysses S. Grant failed miserably as a farmer and a clerk in his father's leather goods store (right). Christmastime of 1857 found him so destitute that he had to pawn his watch (receipt, inset).

most extraordinary collection of talent . . . that has ever been gathered together at the White House—with the possible exception of when Thomas Jefferson dined alone." Far from offending this assembly of genius, Kennedy was merely acknowledging the fact that few individuals, and certainly no other Chief Executives, have matched the accomplishments of the man who was our third President.

Born in Albemarle County, Virginia, in 1743, Jefferson was given every opportunity to indulge his curiosity while his brilliant mind was being cultivated by an encouraging father, competent tutors, and the intellectual mentors of the College of William and Mary. Upon graduation at age 19, he entered an apprenticeship in law. By the time he was 26 he had established himself as a successful lawyer and an outspoken member of the Virginia House of Burgesses.

In addition, the wide range of intellectual interests that Jefferson pursued, and the variety of skills he developed beyond mere proficiency, is simply incredible. Besides becoming a pre-eminent statesman and the author of the Declaration of Independence, this native incarnation of the

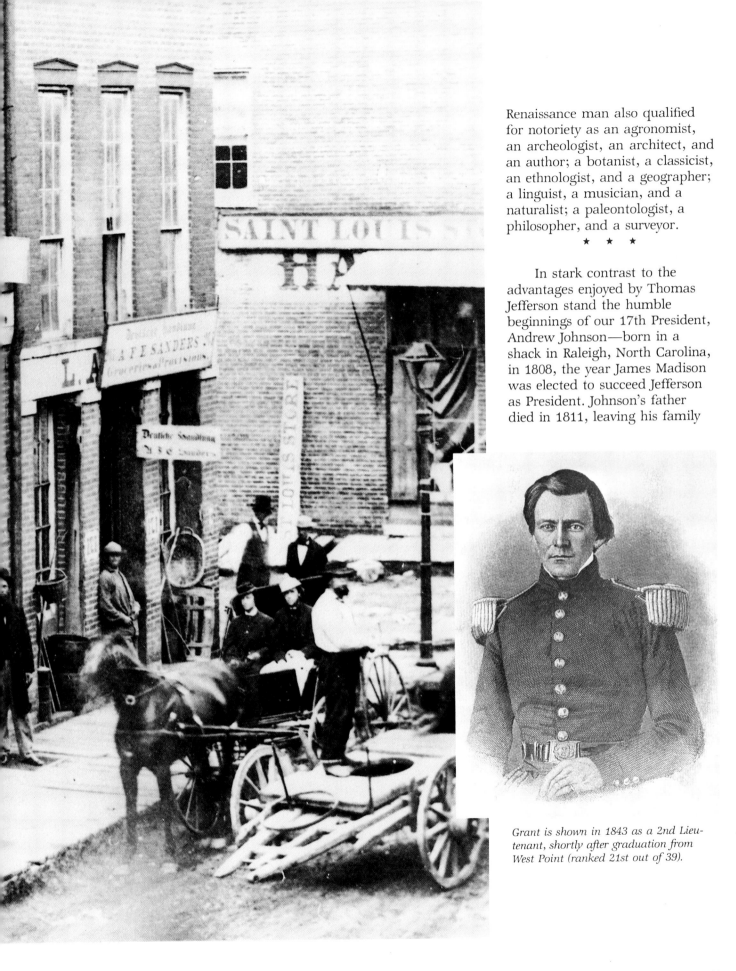

Renaissance man also qualified for notoriety as an agronomist, an archeologist, an architect, and an author; a botanist, a classicist, an ethnologist, and a geographer; a linguist, a musician, and a naturalist; a paleontologist, a philosopher, and a surveyor.

★ ★ ★

In stark contrast to the advantages enjoyed by Thomas Jefferson stand the humble beginnings of our 17th President, Andrew Johnson—born in a shack in Raleigh, North Carolina, in 1808, the year James Madison was elected to succeed Jefferson as President. Johnson's father died in 1811, leaving his family

Grant is shown in 1843 as a 2nd Lieutenant, shortly after graduation from West Point (ranked 21st out of 39).

From 1890 to 1910 Woodrow Wilson was successively a professor at Princeton, then its president.

destitute. When "Andy" was 14, he and his brother Bill were indentured to serve a seven-year apprenticeship to a local tailor. The tailor arranged to have someone read to them while they worked. Thus stimulated, young Johnson gradually taught himself to read and write.

In 1824, Andy and Bill ran away to a nearby town. Their angered master posted a $10 reward for the return of his apprentices but did not bother to search them out. When the boys came back after a two-year absence to apologize and accept their former status, they found that the tailor was not inclined to forgiveness. With the threat of prosecution hanging over their heads, they moved with their mother to the mountains of eastern Tennessee, and finally settled in Greeneville in 1827. Here, at age 18, Andy opened up his own tailor shop in a tiny log cabin and married Eliza McArdle, the daughter of the local shoemaker.

Fascinated with the art of public speaking, Johnson joined two local college debating societies, where his forensic abilities soon began to attract attention. The people of Greeneville elected their tailor to the town council in 1828. Two years later, when he was only 22, they made him their mayor. Johnson's appeal could not be denied. As he continued to grow in skill and stature, his backers sent him to the Tennessee legislature, the governor's mansion, the House of Representatives, and the Senate, before President Lincoln made him his running mate in 1864.

Johnson never lost his identification with the working class or his craftsman's pride in having made his way by the sweat of his brow. Even as governor he insisted on cutting a coat for an old friend. This gift was accompanied by a letter which proclaimed that "the main highway and the surest passport to honesty and useful distinction will soon be through the harvest field and the workshop."

★   ★   ★

Ulysses S. Grant, Johnson's successor as President, did not grow up in abject poverty, yet he showed absolutely no distinction as a youth. Consequently, he surprised everyone by gaining an appointment to the United States Military Academy in 1839. Although he proved to be a slovenly cadet and an indifferent scholar, he was graduated in 1843. After the Mexican War, Grant was promoted to captain and stationed near St. Louis. Here he met and married Julia Dent, the daughter of a local planter.

In 1852, Grant was assigned to the Pacific Coast where he could not afford to bring his family. Lonely and bored, he began to drink compulsively. He had little tolerance for alcohol, and small amounts would transform him into a boisterous rowdy. Unfortunately, his few sprees have served to obscure his many years of quiet sobriety.

Discovered drunk in public by his commanding officer in 1853, Grant quit the service rather than face a court-martial. Returning to his family in Missouri, he accepted a 60-acre farm from his father-in-law, which he hoped to turn into a profitable enterprise. During the panic of 1857 he watched his dreams collapse along with the plummeting crop prices. Grant then took over management of the Dent family's "White Haven" farm, but proved no more successful despite its better land and equipment. Stricken for a year with "fever and ague," he was reduced to squalor. In 1857, two days before Christmas, he was compelled to pawn his watch in order to provide some holiday cheer for his growing family of five.

After he lost two jobs in St. Louis, Grant's younger brothers took pity on him and offered him a clerk's position in the leather goods store they managed for their father in Galena, Illinois. But he grew increasingly withdrawn, unkempt, and forgetful. When entrusted to sell a horse, he let a stranger take it away without paying.

In eight years Grant had shown little ability to adapt to a civilian career. But with the outbreak of the Civil War in 1861, he again came alive, donned his uniform, and began an incredible rise to prominence. Four years later, when—as general in charge of all of the Union armies—he accepted Robert E. Lee's surrender at Appomattox Courthouse, he was second only to Lincoln in the nation's esteem.

★   ★   ★

At 39, the age at which Grant rejoined the Army and began to extricate himself from the depths of failure, our 28th President, Thomas Woodrow Wilson, had already established himself as one of the nation's leading scholars. Professor of jurisprudence and political economy at Princeton, he also was a widely read author and celebrity on the lecture circuit.

Although born amid comfortable circumstances in Virginia in 1856, Wilson was beset by chronic frail health. Like Jefferson, however, he had the compensatory advantage of an encouraging father—a Presbyterian minister who challenged him to set the loftiest moral and intellectual goals for himself.

"Tommy" entered Davidson College at age 16, but fell ill during his first year and had to spend 16 months recuperating. Transferring to Princeton in 1875, he excelled at oratory and debate. Upon graduation he enrolled in law school at the University of Virginia, but delicate health forced him to finish his studies at home.

Wilson was admitted to the bar in Georgia in 1882, and began to practice in Atlanta. He soon found the legal profession unstimulating, however, and decided to enter Johns Hopkins University (then the nation's premier graduate school) to study public administration. Wilson spent two years writing *Congressional Government*, an analysis of the parliamentary system that was published in 1885. This work, which was accepted as Wilson's doctoral dissertation, earned its 29-year-old author immediate esteem as a political scientist.

After teaching at Bryn Mawr and at Wesleyan, Wilson jumped at the opportunity to return to Princeton in 1890 as a full professor. There, he built a reputation at the forefront of American scholarship, and in 1902 he was chosen as Princeton's president. During the next eight years, he enjoyed remarkable success in revamping the curriculum, raising standards, and introducing a new tutorial system.

But he also fought many battles with alumni and faculty, and he ultimately grew disenchanted with academia. Filing as the Democratic candidate for governor of New Jersey, he resigned his position at Princeton in the fall of 1910. After a vigorous campaign, he was elected to his first public office at age 54. He was as successful as a political practitioner as he had been as a

Managing mining enterprises for a British firm, 24-year-old Herbert Hoover (standing) posed in Australia in 1898.

theoretician, and moved from the governor's mansion to the White House in just two years, following his national victory in 1912.

★ ★ ★

Sixteen years after the American people chose as their President a university educator with minimal political experience, they picked an engineer who had never been elected to any public office. Born in West Branch, Iowa, and left an orphan at three, Herbert Hoover was reared by various aunts and uncles in Iowa, Oklahoma, and Oregon. Although he did not complete high school, he was permitted in 1891 to enroll in the new tuition-free university founded by Senator Leland Stanford in California. Here young "Bert" majored in geology and supported himself through various odd jobs. Classmates reported that he "practically lived in the geology lab," but he did find time to date another would-be geologist, Lou Henry, his future bride.

Upon graduation in 1895, Hoover took a job pushing ore cars at a Nevada City gold mine in order to see the operation firsthand. Two years later, impressed by Hoover's combination of training and experience, the British mining firm of Bewick, Moreing, & Co., hired him. First he managed mines in western Australia, then he became the company's representative in China, and in 1901 he was made a junior partner. He spent the next seven years circling the globe in search of profitable mines, introducing and perfect-

ing a number of technological improvements. In Burma in 1904 he discovered the astonishing silver and zinc deposits which later became the chief source of his own fortune.

Internationally recognized by 1908, Hoover went into business on his own as a consultant. His *Principles of Mining* became a standard textbook for a generation of engineers. Having once remarked that if a man "has not made a million dollars by the time he was forty, he was not worth much," this orphaned son of an Iowa blacksmith was reported, at 36, to be worth at least three million.

With the outbreak of World War I, Hoover left engineering to pursue a variety of humanitarian endeavors, first as head of the Commission for Belgian Relief and then as America's wartime food administrator. Gradually he became involved in Republican politics, and served as Secretary of Commerce in the Harding and Coolidge administrations. In 1929 he became the Chief Executive himself after promising to use all of the skills he had acquired as a self-made man to put an end to the nation's poverty.

★ ★ ★

In May of 1919, just as Hoover was winding up his outstanding service as food administrator, Harry S Truman celebrated his 35th birthday. Truman had less to show for those 35 years than any other man who ever became President, his only distinction being his recent service as an artillery captain in France.

Returning to his home town of Independence, Missouri, after his discharge, Truman married Elizabeth Wallace, his sweetheart since fifth grade, and went into

business with his old friend Eddie Jacobson. Having done well running the canteen at an army post, Truman and Jacobson vowed to parlay this experience into operation of a men's furnishings store in Kansas City. In 1919 they leased a choice downtown location and stocked it with quality merchandise. But just as they were beginning to realize a good return on their investment the clothiers Truman

Harry S Truman had served during the war as an artillery officer in France. Back home in 1919, Truman (above, far left) confidently opened a haberdashery with a wartime buddy. But their business failed as a result of the postwar depression.

and Jacobson were hit by the recession of 1921. Falling hopelessly into debt as their sales dwindled, they were forced to close the next year.

Harry Truman seemed even less destined to prominence at 38 than he had three years before. As it turned out, however, one of his good customers, Mike Pendergast, the brother of Kansas City's political boss Tom Pendergast, helped him get elected to a district judgeship in the fall of 1922. From this position, and with the continued support of the Pendergast machine, Truman was able to launch his political career.

★ ★ ★

The fact that Harry S Truman has consistently been rated as one of our finest Presidents begs the question of the relevancy of prior professions to Presidential greatness. No one is surprised that Jefferson is rated near the top or Grant near the bottom, or even that Andrew Johnson is in the average range on most Presidential polls. Yet, would one also expect, based on their prior achievements, to find Wilson among the outstanding and Hoover among the mediocre?

A review of Presidential history might lead to the conclusion that professional soldiers make poor Presidents or that governors make better Chief Executives than do legislators. But, while the basic qualifications may never change, the process by which an individual grows up to be President—as well as individual performance in office—will probably never be predictable.

George
Washington
1732–1799

John
Adams
1735–1826

Thomas
Jefferson
1743–1826

James
Madison
1751–1836

James
Monroe
1758–1831

John Quincy
Adams
1767–1848

Andrew
Jackson
1767–1845

Martin
Van Buren
1782–1862

James Knox
Polk
1795–1849

Zachary
Taylor
1784–1850

Millard
Fillmore
1800–1874

Franklin
Pierce
1804–1869

James
Buchanan
1791–1868

Abraham
Lincoln
1809–1865

Andrew
Johnson
1808–1875

Ulysses S.
Grant
1822–1885

Chester A.
Arthur
1830–1886

Grover
Cleveland
1837–1908

Benjamin
Harrison
1833–1901

Grover
Cleveland
1837–1908

William
McKinley
1843–1901

Theodore
Roosevelt
1858–1919

William Howard
Taft
1857–1930

Woodrow
Wilson
1856–1924

Herbert
Hoover
1874–1964

Franklin Delano
Roosevelt
1882–1945

Harry S
Truman
1884–1972

Dwight D.
Eisenhower
1890–1969

John F.
Kennedy
1917–1963

Lyndon B.
Johnson
1908–1973

Richard M.
Nixon
1913–

Gerald R.
Ford
1913–

William Henry
Harrison
1773–1841

John
Tyler
1790–1862

Rutherford B.
Hayes
1822–1893

James A.
Garfield
1831–1881

Warren G.
Harding
1865–1923

Calvin
Coolidge
1872–1933

Jimmy
Carter
1924–

★ ★ ★ ★ ★ ★ ★ ★ ★ ★ ★ ★ ★

Presidential Stature

James K. Page, Jr.

Most Americans look up to their President, regardless of whether they agree with him. I remember hearing men of my grandfather's time excoriate FDR as "that *man*" and far worse, but still they were very much aware of his authority. A lot more people looked up to Truman—the shortest of modern Presidents— than pollsters in 1948 imagined. Clearly Presidential stature means something other than the incumbent's size.

Or does it? As we have learned from Professor Morris at the beginning of this book, just about everybody looked up to George Washington, yet one cannot help feeling that part of this was, indeed, due to his very imposing size. Remember, in an era before we started growing professional basketball and foot-ball players, a man like Washing-ton—who was six feet-two, with the enormous hands of a farmer and size 13 feet—must have seemed gigantic. The inclination when dealing with giants is to

say, "Yes, sir." In addition, Wash-ington's mien invited little famili-arity: Nobody ever dared tag him with a nickname.

John Adams's manner was every bit as lofty—even haughty— but he was a bookish person, an intellectual, and neither a man of action nor a commanding presence. And he was short, about five-seven. Indeed, when as Vice President he sought the kind of deference that Washington was accorded automatically, people just laughed up their sleeves and dubbed him "His Rotundity." Thomas Jefferson on the other hand was as tall as Washington, though slender and thus not so imposing. As unpre-tentious as Adams was puffy, he was perfectly happy being called "Long Tom."

Tall, short, tall. A pattern emerges that persisted, save for a one-month aberration, until the middle of the 19th century. "Jemmy" Madison, five feet-four, weighed less than 100 pounds. Washington Irving called this ti-niest of American Presidents a

At left, the Presidents are posed against a six-foot line. Dates here indicate life-span; dates on the following pages denote

terms in office. The last of these sil-houettes by Peter Copeland is suggestive of a future victor, still unidentified.

Hickory, Andrew Jackson, was six-one and very lean. The Little Magician, Martin Van Buren, five-six, played Mutt to Jackson's Jeff, a sequence that had remained unbroken as eight Presidents came and went. Only when Old Tippecanoe, Benjamin Harrison, five-eight, thwarted Van Buren's try for a second term in 1840 was a short President succeeded by another short one. The broken pattern was quickly repaired, though, when Harrison died after only 31 days in office, and Vice President John Tyler, an even six feet, took over. James K. Polk, five-eight, had extended its persistence to 60 years by the time he left office to return to Tennessee in 1849.

After Old Rough and Ready, Zachary Taylor, moved into the White House, however, a new pattern emerged—a steady upward curve. Taylor was five-eight, the same as Polk. His successor, Millard Fillmore, was five-nine. Next came Franklin Pierce, five-ten, and James Buchanan, six feet. Then, in 1861, Presidential stature hit a zenith with Abraham Lincoln, six-four, which was not matched until more than a century later, by another westerner, Lyndon Baines Johnson.

Lincoln's postwar successors fit no pattern. Andrew Johnson was five-ten, Grant and Hayes both five-eight, Garfield six feet,

Arthur six-two, Cleveland five-eleven, Harrison five-six, and McKinley five-seven. Teddy Roosevelt, who brought to the office a drive and flamboyancy never before seen, was five-ten. Only one other President in the entire 20th century has been shorter than that (Harry Truman, five-nine), and the average, indeed, has been just shy of six feet.

★   ★   ★

What are we to make of all this? Is it merely trivial? A case can be made (and its maker can also get in a lot of arguments) that those Presidents who have

"withered little apple-john." Next came James Monroe, the last of the Virginia dynasty, an imposing six-footer distinctly reminiscent in appearance of George Washington himself.

Monroe's successor, John Quincy Adams, was the same height as his father, five-seven, and likewise roly-poly. Old

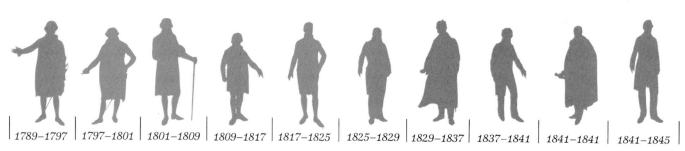

| 1789–1797 | 1797–1801 | 1801–1809 | 1809–1817 | 1817–1825 | 1825–1829 | 1829–1837 | 1837–1841 | 1841–1841 | 1841–1845 |

fundamentally altered the dimensions of the office tend to be tall—or at least (to weasel a bit) robust and strong.

Washington and Lincoln were renowned in their youth for extraordinary physical feats. Teddy Roosevelt, the first Presidential jogger, would have been the envy of today's physical fitness fanatics. An exception: Woodrow Wilson, five-ten, and not what you would call an athlete (he played baseball at the University of Virginia but thought athletics overemphasized at Princeton when he was *its* president). On the other hand, there are those who would not include Wilson among the great, great Presidents, either.

It goes without saying that size does not necessarily confer upon a President the mantle of greatness, for Chester A. Arthur and Warren G. Harding were both strapping six-footers. While Arthur was something more than "a nonentity with side-whiskers" (as Wilson unkindly characterized him), he has never made anyone's pantheon, nor has Harding, with whose own assessment it is hard to quarrel: "I knew that this job would be too much for me."

The two obese Presidents—Grover Cleveland at 260 pounds and William Howard Taft, well over 300—are yet to dominate Presidential histories except in sheer bulk. Taft's feet always hurt, not surprisingly, and he regularly dozed off at meetings. "Taft meant well," said his one-time mentor, Theodore Roosevelt, "but he meant well feebly."

★   ★   ★

To pry any further insight out of this perhaps irrelevant array of data, I headed off for the National Museum of Natural History and, in that milieu, was reminded that the leader of a wolf pack—the alpha male—is generally the largest. War chiefs of preliterate tribes were frequently the big guys and, if not (or even if so), wore large war bonnets of one sort or another that made them all the more awesome. Perhaps, then, there is something atavistic in our genes that makes us inclined to seek, and admire, a big President.

| 1845–1849 | 1849–1850 | 1850–1853 | 1853–1857 | 1857–1861 | 1861–1865 | 1865–1869 | 1869–1877 | 1877–1881 | 1881–1881 |

Yet surely we must have outgrown all these primitive instincts from the dawn of our evolution. We are civilized; more and more of our industry is becoming miniaturized. Furthermore, recent research suggests that, in an energy-and-food-scarce world, we are better off with smaller rather than larger people. Should we not then have a diminutive President? After all, we have television which brings the President into our very living rooms. Who cares how big he is? He is exactly as big as a TV screen, a kind of abstraction, however familiar, and certainly his physical size has nothing to do with the matter. Everything is done with lenses . . . and therein, I soon realized, lies a clue to unraveling the morphology of Presidential leadership.

Returning from the Natural History Museum and passing through the Smithsonian Castle to my office, I was reminded of two incidents which in turn brought me to a brand new post-industrial theory concerning the anatomy of Presidents. The second incident occurred in the Castle nearly a decade ago, the

first in New York City, a few years earlier.

I was walking along Fifth Avenue and saw Lee Marvin, the actor, walking in the same direction. As is my wont when I see celebrities, I trotted up to him and said, "Hello, Mr. Marvin." As I presume is his wont, he glowered at me and I receded back into the throng. But not before noticing something striking. Lee Marvin's face appeared extraordinarily large compared to his overall size (which is itself alarmingly imposing). I wondered if this was simply because his face was so familiar that it appeared large to me, or whether the very quality of being *photogenic* by motion picture and television cameras requires a disproportionately large face. I remembered once being told that TV tends to shrink people's heads.

The other incident took place at the opening ceremony for the Woodrow Wilson International Center for Scholars, a research institution located in the Smithsonian Castle. The celebrants who gathered in the Great Hall included Hubert Humphrey, then the center's chairman of the board. He was joined on the dais by President Richard Nixon. As the two recent combatants sat next to each other, smiling and making apparently cordial noises to one another, I was struck again by the Marvin syndrome. I will swear (until confronted with

1881–1885 | 1885–1889 | 1889–1893 | 1893–1897 | 1897–1901 | 1901–1909 | 1909–1913 | 1913–1921 | 1921–1923 | 1923–1929

evidence to the contrary) that Mr. Nixon's face is larger compared to his body than was Mr. Humphrey's. Both were celebrities, of course, so I ruled out any psychological eye-brain distortion simply because one face was known—like Lee Marvin's—while the other was unknown.

★ ★ ★

So there it is, for what it is worth: the Telegenic Corollary. Electability varies proportionately to the ratio of a candidate's facial size relative to that of his body. This of course demands research of a more precise nature than a layman can perform. It requires a physiognomic analysis more intimate, perhaps, than any candidate would permit, and a

statistical analysis to tax MIT's computers. Yet it might just be the predictive (if not selective) theorem we all are so anxious for.

It applies only to the age of television, of course, so there is no point in considering Presidents prior to Ike. A television critic for *The Washington Post* recently offered the opinion, by the way, that Ike looked great in black and white but probably couldn't have made it on color TV. He missed the point. Eisenhower was a transitional President *vis à vis* television; not until the 1960s did Presidents use, or try to use, the medium to its fullest potential. Ike couldn't have. If examination of photographs of the General serves me right, Eisenhower was the last of the little-faced Presidents.

If the foregoing look at Presidential stature suggests anything, then, it suggests that President makers should be looking for a candidate with an athletic background whose face is telegenically larger than his body would otherwise call for. And then, of course, they should leave it to the voters.

| 1929–1933 | 1933–1945 | 1945–1953 | 1953–1961 | 1961–1963 | 1963–1969 | 1969–1974 | 1974–1977 | 1977– |

$1200
TO
1550 DOLLARS!

NEGROES

H. D. Thoreau

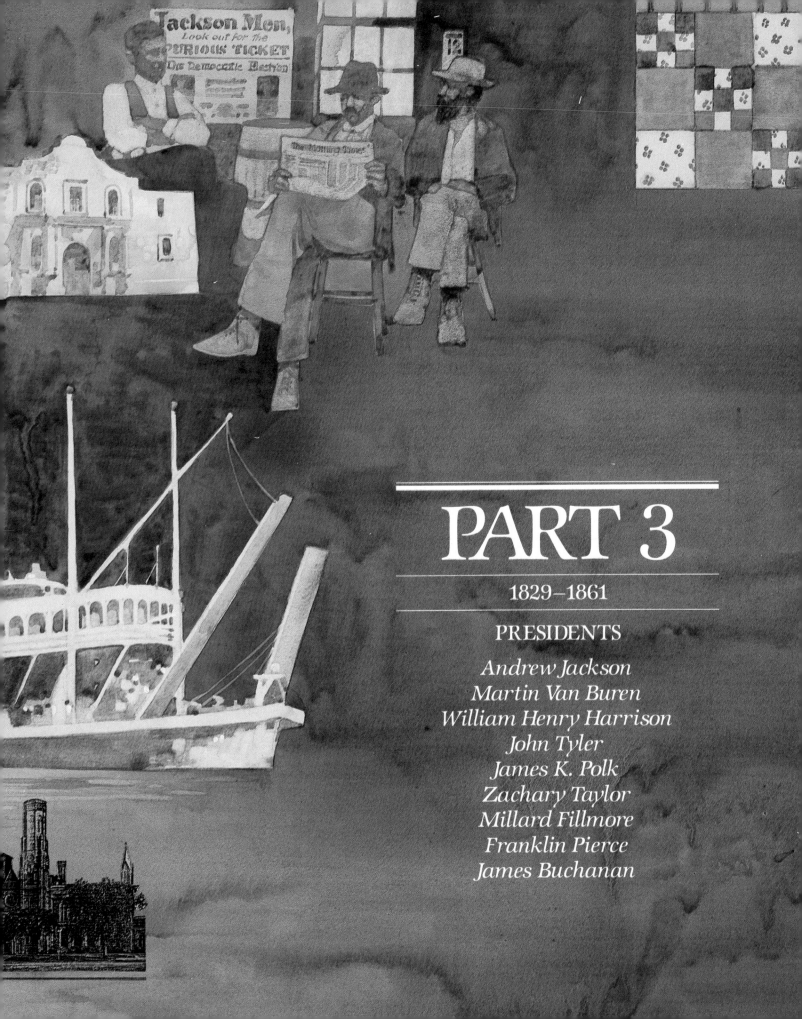

PART 3

1829–1861

PRESIDENTS

Andrew Jackson
Martin Van Buren
William Henry Harrison
John Tyler
James K. Polk
Zachary Taylor
Millard Fillmore
Franklin Pierce
James Buchanan

The President as Popular Tribune

Robert C. Post

In 1831 two young Frenchmen, Alexis de Tocqueville and Gustave de Beaumont, toured the United States. Specifically they came to gather data on American penology, but in their travels they looked at everything. Among the hundreds of citizens they met were Charles Carroll, the last surviving signer of the Declaration of Independence—a man who told them that "a mere democracy is but a mob"—and President Andrew Jackson, who had fought in the Revolution as a small boy, then fought again as major general of volunteers in the second war with England. The President served his guests a glass of Madeira and chatted pleasantly.

Four years later de Tocqueville published *De la Démocratie en Amerique*, a treatise on the American political system that betrayed a nobleman's bias yet remains even today one of the most important books about the U.S. ever written. Toward the end, he told of a dinner party at which he had been seated beside the former President, John Quincy Adams. Adams was 64, the same age as Jackson, but de Tocqueville could see that he still possessed "all his mental and bodily vigour"—as indeed he did, something to which eight terms in Congress would subsequently attest. From the moment that Adams first addressed him "with facility and elegance" in his own language, de Tocqueville was rapt. Clearly men like Adams, and Charles Carroll, were America's aristocrats—not hereditary *à la Française*, of course, but worthy of the appellation nonetheless.

When he wrote *Democracy in America*, though, de Tocqueville said of the "aristocratic element" that "if at the present day it is not actually destroyed, it is at any rate so completely disabled that we can scarcely assign to it any degree of influence on the course of affairs." Whence such pessimism? For one thing, while Adams's successor in the White House had been a proper host, nothing tempered de Tocqueville's feeling that Jackson was "apparently a very mediocre man." Having further pondered the President, he made this remark in his book: "General Jackson is a slave to the majority; he yields to its wishes, its propensities, and its demands— say, rather, anticipates and forestalls them."

Notwithstanding the pejorative, as a thumbnail assessment this is not awry. For Jackson did have a concept of the Presidency different from his six predecessors. When John Adams was defeated in 1800, Thomas Jefferson had come to power amid the rhetoric of a "revolution." Alarmed as the Federalists may have been, it was not much of a revolution, for

A gallant aristocrat to his friends, a rude barbarian to his foes, Andrew Jackson was facile enough a political animal to be many things to many people. Thomas Sully recaptured an exalted image in this portrait completed about the time of Jackson's death.

Jefferson—like Washington and John Adams—was a paragon of a natural aristocracy. When Adams, *fils*, was defeated in 1828, on the other hand, what ensued really was something of a revolution.

John Quincy Adams was the most learned and cosmopolitan President America had ever had. There was Harvard, law practice in Boston, extensive diplomatic service, a term in the Senate, and eight extraordinary years as Secretary of State. His Presidency had been marked by a programmatic vision that was thoroughly remarkable even though thwarted by Congress.

And Andrew Jackson? Well, he had been a lawyer too, but west of the mountains on the Tennessee frontier. Never had he been abroad. Twice he had been elected to the Senate, but each time resigned his public trust to tend to his own affairs. He was a speculator in land and slaves, a fancier of fast horses, a gambler, a fighter—a "hot-head" in de Beaumont's term. But in the War of 1812, a conflict from which the U.S. emerged with dignity mostly by virtue of England's preoccupation with Napoleon, Jackson had provided the nation one moment of genuine pride at the Battle of New Orleans. He was, then, a martial hero, his stature further buoyed by his exploits as "Border Captain" and conqueror of Seminoles in Florida.

Especially since this key to his popularity was similar to Washington's, one wonders why someone like Jefferson thought Jackson "unfit" for the White House. So he was a speculator; Washington had been too. So he had no bent for philosophy and spelled badly; he was no worse than Washington. So he fought duels; had not Washington's closest associate, Alexander Hamilton, done that once? The fundamental contrast begins with the style of the frontier planter. Hamilton and Aaron Burr drew pistols over politics; when Jackson shot Charles Dickenson dead in 1806, the quarrel involved a horse race. Jackson took everything personally. He seemed the embodiment of something we now call "macho." Jackson, wrote Professor Woodrow Wilson in 1896, "came into national party politics like a cyclone from off the Western prairies."

Still, the image of Jackson the "hot-head" may have been deliberately calculated. In 1824 Daniel Webster deemed Jackson's manners "more presidential" than any of the other three candidates. Even the acidulous Mrs. Trollope thought he "looked like a gentleman." Beyond question the majestic figure Thomas Sully depicted in the painting on page 66 was a gentleman of incredible presence, and, in that pose at least, surely aristocratic. And yet Jackson had something else, something of boundless appeal in an epoch when Americans ventured forth as never before to test their

Old Hickory, though hobbled by dropsy and poisoned by bullets lodged in his body, remained a power in Democratic councils until the end. He died on June 8, 1845, less than two months after sitting for this daguerreotype, which was copied and distributed by Mathew Brady, though probably not taken by him. In this chapter we can show a photographic image of each President—albeit sometimes past their incumbency. With photography, there began an interplay of politics and media.

mettle in the wilderness or the marketplace. Jackson was a gentleman who had the common touch.

Other essayists in this book pinpoint moments in history when the new President fit the circumstances so perfectly as to suggest something providential. What Old Hickory's moment called for was a national leader who personified the tenets of a romantic individualism that denied the right of anyone to assume status by dint of birth or education, or to steal a march on his fellows by means of special privilege. Though few Americans had any inkling that romanticism might exist as an abstraction, almost all could have understood a simple assertion of its epistemology such as this one by Jackson's confidant George Bancroft:

> If the sentiment of truth, justice, love, and beauty exists in every one then it follows, as a necessary consequence, that the common judgement in taste, politics, and religion is the highest authority on earth.

However ardent his celebration of the "common judgement," Bancroft was no half-tutored primitivist. In his 10-volume *History of the United States* he disclosed a great cosmic drama of personalized forces—

a world-view that encompassed what he had learned while earning a Ph.D. in Göttingen and sitting at the feet of Hegel himself in Berlin. Cast in romantic terms, Jackson embodied an uncorrupted, intuitive virtue. Insofar as it stressed spontaneity and passion, romanticism was in no way inimical to bellicosity—and thus the power of a contrast between Old Hickory the warrior and Mr. Adams the habitué of effete salons.

Jackson had already outpolled Adams once, in 1824, and it was due only to a peculiarity of the electoral system contrived by the Federalists that he did not become President then. But there was no doubt about victory in 1828, and, as if to confirm the worst fears of the "aristocratic element," Jackson's tenure commenced with a "monstrous crowd" (as Webster put it) having a wild time at the White House.

Decorum had always been a *sine qua non* for the Presidency (Jefferson may have received guests in his bedroom slippers, but to have permitted rowdyism on the premises would have been inconceivable), yet so too had been a record of dedicated public service. By all past standards, Jackson *was* "unfit." To consider why he won is to get to the heart of issues fundamental to Presidential politics ever since. Have the "best men" been bypassed? Or are those who believe this simply unwilling to accept a natural evolution in the criteria by which we choose our leaders? These are questions addressed explicitly elsewhere (pages 173–185 and 216–221). Suffice it to say here that Andrew Jackson—in presuming that his duty was to uphold the "common judgement" rather than the prerogatives of an elite—changed the rules of the game.

Old Hickory was a sick man in 1828, and the death of his beloved Rachel in December left him looking as if he would not live to complete a single term. But, for someone with the most dreadful litany of infirmities, Jackson was incredibly tough. Soon he was contending with a social scandal, the first to impinge directly on the Presidency. Jackson's campaign manager, John Eaton, had carried on a longstanding affair with a barmaid named Peggy O'Neil. When Peggy's husband, a naval officer, died at sea in 1828, Jackson urged Eaton to scotch the incessant gossip. Though Eaton married her at once, tongues kept wagging even after Jackson appointed him Secretary of War. And Peggy was ostracized by the wives of Eaton's Cabinet colleagues.

The President was furious. He demanded the resignation of his entire Cabinet, but had to back off when they protested that they could hardly be held to account for what their wives felt. Jackson suspended Cabinet meetings, turning instead for advice to a "Kitchen Cabinet" comprised mostly of friends in minor government posts. Meanwhile, various members of the administration exploited the controversy for their own ends. Vice President John C. Calhoun assumed the role of moral arbiter. Secretary of State Martin Van Buren rose to Peggy's defense, thereby winning Jackson's favor and ultimately a promise that he would assure his succession to the Presidency in 1836. Jackson broke altogether with Calhoun, once the heir-apparent, and, with Van Buren's help, he was able to revamp the Cabinet. Then he took the political offensive, first against those who flirted with disunion, next against those who upheld special privilege.

Jackson—in fact, nearly every westerner—believed in the sanctity of the Union with a religious fervor. But southerners, distressed by protective tariffs that were inconsonant with the sectional economy, had begun to assert that the federal government was merely a compact between sovereign states, states which therefore could "nullify" federal laws. The chief proponent of nullification was Calhoun, who ultimately went to the extreme of insisting that any state could, if so disposed, withdraw from the Union. Ever since a dramatic confrontation at a Democratic Party dinner on Capitol Hill in April 1830, everybody had known that Jackson and Calhoun—once staunchly allied in their nationalism—were on a collision course.

In 1832, when Calhoun's state declared a newly-enacted tariff null, pledging armed resistance to its enforcement, Jackson issued his most memorable state paper, his "Proclamation to the People of South Carolina." The President concluded that "Disunion by armed forces is *treason*," and proceeded to secure Congressional authority to enforce federal laws by military action, should the need arise. While it was clear he was not bluffing, behind the scenes he did encourage compromise and a measure was devised that South Carolina could tolerate. Token gestures aside, nullification was not pressed again, not in Jackson's time, nor indeed until the election of Abraham Lincoln, when it re-emerged with a new name, secession.

Other controversies that rocked Jackson's Presidency involved using patronage for partisan purposes (the "spoils system"), withholding federal appropriations for "internal improvements" (roads and waterways), and "extinguishing" Indian land titles east of the Mississippi. It was in the last regard, when Chief Justice John Marshall of the Supreme Court denied that the state of Georgia had any jurisdiction in the territory of the Cherokee Nation, that Jackson issued his trenchant retort: "John Marshall has made his decision, now let him enforce it."

Never in all American history was the constitutional principle of separation of powers more ruthlessly defied. Yet, whether the issue be keeping the Union intact or dispossessing the Indians, Jackson simply refused to accept the primacy of an abstract legalism over the will of the majority. Similarly, he refused to accept the legitimacy of an institution that concentrated financial power in the hands of a privileged elite. In 1816, to help liquidate the war debt, Congress had chartered a national bank, the Bank of the United States. The Bank's president, Nicholas Biddle, knew Jackson regarded it as an illegal monopoly and would oppose renewing the charter, which was due to expire in 1836. Taking the offensive, Biddle had Henry Clay sponsor legislation for recharter four years early, thereby compelling the President to take a stand prior to the election of 1832. In rising to the challenge, Jackson affirmed as never before his penchant for taking political issues personally. "The Bank is trying to kill me," he wrote to Van Buren, *"but I will kill it."* After the President vetoed Clay's bill, Biddle responded in kind: The veto was "a manifesto of anarchy, such as Marat or Robespierre might have issued to the mob."

Jackson swamped his opponent Clay in the election, then set out to wreck the Bank by withdrawing all government deposits. Ultimately he accomplished his aim, but failed to devise any satisfactory alternative. "The state banks, the currency, and the credit structure were left without controls, guidance, and protection," laments Biddle's biographer. From Jackson's perspective, however, "controls, guidance, and protection" were simply a ploy for allocating special prerogatives to the few at the expense of the many.

In his annual message at the end of 1833, Jackson assumed full responsibility for removing federal funds deposited with Biddle. Clay immediately introduced a Senatorial resolution charging that the President had "assumed upon himself authority and power not conferred by the constitution and the laws, and in derogation of both." Formal censure was voted in March 1834, and there was even some talk of impeachment. But this came to naught, and Jackson's friend Thomas Hart Benton later got the resolution of censure expunged from the record. The Bank War left a significant residue, however, in the form of a coalition of forces led by Clay, Calhoun, and Daniel Webster that became a party in opposition, the Whig Party.

Sixty years before, people called Whigs had challenged King George. Now Whigs reincarnated challenged "King Andrew." Although they could not defeat his alter ego Van Buren in 1836, four years later victory was theirs with William Henry Harrison. There was an ironic anomaly about the Whigs, however. Ideologically they were champions of Clay's "American System," a program to foster commerce and industry keyed to executive activism. Yet their raison d'être was opposition to Jackson, and so they were bound to advocate executive restraint. In his inaugural, Harrison called it "preposterous" to "suppose that the President . . . could better understand the wants and wishes of the people than their own immediate representatives." Thus, in Jackson's wake came an opposition party committed to the impossible simultaneity of positive government and Presidential passivity!

Andrew Jackson was anything but a would-be king. De Tocqueville was correct in stating that "he takes upon himself the responsibility of measures that no one before him would have ventured to attempt . . . he puts his veto on laws of Congress and frequently neglects even to reply to that powerful body." Yet all that President Jackson did, including his institution of the spoils system, his defiance of Marshall, and his war on Biddle's Bank, he did because he regarded himself as the direct representative of majority opinion. As the right to vote was divorced from property ownership, as parties coalesced in their modern form, and as closed Congressional caucuses gave way to national nominating conventions, he was as indispensable as Washington had been in 1789. As John William Ward emphasizes, to refer to an "Age of Jackson" misstates the reality. "The age was not his. He was the age's." There is no more fitting eulogy than the one composed by William Cullen Bryant:

> Faults he had, undoubtedly; such faults as often belong to an ardent, generous, sincere nature— the weeds that grow in rich soil. Notwithstanding, he was precisely the man for the period, in which he well and nobly discharged duties demanded of him.

Because Old Hickory's martial exploits had been central to his popularity, both parties sought advantage in a proven formula. The Whigs won with Old Tip in 1840 and Old Rough and Ready in 1848. They lost, however, with Old Fuss and Feathers in 1852, and their Republican heirs lost with The Pathfinder in 1856. As for the Democrats, James K. Polk, the winner in 1844, assumed the role of wartime Commander-in-Chief with enormous success; and

Martin Van Buren, above, was Jackson's hand-picked successor. From his nickname, "Old Kinderhook," we get OK. The

Whig Harrison, center, ousted Van Buren in 1841, but died a month later, leaving John Tyler, right, to assume the Presidency.

Franklin Pierce, the winner in 1852, served in the war Polk started with Mexico. Both were sometimes called "Young Hickory," though Polk was the only President between Old Hickory and Lincoln who was completely effective in assuming the mantle of popular tribune.

The election of the first Whig President, William Henry Harrison, constituted one of the great turnabouts in American history, for his party employed the whole panoply of romantic imagery that had served the Democrats so well to depose Jackson's heir, Van Buren. Harrison caught cold while delivering a two-hour inaugural in the rain, and died a month later. Speculation persists about the course his administration might have taken, though, because there is evidence that when confronted with political realities he rescinded his pledge to let Congress call the shots.

There is similar evidence regarding the second Whig elected, Zachary Taylor, who, when he heard talk of disunion in 1850, threatened to take to the field and hang the offenders. Old Rough and Ready is an intriguing character—rumpled, sloppy even, yet one of the most naturally attractive men ever to become President. Patriotic, straightforward, brave, Taylor had been 40 years a professional soldier, but his greatest heroics were fresh in the public mind—victories in Mexico at Palo Alto, Monterrey, and Buena Vista.

If Harrison's Presidential qualifications had seemed thin, however, Taylor's were nonexistent. "The idea that I should become President seems to me too visionary to require a serious answer," he had once said. Still, he was intelligent and principled. Though a slaveholder, he was first and foremost a nationalist. In 1849 there were 30 states, half free and half slave. Taylor believed that any extension of the "peculiar institution" into new territory would exacerbate the danger of disunion, and he adamantly opposed the admission of New Mexico and Utah as territories without restriction on slavery. But he died while the Senate debated, and ultimately an omnibus bill effected under the guidance of Stephen A. Douglas allowed for slavery in all territory acquired from Mexico, except California. That bill, which became known as the Compromise of 1850, would play a significant role in changing the rules of Presidential availability.

Three of the five men elected President between 1828 and 1848 were old soldiers. But there were three other Presidents during those years—what about them? One was the first Vice President to succeed to the office, John Tyler, who had played "Too" to Harrison's Tippecanoe. Tyler was a strange throwback to the old Virginia school. Once a Democrat, he had resigned from the Senate rather than support Benton's resolution to expunge the censure of Jackson. He also had sided with Calhoun in the nullification crisis, and his pairing with Harrison had frankly been a sop to hard-line southern states-righters. After moving to the White House, he lost the support of his own party, as Andrew Johnson did a quarter-century later. In a literal sense, he was a bad politician.

Jackson's immediate successor, on the other hand, was a consummate politician. Martin Van Buren was the product of a "machine"—indeed, a builder of that machine, the Albany Regency, the first in our history. There was no way to cast him as a man of the people, and superficially The Little Magician seemed a strange bedfellow for Old Hickory. But after he showed Jackson how to resolve the Eaton contretemps there was no doubt he would be the successor. Indeed, Jackson's hand was so strong that Van Buren was nominated in 1836 without a dissenting vote. He was true to his word "to tread generally in the footsteps of General Jackson," yet Little Van suffered the fate of all Presidents during a period of Congressional reassertion, and his term was characterized by perpetual stalemate. Running for re-election against Harrison in 1840, he carried only seven of 26 states.

By 1844, Van Buren could not even get the Democratic nomination, primarily because of losing Jackson's support. Polk, whom Jackson backed instead, challenged the British as well as the Mexicans, demanding all of the Oregon Country as far north as Russian America (Alaska)—"54° 40′ or fight!"—but compromised on a 49th-parallel boundary. Even before that he had provoked war with Mexico by ordering Zachary Taylor into disputed territory. Not as much was taken from Mexico as might have been. Still, the U.S. acquired more land as a result of the Treaty of Guadalupe Hidalgo than at any other time except for Jefferson's purchase of the western watershed of the Mississippi in 1803. Louisiana was a splendid coup, but it was Polk who made a truly continental nation.

Insofar as he fulfilled each of his major campaign promises, Polk was one of the most successful of all American Presidents. Moreover, victory in Mexico represented a stunning achievement by a Commander-in-Chief who had never served a day in uniform. There was, however, a dark and tragic side to Polk's attainment of "Manifest Destiny." For always there lurked the question of what to do about slavery in new territory. "Mexico will poison us," said Emerson.

As poison permeated the nation in the 1850s, Presidents Pierce and Buchanan, while both ideological heirs of Jackson, seemed helpless. In the next decade, Lincoln's leadership was of course *sui generis*. Andrew Johnson, after Lincoln, could not lead at all, though he idolized Old Hickory—just as Van Buren had, and Polk, and Buchanan extravagantly, and Pierce with only a few reservations. Pierce's victory in 1852 marked a significant turning point. The incumbent was Millard Fillmore, another accidental President, who had been on the ticket with Taylor as a balance,

like Tyler with Harrison and Johnson with Lincoln. Fillmore held office for well over two years after Taylor's death in 1850, yet experts even have trouble recalling what, if anything, he accomplished. At the Whig convention of 1852 he was given scarcely a nod.

The nomination went instead to Winfield Scott, who had executed a brilliant conquest of Mexico City in 1847 after landing at Vera Cruz. Probably the most able American soldier of his generation, Scott was, like Taylor, an officer with service dating back 40 years, to Chippewa and Lundy's Lane, and he was the first to attain the rank of lieutenant general since George Washington (there would not be another until U.S. Grant). He was not amiable like Taylor, but he had extraordinary presence at six feet-six and 250 pounds. The Whigs had twice been winners with a war hero, and under other circumstances it would have been thrice. Yet Scott was in trouble from the very outset.

While both parties were being sundered by the issue of slavery, the Whigs—a fragile alliance of northern entrepreneurs and southern planters—were bound to disintegrate faster. It took 53 ballots to nom-

In 1844 Jackson withdrew his support of Van Buren, who opposed annexation of Texas, and backed James K. Polk (shown in a Brady photograph), the first "dark horse" to be elected.

The Whigs ran their second war hero, Zachary Taylor, in 1848. After nearly 40 years as a professional soldier, his greatest victory had come at Buena Vista on Washington's birthday, 1847.

inate Scott. His campaign advisors told him to keep altogether silent about slavery, hoping everyone would assume he agreed with them. That strategy backfired completely. Southerners sized him up as a foe and bolted the party. In fact, insofar as he had thought about it at all, Scott supported the Compromise of 1850, which was unacceptable to many northern Whigs. Northerners who suspected Scott's leanings bolted too. The upshot was that the Democrat, who supported the compromise openly, won the election.

Franklin Pierce, too, had fought in Mexico; indeed, he was a brigadier under Scott. In his one combat experience, however, he was thrown from his horse, injured his leg, and was sent home. Or, rather, some said he was thrown. Others thought he had fainted. In either event, had this electoral contest taken place four years earlier, it doubtless would have gone the other way. But in 1852 "Gallant Scott," who had "made his name on many a bloody plain," was soundly trounced by a lawyer from New Hampshire. The formula had failed to work.

Referring to slavery in his inaugural, Pierce said, "I fervently hope the question is at rest." Though it certainly was not, the President had a sterling opportunity for constructive leadership (his was the most resounding mandate of any election between 1840 and 1864). But he let it slip away, and by 1856 the Democratic Party had begun to disintegrate too.

There was in the wings an interesting potential candidate, John C. Frémont, a professional explorer who had made several well publicized western expeditions. In 1856 Frémont was first approached by certain Democrats. But he was not receptive. The Democrats had been responsible for the Kansas-Nebraska Act, which loosed the forces of terrorism on the frontier. The Democrats were not, as he was, unequivocally opposed to the extension of slavery into the territories. And so it was that Frémont agreed to become the candidate of the new Republican Party—the name adopted by a coalition of disaffected Whigs and Democrats when they had met in 1854 in a church in a Michigan town by the name of Jackson.

Frémont was a popular hero quite in accord with the Jacksonian formula. He had been heard to allude to "gradual emancipation" of slaves, however, and it was evident that disunion would result if he became President. The Republican Party was entirely northern, while the Democrats still commanded a nationwide constituency. Some southern Democrats may have wanted disunion, but northerners dreaded it. Frémont's own father-in-law, Thomas Hart Benton, warned, "We are treading on a volcano that is liable at any moment to burst and overwhelm the nation."

In Kansas, pro-slavery mobs were running wild. In Washington, on May 22, 1856, a Congressman from South Carolina took a cane and beat the daylights out of an abolitionist Senator from Massachusetts who had delivered a speech later known as "The Crime Against Kansas." The crimes cut both ways. Two days later, after killing five innocent settlers near Dutch Henry's Crossing at Pottawatomie Creek, an anti-slavery fanatic named John Brown announced that "without the shedding of blood, there is no remission of sins."

Early in June the Democrats nominated James Buchanan. Though he was an old-time Jacksonian with more than four decades of political experience, Buchanan's availability in 1856 stemmed simply from his lack of any direct identification with the Kansas-Nebraska Act (Stephen A. Douglas had introduced it, Pierce had signed it). In terms of campaign strat-

After succeeding Taylor, who died in office, Millard Fillmore, above, lost the 1852 Whig nomination to Winfield Scott, who lost the election.

The Democrats won in 1852 with Franklin Pierce, above, and four years later with James Buchanan, center.

egy, however, things worked out the opposite from 1852. Then, the candidate whose views were most opaque lost. In 1856 the more vaguely committed candidate won. Again, as four years before, the loser was a popular hero. The formula had failed altogether.

Why? In the chaotic 1850s, politics became more crucial than personal style. An uncommitted candidate such as Scott, or a candidate such as Frémont committed to policies unacceptable to the South, could not carry an electorate seeking desperately to forestall the impending crisis. As President, Buchanan appeased the South, to his eternal discredit with anyone wont to compare his style to Lincoln's. Yet the fact remains that peaceable maintenance of unity was terribly important to Lincoln, too, and furthermore he showed residual traces of the Whig concept of the passive Presidency. Nevertheless, as Mark Neely points out, "disunion brought out the Jackson in him."

When, only days after Appomattox, John Wilkes Booth perpetrated his infamous deed, it left the Presidency in the hands of Andrew Johnson, dubbed by one historian "the last Jacksonian." However apposite this may be, Johnson's style was a far cry from Jackson's. Never was any President attacked so viciously for purely political motives, yet Johnson did seem to reflect all of Jackson's shortcomings and nothing of what made him so captivating. He was like a caricature of his hero. In direct contrast to Jackson, he was altogether wrong for the historical moment.

Old Hickory had stood as a clear confutation of Jefferson's prediction that "no man will ever bring out of the Presidency the reputation which carries him in." He returned to Tennessee far more popular than ever, and it is said that there were frontiersmen who kept voting for him long after he was dead. Andrew Johnson, on the other hand, was trampled far worse by Congress than ever Jackson trampled Congress, and *he* returned to Tennessee with only his dignity intact. Yet the same story is told about him, of votes long after his death. This the two men had in common, in addition to holding precisely the same view of their Presidential duty—to fulfill the will of the majority.

In the 40 years after 1829 there were Presidents much like Jackson in personal style but different politically, and there were Presidents unlike him personally but identical in their concept of the Presidency. Only Polk asserted himself fully as popular tribune, but the others adhered to Jackson's precedent partially. Take the veto power. Before Jackson, most Presidents never used it, and just one (Madison) did so more than once. Jackson vetoed a dozen bills, sometimes on constitutional grounds but often on the basis of simple expediency. Tyler wielded the veto on "constitutional and other grounds." Polk, Pierce, and Buchanan vetoed bills for reasons that had nothing to do with constitutionality. Though Tyler's vetoes so infuriated Adams that he began impeachment proceedings, ultimately a new concept of the veto power prevailed. It derived directly from the concept of the President as popular tribune, and was best expressed by James Buchanan. The veto, he said, was a "mere appeal by the President of the people's choice from the decision of Congress to the people themselves."

And take patronage. Aside from Jefferson, who was faced with his Federalist predecessor's "midnight appointments," Presidents had not previously removed appointees out of mere partisanship. But Jackson devised a formal rationale for "rotation in office." He said: "The duties of all public offices are, or at least admit of being made, so plain and simple that men of intelligence may readily qualify themselves for their performance . . . . In a country where offices are created solely for the benefit of the people no one man has any more intrinsic right to official station than another. Offices were not established to give support to particular men at public expense. No individual wrong is, therefore, done by removal . . . ."

Jackson himself was not ruthless about the spoils system, and Van Buren's status as his hand-picked successor inhibited him in this regard. The Whigs officially opposed rotation in office, though both Harrison and Tyler made partisan removals. It was with Polk, however, that sweeping turnovers began. As the Democrats lost, then regained the Presidency in 1849 and 1853, legions of public servants came and went. Buchanan carried spoilsmanship to the ultimate, replacing the appointees of his predecessor Pierce even though everybody was a member of the *same* party, the party of Jackson.

The spoils system is often said to be the worst legacy of Jacksonian politics. Unfortunate or not, it was inevitable. And, with the descent of hordes of office seekers on Washington every four years, the President was given a wieldy political tool. Insofar as the age of the President as popular tribune was rooted in romanticism, with its peculiar affinity for tragedy, the age came to an end with the Civil War. But, insofar as it was rooted in the democratization of Presidential politics, it came to an end when the federal patronage was captured by the politicos after the war, and when party organizations were turned to private benefit.

Andrew Johnson as a Senator in the 1850s. In 1875 Tennessee returned him to the Senate.

No President who succeeded Andrew Jackson in the age that was named for him was his match in charisma, in political savvy, in power to evoke romantic passions—or certainly not his match in all three together. But he did leave a legacy for his successors to draw upon as they would. Its most salient aspect was the evidence that there was inherent in the Presidency an enormous potential for *action*. Ironically, the President who most fully availed himself of that legacy was not a Jacksonian. He cast his first Presidential vote for Henry Clay in 1832, got into politics himself shortly thereafter as a Whig, and remained an orthodox Whig on most issues after he switched to the fledgling Republican Party in 1856. Abraham Lincoln did not invoke the name of Jackson often, for generally they were at odds. But, on one issue, Lincoln agreed with Jackson with all his heart—the issue of preserving the Union intact.

In late April 1861, after the attack on Sumter and after the call for volunteers, though before there had been much combat, a delegation from Baltimore visited Lincoln to tell him that his duty as a Christian statesman was to "recognize the independence of the southern States." This was his reply:

You, gentlemen, come here to me and ask for peace on any terms . . . . You would have me break my oath and surrender the government without a blow. There is no Washington in that— no Jackson in that—there is no manhood or honor in that.

Lincoln had invoked the names of the two Presidents he regarded as most effectively dedicated to their patriotic duty. No matter that one was a proponent of the prerogatives of a natural elite, the other a majoritarian. In 1861, as the nation faced its crisis of survival, the differences between the great patrician and the great popular tribune seemed inconsequential. What truly mattered was the strength of their two traditions combined. That strength, the world would see, was greater by far than the sum of its parts.

Private Lives

Margaret B. Klapthor

The President of the United States is accorded ceaseless pomp and ceremony. A legion of servants, staff advisers, and assistants is at his beck and call, as are all the minions of the media. Even under the worst of political circumstances, no man on earth can command more attention. Under favorable circumstances, no man on earth is more powerful. Yet, there is one thing the President inevitably lacks—privacy. The irony is that he is seldom alone, and never free from an incredible barrage of demands upon his time.

Hints of today's "Imperial Isolation" were perceptible even during the administration of George Washington, who had been in office only a few days before discovering that if he made himself accessible to all the office seekers, the influence peddlers, and the just plain curious, he would have very little time left for his job as President. His advisers all agreed on the necessity of a code indicating that the President was not cut off from the people, yet making it clear that here was a man and an office that demanded respect. The upshot was Washington's decision to hold levees. Tuesday's, between three and four, was the President's own, for men only, with no invitations necessary. But when Martha received, Fridays at eight, the rules were different. This reception was to be attended by men and women "in good society" and by the President as

In accepting the Presidency, George Washington greatly abridged his privacy. A week before inauguration day he crossed New York harbor amid grand festivities. Like her husband, Martha, above, held formal receptions known as levees.

The stream of White House visitors often seems endless. Here, Andrew Johnson receives a contingent of Sioux in 1867.

a private gentleman. Dinner invitations were required.

From time to time Washington permitted less formalized visits by foreign ministers, Cabinet members, Congressmen, and private citizens. But the President paid no social calls himself. And even as he faced the necessity of establishing such a code, he saw the danger of it. He feared that limiting his personal contacts would close "the avenue of useful information from the many and make [him] dependent on the few." Although some of Washington's successors took a more democratic view of their position *vis à vis* the electorate, in the final analysis all have been pretty much "dependent on the few."

President Thomas Jefferson was quick to abolish Federalist

The State Dining Room is shown in Benjamin Harrison's time with its Louis XVI accoutrements. These had been purchased *some 70 years before when the Monroes refurbished the White House after it was set afire by British troops in 1814.*

customs he regarded as monarchial, such as levees. New Year's and the Fourth of July became big public occasions in the White House, and everyone was welcome. At Jefferson's private dinner parties, guests sat at a round table. He termed his social code the "pell-mell" system. Order and formality were re-established by Dolley Madison, though, and reinforced during the terms of James Monroe and John Quincy Adams, both of whom had learned the intricacies of protocol as foreign envoys.

White House social life in the years from Andrew Jackson to the Civil War was characterized by a combination of open functions and more exclusive receptions and dinner parties. The War precipitated a marked change, however. Huge crowds converged on Washington, and the necessity of protecting the President brought soldiers right into his residence. Lincoln found sociability mostly among his family circle, though he did make an occasional public appearance. What happened at Ford's Theatre on April 14, 1865, proved the tragic inadequacy of the measures to insure his safety.

The Grant and Hayes administrations were marked by handsome formal banquets, public receptions, and an expanding range of social activities, but after the assassination of James A. Garfield in 1881 Presidents became ever more conscious of personal danger. The growing proclivity of the press to publicize every facet of the President's activities—whether official or

In an enlarged State Dining Room that accommodates 140 guests, Jimmy Carter toasts Mexico's President López Portillo.

No White House dinner is merely a social affair; political protocol is as important here as at a summit conference.

not—posed another problem. Grover Cleveland actually moved his family out of the White House during his second term to spare them from prying reporters.

After William McKinley was assassinated in 1901—the third President to meet that fate in 36 years—the Secret Service was established, a contingent of agents to accompany the President everywhere, in addition to supervising a special White House police force. Though this force was a source of entertainment for Theodore Roosevelt's younger children, who delighted to join the ranks during roll call,

it naturally diminished any last vestiges of Presidential privacy.

In reaction to the pervasive gloom and secrecy at the end of the Wilson administration, Warren G. Harding had the gates thrown open; once again people could stroll about the White House grounds. This relaxed interlude was brief, however; the Depression, President Franklin D. Roosevelt's handicap, and World

War II all demanded stringent security. Today, the glare of publicity and the whole panoply of precautions against assassination have left Presidents with scarcely any privacy at all. At the same time, the Chief Executive may have real difficulty in maintaining a sense of the nation's mood beyond the walls of the house at 1600 Pennsylvania Avenue. So it is that the character of life within those walls seems all the more significant.

★   ★   ★

John Adams, the first President to occupy the White House, wrote to his wife Abigail the night after arriving there in November 1800: "I pray Heaven to bestow the best of blessings on this house and all that hereafter inhabit it." Some residents of the White House have made it a joyful place, others have been burdened with a sense of tragedy. As for John Adams—the staid, portly President whose prickly disposition and vanity are often all that is remembered about him today—life in the White House was more often happy than not. Adams had a special rapport with children. Abigail writes of him playing "foss" for their young grandson, John Adams Smith, dragging the baby about the room on a chair while being driven with a willow stick. Upon arriving in Washing-

Few first ladies so influenced the social tenor of the White House as Dolley Madison, top. Back in Washington after her husband's death, she played matchmaker, introducing her cousin Angelica, center, to President Van Buren's son. In 1886, another White House wedding united Frances Folsom, 21, and her former guardian, President Cleveland.

ton herself, Abigail had brought the three-year-old daughter of their son Charles, who was dying in New York City. Susanna wore a little black dress and had a bout with whooping cough while in Washington, but her presence cheered the President and Abigail during the bitter election contest of 1800, which the President lost to Thomas Jefferson.

Jefferson, a widower since 1782, moved into the President's House with only the company of his servants and his secretary. He entertained at small, stylish dinner parties and found time for music, architecture, gardening, and natural history. He trained a mockingbird to follow him about and to take food from his lips. Thrilled with the specimens Lewis and Clark brought back, Jefferson displayed them in a special room. He was delighted to have his daughters join him in Washington when they could, but he was an independent man, well-schooled at enjoying life.

Dolley Madison, wife of Secretary of State James Madison, was the reigning lady of Washington society during the Jefferson administration, and when she moved into the President's House with her husband in 1809 she of course kept that role. Dolley's social schedule was a busy one: Wednesday night drawing rooms, dinner parties, luncheons, and teas, as well as huge public receptions on the Fourth of July and New Year's Day. Gregarious and full of *joie de vivre,* she surrounded herself with people and, in doing so, she provided James an opportunity to relax with individuals with whom he felt comfortable.

★   ★   ★

From time to time there have been weddings in the White House. In 1837, when Martin Van Buren moved in along with his three sons, he had been a widower for many years. All the sons were bachelors. It was a situation to set any matchmaker scheming—four potential grooms under one roof and the first house in the land without a hostess. Dolley Madison, who was again living in the capital after the death of her husband James, was

the one to solve the problem. She introduced a lovely young cousin from South Carolina to the prospects in the White House, and the next year Angelica Singleton married the President's oldest son, taking the role of First Lady for the rest of Van Buren's term.

John Tyler was left a widower in 1842. By the next winter, though, the President was plainly infatuated with young Miss Julia Gardiner of New York, who was enjoying a social season in Washington. Dire predictions were heard when they married, especially since the bride was 24 and the groom 30 years older. Theirs

was, nevertheless, a fruitful union. Seven children were added to the eight which the President's first wife had borne, giving Tyler the distinction of having more children than any other man ever to serve as President.

Chester A. Arthur, who became President less than a year after the death of his beloved wife Nell, was not so readily consoled. Each day he placed a fresh bouquet before her picture, which he kept by his bed. Arthur sought relaxation with good friends, entertaining them most elegantly, but he left the White House as he had come, a widower.

Last-minute preparations are made for the wedding of Lynda Bird Johnson and Marine Corps Captain Charles S. Robb, *on December 9, 1967. The first White House wedding in 53 years took place in the East Room resplendent with evergreens.*

land wedding and that of President Theodore Roosevelt's daughter, Alice, the marriage of President Woodrow Wilson and Edith Bolling Galt in December 1915 took place at the bride's home. After his first wife, Ellen, died at the White House in the summer of 1914, Wilson had "lived a lifetime of loneliness and heartache" in the months before he met Edith. Wilson's companion and confidante during World War I, Edith then became his protector and channel of command at the end of his administration, when he was so ill.

★ ★ ★

Those Presidents who lived in the White House when their children were still young enjoyed a unique source of pleasure and relaxation. Abraham Lincoln and his wife, Mary, spoiled their boys shamelessly. Willie and Tad were welcome visitors to the President's office whenever it struck their fancy. Somewhat to the dismay of his Cabinet, the President did not even scold Tad when he bombarded the office door with his toy cannon during a meeting. After the death of Willie in 1862, the Lincolns were inconsolable and Tad seemed to become more spoiled than ever. When his goat ate up the flowers on the White House lawn, his father suggested letting it inside, and it was subsequently found resting comfortably on Tad's bed.

The U.S. Grants brought a spirited family to the White House. Dinner with the children was happy and spontaneous, and sometimes the President rolled

Top, visitors wait in the East Room during Benjamin Harrison's administration. After refurbishing the White House with art works and antiques, Jackie Kennedy invited TV cameras inside for an intimate view, above.

Arthur's successor Grover Cleveland was the first President to be married in the White House. Cleveland was a bachelor of 49, his bride Frances Folsom was 21. Popular interest in the wedding, which took place in the Blue Room, foretold the fascination with White House weddings in our own day. Though only a small number of guests were invited, the gates were open to all who wished to peer in the windows. A crowd of several hundred gathered to watch the guests arriving, to listen to the music, and to give a hearty cheer when the Presidential salute was fired from the Navy Yard and wedding bells rang out from churches all over the city.

Perhaps because of the publicity attendant upon the Cleve-

Several Presidents had seashore cottages. President Grant and his family enjoyed their vacation retreat at Long Branch.

bread into little balls and threw them at Nellie and Jessie. If he hit them with a bread ball, they got a kiss in apology.

Rutherford and Lucy Hayes had five children, ranging in age from their son Webb, who served as his father's secretary, to the baby Scott, who was only six in 1877. Theirs was a closely knit family. The parents believed in loving discipline and good education. No bread balls or nanny goats for the Hayes children; instead, each evening the family gathered in the Red Room to sing sentimental ballads. A few hymns

and family prayers followed, then the children were sent upstairs to study while the President and his wife received guests.

The White House during Theodore Roosevelt's years was a veritable beehive of activity. Edith Roosevelt was a calm and tolerant wife and mother, and sometimes seemed to be the only one capable of keeping everyone from going berserk. The President, with his philosophy of "the strenuous life," was the catalyst for the family's exuberance. He liked nothing better than gathering all six of the children together for some sort of challenge, whether it be playing tag

in the attic or scaling a cliff in Rock Creek Park.

The public, always fascinated by White House children, was especially captivated by the children of John and Jacqueline Kennedy. On one famous occasion, reporters in the West Lobby greeted Caroline with glee when the three-year-old teetered into the room in her mother's high heels. Asked about her father, Caroline replied, "Oh, he's upstairs with his shoes and socks off, not doing anything."

White House children are as much public figures as their parents are. At the reins of a goat cart, above, is Baby McKee, grandchild of Benjamin Harrison, joined here by a sister, uncle, and cousin. Thomas "Tad" Lincoln posed with alacrity in an officer's uniform in 1864. Far left, during the Hoover administration, children danced around a maypole during the annual Easter-egg roll on the lawn at the White House.

enjoyed the arts. Washington had his own box in theaters in New York and Philadelphia; today, there is a reserved Presidential box in Washington's Kennedy Center. Jenny Lind visited the capital to the pleasure of Millard Fillmore and his family. Ole Bull, the Swedish violinist, performed for Tyler. Lincoln welcomed the Hutchison family, popular Abolitionist performers from New Hampshire, to the White House. William Howard Taft's wife Helen had been active in supporting the symphony in Cincinnati, and the best of classical performers appeared at the White House during the Taft Presidency. The Kennedys applauded Pablo Casals in an East Room concert in 1961, while the Carters invited Vladimir Horowitz to perform, and shared the occasion with the American people via the Public Broadcasting System.

Presidents have had favorite recreational activities too. John Adams wrote home to Abigail, in Quincy, that he and his nephew rode 14 miles across the countryside on Christmas Eve of 1798, and again on Christmas Day they enjoyed the winter landscape and the escape from official duties. James Madison and Andrew Jackson especially enjoyed the horse races that were held to celebrate the adjournment of Congress.

Hunting was popular with many Presidents, especially during the late 19th century, and fishing has been a perennial Presidential hobby. Herbert Hoover had delighted in casting for trout since his California youth, so after moving to the White House in 1929 he and his wife Lou established a fishing camp on the Rapidan River about an hour's drive from Washington.

Other Presidents have known the same grief the Lincolns felt at the loss of their Willie. Bennie Pierce, a boy of eleven, was killed in a train wreck prior to his father's inauguration. The Coolidge administration, too, was saddened by the loss of a son, 16-year-old Calvin, Jr., who died of blood poisoning from a blister he got playing tennis. "When he went," Coolidge wrote, "the power and the glory of the Presidency went with him."

★   ★   ★

From George Washington to Jimmy Carter, Presidents have

Amy Carter and her friends kick off their shoes and retreat to a tree house on the White House grounds. Below, Amy accompanies her parents on a state visit to South Korea in June 1979.

Two Presidents, two recreational preferences. After the intensity of his Hundred Days, Franklin D. Roosevelt sails Amberjack II from Massachusetts to his summer home at Campobello in Canada. A less swashbuckling William Howard Taft tallies his score after a round of golf.

aboard the Presidential yacht. So it was with John F. Kennedy: He too used the pool for exercise, but his real passion was sailing the waters off Hyannisport. The first White House pool was filled in during the administration of Richard Nixon, but a new Olympic-size pool on the South Lawn was presented to his successor, Gerald Ford, who used it both for exercise and pleasure.

Nixon's preferred recreation was golf, a sport enjoyed by many 20th-century Presidents. Warren G. Harding trained his Airedale "Laddie Boy" to retrieve balls when he practiced shots on the South Lawn, where President Eisenhower later had a putting green installed so he might practice whenever he could steal a few minutes from his desk.

Many Presidents have gone home at regular intervals to refresh themselves in familiar surroundings. Others have preferred the ocean or the mountains for a change of scenery. Before the Civil War, the seashore had become a favorite retreat and Presidential cottages were to be found along the Jersey coast from Cape May to Long Branch. But, whether retreating to the springs of Virginia, to the Black Hills of South Dakota, to Key West, or simply to a cottage on the grounds of the Soldiers' Home in Washington, the net gain for any President includes a break in routine, a semblance of privacy, and a respite from the pressures of his job.

One President refused to be tempted by any such distractions. In his four years, James K. Polk

John Quincy Adams's favorite recreation was swimming. One morning, as he and his servant were crossing to the Virginia shore of the Potomac, their canoe swamped and both were dumped into the water. Though the President had trouble with the loose sleeves of his shirt, which filled with water and hung like weights, he finally reached safety and stripped off his clothes. Then he and his son John—who had swum frantically to join his father when he saw the accident—sat "naked, basking on the bank" awaiting rescue.

The first White House swimming pool was installed through a public subscription sponsored by a New York newspaper during the administration of Franklin D. Roosevelt. FDR thought of swimming simply as exercise; his favorite pastime was cruising

Lyndon Johnson's favorite retreat was his LBJ ranch in Texas. Gerald Ford, below, an outstanding football player in college, kept in shape as President by swimming laps in an Olympic pool, newly installed on the South Lawn of the White House.

devoted an incredible amount of time to official duties. He considered his election tantamount to being "hired to work." Totally exhausted when he left office in 1849, Polk died in Nashville a few weeks after returning home.

★　★　★

While individual religious beliefs are ordinarily a most private matter, a President's church membership inevitably makes an explicit statement to the electorate. Sometimes, affiliation has simply been determined by regional ties or family background. The Virginia Presidents of the late 18th and early 19th centuries were Episcopalians, the established church in colonial days. Only Jefferson ranged beyond tradition; finally rewriting the New Testament, this President left a record of his own brand of deism. John Adams and his son John Quincy were Unitarians, a reflection both on the Congregationalism of their forefathers and the liberal influences of their years abroad. Martin Van Buren's affiliation with the Dutch Reformed Church sprang from his New York state origins.

As the nation expanded westward, our Presidents reflected a greater diversity of religious background. The forebears of Andrew Jackson, James K. Polk, and James Buchanan were Scotch-Irish Presbyterians. Abraham Lincoln, though he never formally joined a church during his Presidency, often attended the New York Avenue Presbyterian Church near the White House. Our several Presidents from Ohio were predominately Methodists, though James A. Garfield had been a lay preacher in the Disciples of Christ before entering politics. The 20th century added to the roll of Baptists and Quakers, and the first Roman Catholic was elected. Revivalists such as Billy Sunday and Billy Graham have influenced Presidents both spiritually and politically.

★　★　★

Today, even though the attention focused on the family living at 1600 Pennsylvania Avenue permits little privacy, Americans retain an image of the White House as the epitome of domesticity. This involves no necessary contradiction, of course. Moreover, nobody in public life gets to the White House without having become gradually accustomed to his past and present being treated as an open book. It is perhaps fortunate that Presidential candidates and their families are well conditioned to a state of peopled isolation. It is definitely fortunate that, despite everything, the image of domesticity is not entirely illusory.

★ ★ ★ ★ ★ ★ ★ ★ ★ ★ ★ ★ ★ ★ ★

His Superfluous Excellency

Edwards Park

The most insignificant office that ever the invention of man contrived or his imagination conceived." This was the assessment of the Vice Presidency of the United States by the first person to hold the job, John Adams.

George Washington had been a shoo-in for the Presidency when the Electoral College met for the first time in 1789. Adams was the natural second choice and would have garnered even more votes had not Alexander Hamilton arranged to diminish his majority so that Washington's unanimous vote would seem all the more impressive.

Adams, of course, was furious. "Is not my election to this office, in the scurvy manner in which it was done, a curse rather than a blessing?" he wrote. But, cursed or not, this first Vice President carried out his few required duties with skill and dedication. These included

presiding over the Senate and breaking ties. Since the Senate was small, ties were frequent, and Adams had the chance to decide issues 29 times. Yet too often he became engrossed in petty matters like proper modes of address, and people recalled Ben Franklin's suggestion that Adams's office merited the title

President Nixon delivers 1974 State of the Union message. Behind are Vice President Gerald Ford and Speaker Carl Albert,

third in line of succession. Aaron Burr, above, tied Jefferson's electoral vote in 1800, but had to accept Vice Presidency.

of "Your Superfluous Excellency."

Moving up to the Presidency by the turn of the hierarchical wheel in 1797, Adams found himself saddled with a Vice President from the opposing faction—Thomas Jefferson. Adams had been supported by the Federalists; Jefferson was the torchbearer of the Antifederalists—called Republicans or, later, Democratic-Republicans. From 1797 to 1801 the two men hardly communicated.

When Jefferson himself moved up, he was teamed with the enigmatic Aaron Burr. Burr, grandson of Jonathan Edwards, son of the president of the College of New Jersey (later Princeton), was brilliantly endowed and strangely devoid of personal standards. In 1800 he was only 44 and still something of a gallant. He had a large helping of ambition and enough charm to get away with almost anything.

What Burr almost got away with was the Presidency itself, for the Electoral College had declared a tie with Jefferson. Instead of politely stepping aside and accepting the second slot, Burr sat back and watched the House of Representatives sweat through 35 ballotings until vigorous wire-pulling by the ubiquitous Hamilton established Jefferson as President. (Hamilton considered him the lesser of two evils.) As Vice President, Burr, surprisingly, served with dignity and even statesmanship. Knowing he would be dumped in 1804, however, he aimed at the governorship of New York and was again foiled by Hamilton. There followed the infamous duel in which Hamilton died—inducing one Senator to note that he was being presided over by "a man indicted for murder."

Burr's further adventures—his scheme for a Louisiana empire—resulted in a charge of treason which he ducked on a technicality. He remains a mystery. He has been labeled a traitor, and been defended on the grounds that he was curiously naive about politics. Whatever the case, Burr died in disgrace. Among the many reminders of his career is the 12th Amendment, ratified in 1804, which provided that there would be separate balloting for the Vice President. Let there be no more Burrs who might stumble right into the White House through an imperfect electoral system.

Nevertheless, it is also true that Aaron Burr was the last "top echelon" contender for the Vice Presidency. By lowering sights half a notch, the nation now aimed at getting Vice Presidents from the second echelon—often men just as able as those of the first, but lacking a consuming ambition to become

Chief Executive (or at least concealing it effectively).

★　★　★

First of the second echelon was Governor George Clinton of New York. Clinton was overaged and safely noncontroversial. He served during Jefferson's second term and part of another term under James Madison, then died in office. No one bothered to replace him.

As the years passed, so did a parade of Vice Presidents whose names are barely known today. Richard M. Johnson, for example, was the first of three Johnsons to fill the position. He was Vice President under Martin Van Buren, who had himself been a Vice President. Johnson was born in Beargrass, Kentucky. He led a group of mounted riflemen in the War of 1812 and later sired an act that allowed Congressmen an annual salary of $1,500 instead of a per diem. He also sired two daughters by the first of three slave mistresses and tried to get them accepted in society. Johnson's peccadillos didn't help his political image and he was dropped from the Democratic ticket prior to the 1840 campaign. The party went into the election without a Vice Presidential candidate—a suggestion of how important the job was considered. By a twist of fate, however, it was the 1840 election that produced the first Vice President to be elevated to the top when the President died.

In 1840 Van Buren was soundly beaten by the new Whig party and its team of William Henry Harrison and John Tyler— "Tippecanoe and Tyler too!" But one month after Inauguration Day, old Tippecanoe was dead. Tyler was down in Williamsburg,

Virginia, when the tragedy struck, and remained uninformed for some time. When he finally reached Washington, after a tedious ride, the nation had gone 53 hours without a President—the longest such hiatus ever.

Then the question arose of exactly what it was that Tyler was taking over. The Constitution says, "In Case of the Removal of the President from Office, or of his Death, Resignation, or Inability to discharge the Powers and Duties of the said Office, the Same shall devolve on the Vice President. . . ." The same what? If just the powers and duties, then Tyler would remain Vice President, but take over those powers and duties. Many impor-

tant Congressional figures considered this the correct answer. Not Tyler. He interpreted the Constitution to mean the same *office*—that is, the office of the Presidency. Tyler took the Presidential oath, informed the Cabinet that he was the man in charge, and finally even broke with the Whigs in order to follow his Presidential conscience. Ever since that time, the death of a President has always meant that the Vice President assumed both his office and his duties.

After Tyler, the list of forgotten Vice Presidents resumes. George M. Dallas, a Philadelphian, served from 1845 to 1849 under Polk. The Democrats nominated him because of his

Vice President Lyndon B. Johnson is sworn in as President aboard Air Force One at Love Field, Dallas, on November 22, 1963. Lady Bird and Jacqueline Kennedy look on as District Court Judge Sarah Hughes administers oath. Spirit of the late President John F. Kennedy lingers on, right.

favorable attitude regarding statehood for Texas. Dallas was bright and honest and loyal to Polk. But this loyalty cost him his home-state backing, and one editor voiced popular opinion by vowing that never again would a Vice President come from Pennsylvania. None has. Yet, in Texas, Dallas is well memorialized.

★   ★   ★

Andrew Johnson—the second Vice President Johnson—is well known. But jump ahead a bit to another name: Levi P. Morton. He was a Vermonter by birth, a Republican New York banker by profession when Benjamin Harrison hitched him to the team for his term beginning in 1889. Although Morton bore the stigma of friendship with Roscoe Conkling, one-time political boss of New York, he proved so fair-minded in his administration of the Senate that he won universal respect. He would not allow the Republican majority to get away with the slightest procedural dirty trick. It is said that he even went without lunch so no hanky-panky would be perpetrated on the Democratic minority during his absence.

Adlai E. Stevenson is a well-remembered name today. But the Stevenson who twice lost Presidential contests against Dwight D. Eisenhower was named for his grandfather, likewise a figure in national politics. Stevenson was a country lawyer from Illinois who had campaigned against Lincoln in 1858 and again in 1860, and strongly backed George McClellan, the general-turned-politician, in

1864. With such a track record, Stevenson might have been judged a bad risk. But he served as Postmaster General during President Cleveland's first term and was a popular Vice President during his second, 1893–1897.

★   ★   ★

Jumping into the 20th century, who remembers Charles Curtis? He was Herbert Hoover's Vice President, a Kansas Senator—majority leader, actually—rung in with the liberal Republican Hoover because he was a farm-state reactionary. Curtis was called "Indian" because his mother was a Kaw.

And then there was John Nance Garner, "Cactus Jack" from Texas. Garner was unfortunately regarded as a sort of clown—perhaps because he described the Vice Presidency as not worth "a pitcher of warm spit"—but he was imbued with a lot of common sense. "Men who have known how to compromise intelligently have rendered great service to their country," he said, and other Texans who reached Congress—including Sam Rayburn and Lyndon B. Johnson—listened. Garner put country before party, a refreshing idea, and admitted it openly—even more startling. At age 63, Garner finally made Speaker of the House and a year later he was nominated to run with Franklin Delano Roosevelt.

At first Cactus Jack did his job with aplomb, though openly disdainful of it. But two terms with Roosevelt were more than enough for Garner. He could not easily forgive the President for trying to "pack" the Supreme Court in 1937. Cordiality between the two men eroded. Garner found himself castigated by labor

Vice Presidents whose names and faces have been lost in the sands of time. Levi P. Morton, top, was a New York banker, a Congressman, and Minister to France before serving under Benjamin Harrison, 1889-93. Charles Curtis, part Indian, sat 38 years in Congress and was Senate Majority Leader when tapped for the Republican ticket with Herbert Hoover in 1928.

John Nance Garner, "Cactus Jack," was one of the most colorful Vice Presidents. He had accepted second place on the 1932 Democratic ticket in return for releasing the Texas and California convention votes to Franklin D. Roosevelt.

leader John L. Lewis as a "poker-playing, whisky-drinking, evil old man," and he was replaced as FDR's running mate in 1940 by Henry A. Wallace.

Years later, on his 95th birthday, Garner got a call from another President who happened to be in Texas and had seized a moment to pay his respects to the old man. The President was John F. Kennedy and the date was November 22, 1963.

★ ★ ★

Garner, born during the Presidency of Andrew Johnson, was old enough to remember some of the problems a Vice-Presidential succession could entail. James A. Garfield had been in the White House only four months when he was shot by a crank who felt he was doing God's will. For 11 weeks Garfield lingered on. He conducted no business save for signing one extradition order.

Garfield's Vice President was a big, handsome Vermonter-turned-New Yorker, Chester A. Arthur. What was he to do? According to the Constitution, the Vice President was supposed to assume the Presidential job if the President was unable to do so. Yet Arthur would not step in. He kept out of sight—aware, perhaps, of his own unpopularity because of his association with Garfield's foe, the nefarious Roscoe Conkling. He also was aware of rumors that he himself had somehow engineered the shooting of Garfield.

Thomas R. Marshall, a Hoosier well liked for his modesty and wit, was Vice President for Woodrow Wilson's eight years.

Leaderless, the nation drifted. Then at 10:30 p.m. on September 19, 1881, Arthur got the word that Garfield had died, and a few hours later he took the Presidential oath. In office, he astonished everyone by being completely his own man. He conducted Presidential business fairly and sensibly, and inspired this comment from Henry Ward Beecher: "I can hardly imagine how he could have done better."

There was, of course, considerable debate about what the framers of the Constitution had in mind when they talked about Presidential "inability." Did the inability have to be permanent? If not, would the Vice President have to give up the Presidency should a Presidential "inability" prove temporary? How could he be forced to do so? As President, Arthur tried to get a Congressional ruling on these questions, but, typically, once no crisis was imminent, Congress lost interest.

Then, some 38 years later there came about an even more devastating period of Presidential inability. In September 1919, Woodrow Wilson fell ill while crusading on behalf of the League of Nations. For the rest of his term, over a year, he spent most of the time in a darkened room, flat on his back.

Wilson's Vice President was a small, bright Hoosier, remembered mostly for a remark he made while listening to a long-winded harangue in the Senate about what the country needed. What the country needed, he said out of the side of his mouth, "is a really good five cent cigar." It was a wonderful statement, yet Thomas R. Marshall should be remembered for other things too. While gossip reverberated concerning the President's condition Marshall carried on, always prepared for the fateful phone call. It came once, while he was lecturing in Georgia, and he steeled himself to face the giant task of running the nation. But the call was a hoax, perhaps the cruelest in our history.

Wilson, almost totally incapacitated, did not seek Marshall. Mrs. Wilson, selecting out those few bits of business that she thought Wilson should consider, did not confer with Marshall. The Vice President, like everyone else, simply read the newspapers and learned what he could about the President's condition.

Secretary of State Robert Lansing tried to get Wilson's physician and his private secretary to certify the President's inability to serve. Both refused. Lansing asked the Cabinet about calling upon Marshall to take over. But the decision had to be referred back to Wilson's "palace guard," who wouldn't budge.

Marshall himself was too scrupulous a constitutionalist to move in without a proper mandate. And so he remained in the background, carrying on with his meager slate of duties. One of these entailed serving in an honorary capacity as a Regent of the Smithsonian Institution. In his memoirs, *A Hoosier Salad,* he explained that this was the sort of "innocuous" task provided because "since the days of John Adams there has been a dread and fear that some vice-president of the United States would break loose and raise hell and Maria with the administration. . . ."

Marshall recalled that at his first meeting of the Regents he met Chief Justice Edward White, Alexander Graham Bell, Senator Henry Cabot Lodge, Sr., "and others of like caliber." He kept a modest silence until the Regents began considering an appropriation for an expedition to seek traces of prehistoric man in Guatemala. Then he broke in: "I ventured to inquire whether they had dug in Washington yet. A look of amazement came over the countenances of all these distinguished gentlemen, and somebody asked me what I meant. The reply was that from some of the specimens walking the streets I thought they would not need to go more than six feet down to discover the prehistoric man." Not a soul smiled. Marshall wrote that "it was a year before I had courage to open my mouth again."

Though well prepared for the critical moment, Marshall never met it. Yet others have, under widely varying circumstances. When President McKinley was assassinated, Theodore Roosevelt was hiking in the Adirondacks. A courier chased him through the mountains to bring him the news. Calvin Coolidge, visiting his father in Vermont, got a hand-delivered telegram in the middle of the night informing him of President Harding's sudden death. Since his father's telephone was for local use only, Coolidge had to go across the road to a store to make a long-distance call. He needed to know the form of oath for the swearing in so that the elder Coolidge, a notary public, could administer it. Just to make sure everything was legal, President Coolidge was secretly sworn in a second time, down in Washington, by a Justice of the Supreme Court.

★　★　★

Whether our Vice Presidents have moved on to the White House or receded into obscurity, they have mostly proved to be pretty good men. Look at the recent losers—would-be Vice Presidents only: Earl Warren, Governor of California and later Chief Justice of the Supreme Court, ran with Dewey against victorious Harry S Truman in 1948. John Sparkman, Senator from Alabama, ran with Adlai E. Stevenson against Eisenhower in 1952. Estes Kefauver, Senator from Tennessee, campaigned in a coonskin hat alongside Stevenson in 1956. Henry Cabot Lodge, Jr., son of Wilson's nemesis, teamed with Richard M. Nixon in 1960. Congressman William Miller of New York went down to defeat with Barry Goldwater in '64. Edmund S. Muskie ran with Hubert Humphrey in 1968 and Sargeant Shriver with George McGovern in '72. Senator Robert Dole of Kansas joined President Ford in the '76 campaign and lost to the Carter team.

How quickly the names of the "veeps" (a term coined by Vice President Alben W. Barkley) drop from our minds—even when they are in office. In the time of John Kennedy's Camelot, people would break each other up by asking what ever became of Lyndon Johnson. Tom Marshall used to say he was too small to wear a Prince Albert the way protocol demanded in the early 20th century. But it was only Marshall's job that was small. He showed himself to be extra large in a number of ways—capability, patience, diplomacy, humor, ethics, integrity, and human decency. And in that ghostly brigade of Vice Presidents, he was not alone in his bigness. There were many, many more.

PART 4

1861–1865

PRESIDENT

Abraham Lincoln

★ ★ ★ ★ ★ ★ ★ ★ ★ ★ ★ ★ ★ ★ ★

The Presidential Apotheosis

Mark E. Neely, Jr.

When he became President of the United States, Abraham Lincoln had absolutely no executive or administrative experience. His only previous term in national office, as a member of the House of Representatives from 1847 to 1849, hardly constituted a Presidential apprenticeship. Congressmen had no staff in those days, and Lincoln answered all his mail himself, either in his lonely room in a Washington boarding house or at his desk in the Capitol while he awaited votes or debates. His law practice in Illinois, though large and lucrative, depended little on organization or management. Lincoln never had more than one partner in the office—after 1844, William H. Herndon—and never employed even a secretary. Occasionally a young man studying for the bar worked in the office briefly and bore some of the burden of book fetching and precedent searching, but for the most part Lincoln and Herndon did everything.

Lincoln had no illusions about the Presidential office. "The Presidency," he remarked in 1850, "even to the most experienced politicians, is no bed of roses. . . . No human being can fill that station and escape censure." When he took office, Lincoln had been a Republican for five years. Before that he had been a Whig for 20. The Whig Party—born of opposition to a strong President (Andrew Jackson) and nearly always set against the administration in power—did not consider grandeur as a proper attribute of the office. Lincoln came rather late to this Whig conception of a weak Presidency. Only in 1848, when he campaigned for Zachary Taylor—who had no platform, a very tenuous partisan identification, and a disinclination to counter the aims of Congress—did Lincoln extol the virtues of the Whig viewpoint. He was not insincere, yet he thought Taylor carried the idea too far. He warned Secretary of State John M. Clayton that the President must not appear "a mere man of straw." Lincoln understood the popular power of Jackson's concept of the office. Taylor, Lincoln said, "must occasionally say . . . , 'by the Eternal,' 'I take the responsibility,' " as Jackson had done, and done most effectively. President Lincoln proved to be Whiggishly reluctant to use the veto, or even threaten to use it, and he interfered little with Congress. But disunion brought out the Jackson in him.

A modern biographer of Jackson explains his undistinguished Cabinet by saying that strong Presidents choose weak Cabinets. Lincoln was so

---

Alexander Gardner's photograph of Abraham Lincoln, taken on April 10, 1865, reveals the President's careworn face the day after Appomattox and four days before he was shot by John Wilkes Booth at Ford's Theatre. Lincoln had been Gardner's first sitter.

Lincoln presents the Emancipation Proclamation to his Cabinet in 1862. Left to right: Stanton, Secretary of War; Chase, Treasury; the President; Welles, Navy; Seward, State; Smith, Interior; Blair, Postmaster General; and Bates, Attorney General. Artist Francis B. Carpenter made the painting from a number of original sketches and photographs.

strong a President that the Democratic opposition insisted he was a tyrant, yet no stronger Cabinet than Lincoln's is imaginable. He daringly absorbed into his own official family all his rivals for the Republican nomination—William H. Seward, who assumed that he would become a sort of prime minister for a figurehead President; Edward Bates, who had thought so little of Lincoln's chances at the convention that he ignored the crucial second-ballot votes which Lincoln's managers gobbled up to make him everybody's second choice; Simon Cameron, whose reputation for corruption many timid Republicans thought sure to ruin a President known to the public mostly for his honesty; and Salmon P. Chase, so ambitious for the Presidency himself that Lincoln finally had to dismiss him in 1864.

Lincoln could risk such a concentration of egos, talent, and independent political strength because he planned to make the important decisions himself. More than 10 years earlier he recognized the importance of executive will:

> It is said Gen. Taylor and his officers held a council of war, at Palo Alto (I believe); and that he then fought the battle against unanimous opinion of those officers. This fact (no matter whether rightfully or wrongfully) gives him more popularity than ten thousand submissions, however really wise and magnanimous those submissions may be.

Though there was grandeur in President Lincoln's will, there was nothing grand about the way he conducted his day-to-day business. That varied as little from the model of his law office as the enormous increase in the volume of work would allow. For much of the time, he employed only two private secretaries, John Nicolay and John Hay. The White House budget was so meager that Hay was appointed to a clerkship in the Interior Department and lent to the White House. These two talented and humorous young men, who had rooms in the executive mansion but took their meals in a Washington hotel, worked hard. They screened the visitors and the mail, prepared a daily news summary, drafted routine letters, ran errands, and handled matters of social protocol (Secretary of State William H. Seward handled diplomatic protocol).

Lincoln attended to a vast amount of correspondence personally, and regularly signed piles of slippery vellum documents which constituted the official appointments to high ranking offices. He put his signature to the military appointments without reading them, assuming they were all right as long as his efficient Secretary of War Edwin Stanton had already signed them. The President drew the line at land grants, however, and William O. Stoddard signed these for Lincoln. Though "Stod," like Hay, was officially a clerk in a Cabinet department, he worked in the executive mansion and provided assistance to the overworked secretaries screening mail and running errands for them and for the President.

What Lincoln lacked in administrative expertise, he made up for in political experience, native intelligence, and sheer energy. His Presidency predated civil service reform, and this first Republican administration swept the ranks of incumbent bureaucrats nearly clean, reassigning their jobs in the traditional way to strengthen the party. By his own admission Lincoln "distributed to . . . party friends as nearly all the civil patronage as any administration ever did." Of 1,520 Presidentially appointed office holders, all but 325 were removed. Since Southern offices naturally remained vacant, this constituted almost a complete overturn of the civil service.

Republican office seekers, hungry for their first taste of the federal patronage, flocked to Lincoln's door. It was almost always open to them—and anyone else who wanted to see him. Early in his administration, in fact, the President's office hours were unlimited. But five weeks after Lincoln took office Fort Sumter was attacked, and the exigencies of overseeing the greatest war in American history necessitated limiting office hours: 10 to one on Mondays, Wednesdays, and Thursdays and, on Tuesdays and Fridays (when the Cabinet met), 10 to noon. Some gained admittance before others, of course. Cabinet members had first priority, followed by Senators and then Representatives. Any ordinary citizen who waited for those privileged visitors to finish their business could see the President. The waits were often long and frustrating, but ordinary citizens came in large numbers, not only to seek office, but also to beg favors, to call attention to local or personal problems, and to give advice. Such openness made Lincoln's day an ordeal, but his accessibility was not simply a matter of slipshod administration born of a westerner's friendly ways and casual manner. It was a matter of deliberate policy to take his "public opinion baths." There was more than mere absence of style in this; here was the Presidency in democratic style.

While Lincoln intentionally kept official Presidential business on a low key, White House social life lacked grandeur despite Mrs. Lincoln's best efforts. The executive mansion was so dilapidated when the Lincolns arrived that Congress appropriated $20,000 to fix it up. Mary Todd Lincoln overspent the appropriation by $6,700, and the press focused less on the decorative results than on the impropriety of such attention to "show" in the midst of war. Lincoln sensed the problem the moment the commissioner of public buildings informed him of the excessive expenditures. The President exploded, "It would stink in the nostrils of the American people to have it said that the President of the United States had approved a bill overrunning an appropriation of $20,000 for *flub dubs*, for this damned old house, when the soldiers cannot have blankets." Social events at the White House were always subject to criticism. For example, Massachusetts Governor John Andrew refused to attend a White House ball, taking a huffy swipe at "the improper levity of such a proceeding in the present awful condition of the country." Critics were silenced after February 1862, however, when Willie Lincoln died and the executive mansion was plunged for months into the darkness of official Victorian mourning. Rarely afterwards was there much "levity" in the White House. Mrs. Lincoln was never quite the same again.

The President never shared his wife's interest in the trappings of his high station. During his previous stay in Washington as a Congressman, he had asked Mary to drop the title "Hon." before his name on letters she addressed to him. He was no more given to formality when he entered the White House some 12 years later. The Lincoln children, Willie and Tad (Robert was away at Harvard during most of the war), were notoriously undisciplined. Their numerous pets, including goats, were often found inside the executive mansion. The children, the animals, and the souvenir hunters who cut pieces from draperies and carpets gave the mansion anything but a regal air.

The President dressed well and maintained a generally dignified appearance in his office, but the office itself was rather plain. A table and chairs for Cabinet meetings and a large desk—its pigeonholes stuffed with letters and papers—were the principal furnishings. Ceiling gas jets lighted the room, and a marble-manteled fireplace heated it. The only decoration was an oil portrait of Andrew Jackson which Mrs. Lincoln had ordered cleaned when she was refurbishing.

Despite the President's usually dignified appearance, the aspect of his personal style that most preoccupied the public was his humor, a legendary trait even in his own time. Robert M. DeWitt's *Old Abe's Joker or Wit at the White House*, published in New York in 1863, was a miserable little paperback which sold for 10 cents at railway stations, but it was the first book to capitalize on the fact that " 'Wit at the White House' is in full blow." These were not even Lincoln's jokes. DeWitt did little more than try "to associate" some standard minstrel and Irish jokes with "the name of one who so greatly enjoys and successfully perpetrates the fine old, full-flavored joke." A more distinguished effort in a generally undistinguished genre was *Lincolniana; or the Humors of Uncle Abe*, by "Andrew Adderup" of Springfield, published in New York in 1864. *Lincolniana* did not merely attach Lincoln's name to stock jokes. It was heavily—and somewhat artfully—flavored with the facts of Lincoln's early life in "Suckerdom" (Illinois is the Sucker state) and with the lore of Washington politics. It showed some effort to present jokes Lincoln had really told. *Old Abe's Jokes, Fresh from Abraham's Bosom, Containing All His Issues, Excepting the "Greenbacks," to Call in Some of Which This Work Is Issued*, also published in New York in 1864, was more than a joke book. It was practically a campaign biography, for the humorous stories and quips were interspersed with favorable comments about the President quoted from the contemporary press.

James G. Randall, Lincoln's greatest biographer, wrote that "the continual interweaving of good fun in his [Lincoln's] writings and speeches shows that humor was no mere technique, but a habit of his mind." Lincoln's wit gained mythic status with Americans, yet, as White House secretary Stoddard noted, the President had never even heard of "a vast number of so-called jokes, attributed to him." The trait, in other words, proved so endearing that it was quickly exaggerated. When, after his death, Lincoln became America's patron saint and eventually outranked George Washington in the national pantheon, his humor remained an essential component of his image. Along with his democratic ways, it made him an approachable and lovable god.

To modern sensibilities, Lincoln's humor is one of his most endearing attributes—so much so that it is hard to recapture a sense that in his own time it was not universally admired. Lincoln lived in the Victorian era when earnestness was so cardinal a virtue that no one wished to be seen smiling in a portrait or photograph. (Lincoln never smiled in his sittings, and, as a result, no one has any idea what his teeth looked like.) Conversely, humorlessness was not a cardinal failing, and levity seemed to smack of a lack of earnest purpose. In sum, Lincoln's wit was probably as much a political liability as an asset.

The opposition, at any rate, proved willing to make a political issue of the President's humor. It was repeatedly cited as proof that Lincoln was too small a man for the job, a mere frontier jokester incapable of even grasping the national crisis, much less surmounting it. The most controversial incident occurred when Lincoln visited the Antietam battlefield early in October 1862. As he was being taken in an ambulance to troops he was to review, the President asked Ward Hill Lamon—an old Illinois friend blessed with a wonderful voice for ballads—to "sing one of your sad little songs." Lamon sang a melancholy favorite of Lincoln's and followed it with a couple of nonsense tunes to cheer him up. One was a song in Negro dialect called "Picayune Butler." Two months later, a New York newspaper reported that the President had shockingly called for a "jolly" song while on the "sanguinary" field of Antietam. Soon thereafter another version of the story appeared in a London newspaper. By 1864 accounts had circulated widely that Lincoln had requested a vulgar Negro tune in the midst of the dead bodies littering the Antietam battlefield.

The problem reached significant proportions as the election drew near. On September 9, 1864, the Democratic *New York World* published "One of Mr. Lincoln's Jokes," recounting the "Picayune Butler" story. Lincoln took the matter seriously enough to draft a lengthy refutation. He had not been on the battlefield at the time. He had asked for the sad song, but someone else suggested the comic relief. He had examined the battlefield *after* he reviewed the troops. The whole incident occurred 16 days after the battle, and there had not been a body to be seen, "nor even a grave that had not been rained on since it was made." Written to be given to the press over Ward Hill Lamon's signature, the explanation was never actually sent out (and was not even revealed until 1895, more than 30 years later).

The Lincoln wit was not always an asset even among Republican friends. When Ozias M. Hatch and Jesse K. Dubois, old Illinois cronies of the President's, heard that Montgomery Meigs had been removed as quartermaster general, they wasted no time in recommending Robert Allen for the post. Unfortunately, the newspaper report of Meigs's removal was erroneous. Lincoln, not knowing anything about the report, fired back a brief reply: "What nation do you desire Gen. Allen to be made Quarter-Master-General of? This nation already has a Quarter-Master-General." Hatch and Dubois thought Lincoln's letter "read harshly," and they were considerably mortified. The President apologized: "The particular form of my dispatch was jocular, which I supposed you gentlemen knew me well enough to understand."

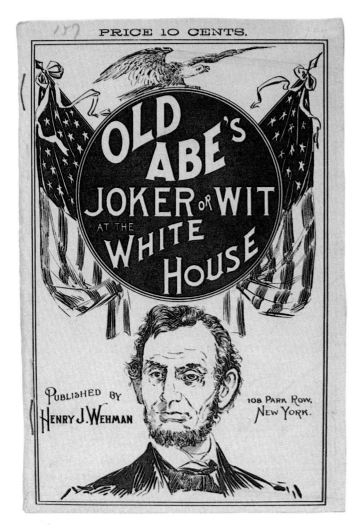

Lincoln's legendary humor was as much a political liability as an asset. Cartoon above, for example, cruelly misrepresents the President during his visit to the Antietam battlefield. Robert M. DeWitt's paperback, left, was the first to capitalize on public preoccupation with Lincoln's humor. Purporting to be a collection of White House wit, its jokes were not actually Lincoln's.

An anticipation of Lincoln's apotheosis while he was still alive was the mythic treatment of his reputation for clemency. This aspect of his Presidential style was, unlike his wit, quite appropriate for a war weary nation. Out of 456 requests for pardons in civil cases, Lincoln granted all but 81. Even excluding war related cases, Lincoln's pardons practically equaled the number granted by his two predecessors, James Buchanan and Franklin Pierce, put together.

Pardons in military cases made Lincoln famous for clemency. Although there is no accurate record of the total count, he suspended sentences or requested information in easily 100 such cases a year, considering most of them individually. Youth was always an extenuating factor: "I am unwilling for any boy under eighteen to be shot," he told General Meade on October 8, 1863. So was economic distress: "I do not like the punishment of withholding pay," he said, "it falls so very hard upon poor families."

President Lincoln saved so many soldiers from the firing squad that in 1863 Francis DeHaes Janvier wrote a poem called "The Sleeping Sentinel" about William Scott, a Vermont soldier sentenced to die for sleeping on guard duty. As young Scott trembled by his coffin,

. . . In double file, advancing, then, he saw
Twelve comrades, sternly set apart to execute the law—
But saw no more:—his senses swam—deep darkness settled round—
And, shuddering, he awaited now the fatal volley's sound!
Then suddenly was heard the noise of steeds and wheels approach,—
And, rolling through a cloud of dust, appeared a stately coach.
On, past the guards, and through the field, its rapid course was bent,
Till, halting, 'mid the lines was seen the nation's President!
He came to save that stricken soul, now waking from despair;
And from a thousand voices rose a shout which rent the air!
The pardoned soldier understood the tones of jubilee,
And, bounding from his fetters, blessed the hand that made him free!

T.B. Peterson & Brothers of Philadelphia published Janvier's poem as a pamphlet that sold for 10 cents, and the poem was widely declaimed in patriotic readings by James E. Murdoch (one of which Lincoln himself apparently heard). This was the stuff of myth, and indeed the case of William Scott appears to have been heavily encrusted with myth. Scott was sentenced to die for sleeping on guard duty, but no soldier was ever shot for that offense during the war. The pardon may well have been granted by General McClellan, not Lincoln. Yet, no matter the facts, the anecdote is significant. As Lord Charnwood, the able biographer of Lincoln from the era of World War I, explained: "If the story is not true . . . still it is a remarkable man of whom people spin yarns of that kind."

Lincoln was famed, not only among sentimental common people but also among hard-bitten generals and politicians, for pardoning convicted soldiers. General William T. Sherman noted in 1864 that "we all know that it is very hard for the President to hang spies, even after conviction, when a troop of friends follow the sentences with earnest exparte appeals." The crusty Secretary of the Navy, Gideon Welles, characterized the President's disposition to mitigate punishment "as, at times, a weakness." And the pardon clerk in the Justice Department stated that his chief,

the Attorney General, "soon discovered that my most important duty was to keep all but the most deserving cases from coming before the kind Mr. Lincoln at all; since there was nothing harder for him to do than to put aside a prisoner's application and he could not resist it when it was urged by a pleading wife and a weeping child." Cynics like reporter Donn Piatt had another view:

There was far more policy in this course than kind feeling. To assert the contrary is to detract from Lincoln's force of character, as well as intellect. . . . He knew that he was dependent upon volunteers for soldiers, and to force upon such men as those the stern discipline of the Regular Army was to render the service unpopular. And it pleased him to be the source of mercy, as well as the fountain of honor, in this direction.

Yet Lincoln was too often on record—in private as well as in public—as opposing revenge in all matters, to be judged as calculating in his mercy. There should be "no motive of revenge, no purpose to punish merely for punishment's sake" in handling prisoners of war, Lincoln told Stanton in a long private letter. When the subject of Confederate war crimes came up in a Cabinet meeting near the end of the war, Lincoln, according to Welles, stated characteristically that he:

Lincoln visits Army of the Potomac headquarters in October 1862 at Sharpsburg, Maryland, site of the battle of Antietam. Facing Lincoln, sixth from left, is General George B. McClellan, *who would run against him in the 1864 election. Though popular with his troops, McClellan was too cautious for Lincoln's taste, and was removed from command in November 1862.*

This Alexander Gardner photograph portrays Lincoln with his two young secretaries, John Nicolay, left, and John Hay. Hay had met Lincoln while practicing law in Springfield, Illinois. Nicolay had been editor of the Pittsfield, Illinois, Free Press. They began gathering historical and biographical material on Lincoln in 1861, and published a 10-volume biography in 1890.

was particularly desirous to avoid the shedding of blood, or any vindictiveness of punishment. He gave plain notice that morning that he would have none of it. No one need expect that he would take any part in hanging or killing these men, even the worst of them. "Frighten them out of the country, open the gates, let down the bars, scare them off," he said, throwing up his hands as if scaring sheep.

The Second Inaugural Address's tone of "malice toward none" was the public statement of Lincoln's personal penchant for mercy.

Like humor, forgiving was a habit of Lincoln's mind, an important aspect of his personal style. After his death it became a major component of his apotheosis, but in life it rarely interfered with his determination to win the war. Lincoln was quite capable of showing the mailed fist. Nothing could induce him to commute Nathaniel Gordon's death sentence to life imprisonment. Gordon had been convicted of engag-

ing in the slave trade, a form of commerce Lincoln found loathsome. Besides, antislavery Republicans would never have forgiven toleration of this crime. Lincoln let him hang despite earnest appeals from "a large number of respectable citizens." He likewise ignored the appeals of six Senators and 91 Representatives and let the young son of a socially prominent Virginia family, John Y. Beall, hang for sabotage on February 25, 1865. And he was usually tougher on officers than on enlisted men. Fifty-nine convictions involving officers reached Lincoln's desk in the last half of 1863; in 14 instances punishment by Presidential decree was more severe than had been recommended by the courts-martial.

Many requests for pardon were the result of Lincoln's own tough wartime policies, especially his suspension of the privilege of the writ of *habeas corpus.* In doing so, the administration allowed arbitrary arrests and imprisonment without preferring charges. Rarified and legalistic debates over the constitutionality of this policy raged throughout the war, but the abstractness of these debates should not obscure its practical impact. Although no complete records exist, the commissary general of prisoners listed 13,535 citizens so arrested from February 1862 to April 1865. At least one American out of every 2,000 was arrested, sometimes in the night, and quickly bundled off to Fort Lafayette, Fort McHenry, Fort Warren, or another of the prisons that the Democratic opposition dubbed "American bastilles." Lincoln urged sparing use of the power except in *"manifest* and *urgent"* cases, though he had little control over faraway military authorities.

Still, the President was never reticent to defend the policy. In June 1863 a public letter written by Lincoln characterized libertarian criticism of his administration as something on which the seceding states had counted:

> . . . under cover of "Liberty of speech" "Liberty of the press" and *"Habeas corpus"* they hoped to keep on foot among us a most efficient corps of spies, informers, suppliers, and aiders and abettors of their cause in a thousand ways. They knew that in times such as they were inaugurating, by the constitution itself, the "Habeas Corpus" might be suspended; but they also knew they had friends who would make a question as to *who* [Congress or President] was to suspend it; meanwhile their spies and others might remain at large to help on their cause. Or if, as has happened, the executive should suspend the writ, without ruinous waste of time, instances of arresting innocent persons might occur, as are al-

ways likely to occur in such cases; and then a clamor could be raised . . . which might be, at least, of some service to the insurgent cause. "I think the time not unlikely to come," the President concluded boldly, "when I shall be blamed for having made too few arrests rather than too many."

In defending administration policy, Lincoln could even exploit his own reputation for sparing the lives of court-martialed common soldiers. "Must I shoot a simple-minded soldier boy who deserts," he asked, "while I must not touch a hair of a wiley agitator who induces him to desert? . . . I think that in such a case, to silence the agitator, and save the boy, is not only constitutional, but, withal, a great mercy."

Lincoln was equally tough in defending the unpopular draft. His unpublished opinion on the conscription law asked: "Shall we shrink from the necessary means to maintain our free government, which our grand-fathers employed to establish it, and our own fathers have already employed once to maintain it? Are we degenerate? Has the manhood of our race run out?" Nor did Lincoln shrink from the dreadful cost of victory on the battlefield. William O. Stoddard recounted the mood of the White House immediately after hearing of the appalling losses at the Battle of Fredericksburg:

We lost fifty percent more men than did the enemy, and yet there is a sense in the awful arithmetic propounded by Mr. Lincoln. He says that if the same battle were to be fought over again, every day, through a week of days, with the same relative results, the army under Lee would be wiped out to its last man, the Army of the Potomac would still be a mighty host, the war would be over, the Confederacy gone. . . .

The grim arithmetic of war, which the President understood very well, dictated an approach to military appointments different from the rest of the patronage. "The administration," he explained to an unhappy and narrowly partisan Republican, "could not even start in this [war], without assistance outside of its party." Lincoln knew that "the war should be conducted on military knowledge" rather than "on political affinity." Democrats got their share of generalships, and Lincoln was never guilty of accepting the fallacy that generals fought better when their hearts were in the war politically (most generals educated at West Point had never voted). Just as he was willing to risk political competition from a strong

Cabinet, Lincoln was equally ready to risk it from strong generals—hence the fame of his letter written on the occasion of appointing General Joseph E. Hooker to command the Army of the Potomac:

I have heard, in such way as to believe it, of your recently saying that both the Army and the Government needed a Dictator. Of course it was not *for* this, but in spite of it, that I have given you the command. Only those generals who gain success, can set up dictators. What I now ask of you is military success, and I will risk the dictatorship.

The Hooker letter is a reminder that a crucial aspect of Lincoln's Presidential style was his writing. Lincoln was fortunate in having a splendid literary style. In neither of his campaigns for the Presidency did he make any speeches (the office was supposed to seek the man and not the other way around), nor did he hold any Presidential press conferences or public briefings. The White House budget, inadequate even to pay secretaries to open the mail, did not include press secretaries or any of the modern appurtenances of public relations. Lincoln rarely left Washington and he made no speeches of any substantial length during the war. So the American public knew the President almost wholly through his writings—his inaugural addresses, annual messages to Congress, proclamations, and occasional public letters.

As many critics have learned to their sorrow, Lincoln's literary style almost defies analysis, but some traits are obvious. His legal training gave his writing precision and clarity (as well as a penchant for split infinitives). His style was economical, compact, at times even terse. The Gettysburg Address is justifiably famous for its brevity. Try to paraphrase it or any famous Lincoln letter; not only will the result be stylelessly flat, it will not be much shorter and it will probably sacrifice precision. Lincoln spoke the common idiom and he avoided abstractions. "Mr. Lincoln was a very patient man generally," his old law partner Herndon recalled, "but if you wished to be cut off at the knee, just go at Lincoln with abstractions, glittering generalities, indefiniteness, mistiness of idea or expression." As a result of decades of experience in political oratory, Lincoln was quite conscious of how his writing would sound if spoken aloud. For example, when he entrusted James Cook Conkling—an old Springfield friend and "one of the best public readers"—with presenting an important public letter to a mass meeting in Illinois late in the summer of

1863, he had just one suggestion: "Read it very slowly." Lincoln knew how the letter should sound.

Finally, it is essential to remember that Lincoln *had* a style and was conscious of it. There was nothing "natural" about his literary efforts. The Gettysburg Address was not the result of spontaneous genius or momentary inspiration, jotted on an old envelope on the train ride to Pennsylvania. The neatness of the writing and the straight lines on the early drafts (as well as the White House stationery) show he composed most of it in advance of the occasion, in Washington. That it required careful consideration and effort is obvious from a comparison of the famous first sentence with an earlier expression of the same idea. At Gettysburg, the President said: "Four score and seven years ago our fathers brought forth, upon this continent, a new nation, conceived in liberty, and dedicated to the proposition that 'all men are created equal.'" Four months previously, Lincoln had given the same idea spontaneous expression in an impromptu response to a group of serenaders at the White House: "How long ago is it?—eighty odd years—since on the Fourth of July for the first time in the history of the world a nation by its representatives, assembled and declared as a self-evident truth that 'all men are created equal.'

Flower bedecked Mary Todd Lincoln posed for photographer Mathew Brady in one of several new gowns she wore for her husband's 1861 inauguration.

That was the birthday of the United States of America."

With consciousness of style came confidence. Unlike other frontier Presidents—Jackson and Taylor, for example—Lincoln never resorted to ghost writers. Instances in which someone else wrote Lincoln's words are practically all common knowledge to Lincoln students. The only notable examples are the closing of the first inaugural address (suggested by Seward but considerably improved by Lincoln) and a routine proclamation of thanksgiving.

Lincoln wrote his own speeches and took quiet pride in them. Of his second inaugural address Lincoln said: "I expect [it] . . . to wear as well as—perhaps better than—any thing I have produced; but I believe it is not immediately popular. Men are not flattered by being shown that there has been a difference of purpose between the Almighty and them. To deny it, however, in this case, is to deny that there is a God governing the world. It is a truth which I thought needed to be told; and as whatever of humiliation there is in it, falls most directly on myself, I thought others might afford for me to tell it."

Lincoln's was not the "managed" style of an executive ever conscious of public relations; he wrote and spoke for the ages.

★ ★ ★ ★ ★ ★ ★ ★ ★ ★ ★ ★ ★ ★ ★ ★ ★

The Assassins

Robert J. Donovan

On the press bus in Dallas on November 22, 1963, I was talking with a newspaper colleague about the political situation in Texas when, at about 12:30 p.m., the bus suddenly stopped in Dealey Plaza. Glancing up, I saw a drab brick building ahead with a sign: Texas School Book Depository. Someone was demanding to be let off the bus, and someone was exclaiming about having heard a shot. The commotion struck me as absurd. Having covered Presidents extensively, beginning with Harry Truman, I had ridden in scores of press buses in Presidential motorcades around the country. False alarms were familiar experiences.

The bus door was opened. A person outside called in to say that a couple had thrown a child to the ground and covered it with their bodies at the sound of the shots.

"President Kennedy's car has left the motorcade," a reporter in the bus shouted just as the motorcade began to move again. The bus turned left in front of the

book depository and dipped through a railroad underpass. Startlingly, a motorcycle policeman roared by us and swung up the grassy embankment toward the railroad tracks. When the incline became too steep he leaped off the motorcycle and, drawing his revolver, ran along the tracks. The sight of the revolver told us all that something serious had happened.

Tragedy was the last thing imaginable that day. When Air Force One had arrived 50 minutes earlier at Love Field, Dallas, on a flight from Fort Worth, I stood within 10 feet of John and

Homage to martyred Presidents, 1865 and 1963. At left, Abraham Lincoln's cortege in New York City; right, John F. Kennedy's funeral procession in Washington, D.C., with a time-honored symbol, a riderless horse, boots backward in the stirrups.

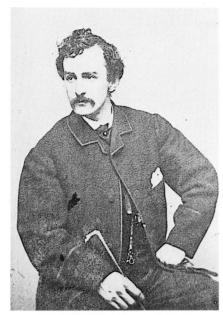

He wanted his face and name to be known . . . John Wilkes Booth. Thus the dapper assassin posed for a photograph.

Jacqueline Kennedy. In the brilliant sunshine they had never looked more stunning. Hollywood could not have cast such a glamorous pair. They were two people with everything to live for: power, money, fame, popularity, youthfulness, good health, beautiful children, a seemingly splendid future.

At each previous stop on the two-day tour in Texas Mrs. Kennedy had been handed, appropriately, yellow roses. Indeed, a day earlier I had filed a small feature to my paper, the *Los Angeles Times*, on the amusing fact that something was amiss with the supply of yellow roses in Texas; the ones given to Mrs. Kennedy had been imported from California.

With the yellow rose situation in the back of my mind, I was not altogether surprised that morning in Dallas to see a member of the welcoming committee hand Mrs. Kennedy a bunch of blood-red roses. The

next time I was to see those red roses they lay crumpled in the back seat of the President's limousine standing outside Parkland Hospital. Inside the hospital John F. Kennedy lay dead.

Everywhere in the anguished corridors the question was being asked: Who could have done a thing like this? Even though the assassin had not yet been caught, I felt I knew almost exactly the kind of person he would turn out to be. For Dallas was not my first exposure to an attempt on the life of a President. On November 1, 1950, I was walking to the White House to cover a story when, in the block beyond, I saw a commotion in front of Blair House, where President and Mrs. Truman were living while the family quarters of the White House were under renovation. As the President was napping after lunch, Oscar Collazo and Griselio Torresola, who lived in the Bronx and were members of the Puerto Rican Nationalist party, tried to shoot their way inside to assassinate him. In the ensuing gun battle with the Secret Service and White House police, Torresola was killed and Collazo felled by minor head wounds.

My curiosity about the motives of these two men led me into a long study not only of the Blair House incident but also of other assassinations and assassination attempts. The result was a series of articles and a book, published in 1955, titled *The Assassins*, which was subsequently cited numerous times in the Warren Commission report on the Kennedy assassination.

In the bedlam of Parkland Hospital, therefore, a profile of the still-unapprehended assassin formed in my mind. He would be a man of slight stature and

medium height. He would not have been known as a criminal; at worst he would be a petty offender. His name would mean nothing to the world. Poorly educated, he would have had a job such as saloonkeeper, dishwasher, debt collector, house painter, factory worker, bricklayer, or metal polisher—jobs held by previous Presidential assassins or would-be assassins.

Presidential limousine with removable top and bulletproof windows speeds from assassination scene in Dallas.

Lee Harvey Oswald reels from Jack Ruby's bullet as detective's face reflects horror.

After President Garfield was shot in a Washington railway station, above, he lived 80 agonized days.

Garfield's killer, Charles Guiteau, forever known as a "disappointed office seeker," had hoped to be consul in Paris.

Kennedy's killer would be a drifter and, above all, a loner. Moody, withdrawn, discontented, disappointed, maladjusted, loveless, he would in all probability be mentally ill and perhaps subject to delusion. He would be the kind of disturbed human being who might feel a great sense of aggrandizement at the thought of murdering a ruler and thus winning notoriety unattainable otherwise.

If the historical pattern were to hold true in Dallas, the assassin probably would have borne no hatred for the President personally—John Wilkes Booth was an exception in this regard. Indeed, the assassin might even have felt a distant admiration for his intended victim, as Collazo did for Truman. But he would have acted in a fanatical expectation that his bullets could further

a cause to which he felt himself devoted. With previous Presidential assassins, that cause had ranged from the independence of Puerto Rico, to vengeance for the Confederacy, to the welfare of the working man.

When Dallas police arrested Lee Harvey Oswald two hours and twenty minutes after Kennedy was shot, parts of the familiar pattern began to fall into place. Oswald was slim and of moderate height—about the size of Booth. Acquaintances were to describe him as maladjusted and secretive. He had been found to have serious emotional and psychological problems. A high school dropout, he had been a drifter, serving in the Marine Corps, then living in the Soviet Union, traveling to Mexico, seeking a visa to Cuba, going from job to job and winding up stacking school books. Hardly anyone had ever heard of him.

According to the Warren Commission report (whose findings in this respect have been supported by independent research), Oswald was unable "to enter into meaningful relationships with people." He harbored "deep-rooted resentment of all authority which was expressed in a hostility toward every society in which he lived." His "urge to try to find a place in history" alternated with recurring despair "over the failures in his undertakings." He was living alone, estranged from his wife. Beneath his doleful exterior lurked a violent streak. In *The Death of a President* William Manchester concluded that at the time of the assassination the 24-year-old Oswald was insane.

Largely because the subsequent bizarre murder of Oswald by Jack Ruby precluded an inquiry into Oswald's mental condition and motives, theories about the crime proliferated. With all due respect to the 1979 report of the House Special Committee on Assassinations, none of these theories has convincingly refuted the Warren Commission's conclusion that Lee Harvey Oswald, acting alone, killed John F. Kennedy. It is possible, of course, that in the future new evidence will warrant a new conclusion.

★   ★   ★

What is pertinent here, however, is that everything known about Oswald fits the general pattern for assassins and would-be assassins of American Presidents. It is a seedy roster that includes Richard Lawrence, Charles J. Guiteau, Leon F. Czolgosz, John Nepomuk Schrank, and Giuseppe Zangara. It also includes two eccentric women with fuzzy motives, who, separately, threatened the life of President Gerald R. Ford in 1975—Lynette Alice ("Squeaky") Fromme, who pointed a loaded pistol at Ford in Sacramento but failed to make it fire, and Sara Jane Moore, who 17 days later fired an ineffectual shot at the President in San Francisco.

In such company Booth, a prominent actor from a famous theatrical family, is distinctive. Collazo and Torresola were nationalistic fanatics, not mental cases. But, on the whole, Presidential assassins and would-be assassins have been obscure people whose

Purveyors of Presidential memorabilia are always ready to capitalize on even the ultimate tragedy, assassination.

murky motives seeped from the crevices of their emotions or delusions. Excepting Collazo and Torresola, and perhaps Booth, theirs were not crimes undertaken for political ends. The assassinations of Lincoln, Garfield, McKinley, and Kennedy each had a dramatic impact on history, especially Lincoln's succession by Andrew Johnson at the outset of Reconstruction and Kennedy's by Lyndon Johnson at a crucial juncture in relations with Vietnam. Nevertheless, assassinations have not precipitated fundamental shifts in political power, and certainly not changes in the structure of the nation's government.

The United States has experienced much violence of many

Leon Czolgosz peers from behind bars. With a concealed revolver, he had fired at President McKinley almost point-blank.

Scene at Blair House following attempt on President Truman's life, November 1, 1950. Would-be assassin Griselio Torresola was killed. His accomplice, Oscar Collazo, is shown lying wounded at foot of steps. Collazo's death sentence was commuted by Truman in 1952.

Kennedy—were shot and killed. Still, there exists no tradition of political assassination as there has been at times in parts of Asia, the Balkans, and the Middle East (whence the word assassin derives). Happily, the United States has been free of fanatical sects and conspiratorial organizations such as the Black Hand in Serbia, which was instrumental in the murder of the Austrian archduke, Franz Ferdinand, and thus in precipitating World War I.

★　★　★

The American people have learned to their sorrow, however, that in certain circumstances a madman can be quite as lethal as a cold-blooded conspirator. In 1881 Charles Guiteau, with a bone-handled British bulldog revolver in his pocket followed President Garfield around Washington freely, waiting for the moment of inspiration from God to pull the trigger. Twenty years later, after William McKinley was felled by Leon Czolgosz in Buffalo—thereby becoming the third President to die by assassination within 37 years—the United States Secret Service was assigned full responsibility for protecting the life of the President. Secret Service methods have grown increasingly sophisticated—since Dallas, particularly—and, fortunately for the peace of mind of all concerned, the odds against a Presidential assassination today are long.

In slightly less than a century four Presidents were murdered. The first three of these crimes, however, could have been averted by what would now be considered the most rudimentary

kinds, yet every society has passed through violent epochs. History is filled with assassinations of kings, emperors, premiers, chancellors, imams, and czars. Assassinations of American Presidents have been so sensational that the uproar has tended to obscure reality: Such crimes are rare compared to other kinds of violence, and, overall, assassination has been uncommon in America. A couple of famous men who happened to be Senators—Huey Long and Robert F.

protective procedures. Preventing the murder of John Kennedy would have taken more luck and better police work, yet that too might have been accomplished if the book depository had only been searched before the motorcade passed.

★   ★   ★

To kill a President and get away with it would seem next to impossible. But, so long as the President goes out in public at all, there always remains the chance of another Dallas or Ford's Theatre. Inevitably, the danger of assassination is on the mind of any President. "A President has to expect those things," Truman remarked after the Blair House shooting. Abraham Lincoln —like all Presidents and probably more than most—was the recipient of written threats. He kept an envelope marked "Assassination" which once contained 80 threatening letters. Not a month before his death he dreamed of hearing a wailing in the White House and of discovering a coffin in the East Room. When he asked a soldier who was dead, the answer came back, "The President. He was killed by an assassin." In Fort Worth, before the final flight to Dallas, Kennedy mused about the possibility of assassination. "You know, last night would have been a hell of a night to assassinate a President," he said to an aide.

Still, men who have reached the White House are so familiar with the hazards and vicissitudes of a political career that they

tend to be fatalistic. The intensity of ambition that spurs somebody toward the Presidency will not be deterred by the chance of death from an assassin's bullet. Nor will a President readily accede to doing everything necessary to minimize the likelihood of assassination, such as campaigning from the safety of television studios. The fate of four martyred Presidents underscores the risks of mingling in crowds. Yet it is the nature of men in high office to want to do so. Crowds are part of the essential environment of political leadership. Politicians do not want to be walled off. "I am not going to live in the shadows," Robert Kennedy said when his friends urged him to seek more protection in public after the death of his brother.

Nevertheless, Presidents and Presidential candidates have had to accept the stern reality that there are some things they simply cannot do. They have learned

After pleading guilty to an assassination attempt on President Ford, Sara Jane Moore is led from Hall of Justice.

Seconds after "Squeaky" Fromme's attempt to kill President Ford, she is subdued by Secret Service, left.

that lesson through the fate, for one, of Robert Kennedy in the kitchen of the Ambassador Hotel in Los Angeles.

The encouraging lesson is that the government of the United States has demonstrated remarkable stability, or at least remarkable resilience. Even after the assassination of Lincoln at a critical hour. Even in the violent, almost revolutionary spring of 1968 when the Reverend Martin Luther King, Jr., and Robert Kennedy were murdered within 62 days of one another. No one has proved indispensible to the republic. In that sense the United States has truly been a government of laws and not of men.

Describing the man picked by the Confederate Constitutional Convention to lead the South, a delegate remarked, "He looked like a President." John Roy Robertson's portrait of Jefferson Davis, above, was painted during the war. G.P.A. Healy portrayed Vice President Alexander Hamilton Stephens in an unusually candid manner, right. The flag of the Confederate States of America, far right, was first raised in Savannah on November 18, 1860.

A President in Richmond

Russell Bourne

The first Presidency began on April 30, 1789, when George Washington took the oath of office in New York City. Another first Presidency began some 73 years later, on Washington's birthday 1862, when Jefferson Davis took the oath of office in Richmond, Virginia, to become President of the Confederate States of America.

The two men had little in common save their southern background. General Washington had been elected President having first led a revolution, while Senator Davis had served in the government for many years before he was chosen to lead a rebellion. Yet, despite this difference, and many others of style and personality, the two men are quite alike in one key regard—the real person is virtually impossible to discern.

★   ★   ★

That rainy 1862 inauguration was the second for Davis. A year earlier he had been summoned from his Mississippi plantation to Montgomery, Alabama, to be sworn in as Provisional President of the Confederacy. It had taken Davis six days to travel from Vicksburg via the South's poorly developed rail system, an inauspicious portent for the Confederacy. And perhaps nobody in the South was more cognizant of its weakness *vis à vis* the Union than Davis, who had been Secretary of War between 1853 and 1857. His perception of the Confederacy's military limitations, both in terms of numbers and materiel, goes far to explain his cautious secessionism compared to that of the so-called "fire-eaters."

Yet, at first it seemed like the most glorious of reigns. Every railroad station between Vicksburg and Montgomery turned out crowds, turned on bonfires to hail the chief. It was reminiscent of Washington's trip from Mount Vernon to New York in 1789. When Davis finally arrived at Montgomery's Exchange Hotel (having given some 25 speeches en route), he was celebrated

JEFFY'S DREAM.

Jefferson Davis's dream, as parodied above, was that foreign nations would support the Confederacy in order to obtain cotton. Another broken dream was internal unity: Robert Barnwell Rhett, whose Charleston Mercury *had hailed secession on December 20, 1860, left, subsequently led the press campaign against Davis's conduct of the war.*

CHARLESTON MERCURY

EXTRA:

Passed unanimously at 1.15 o'clock, P. M., December 20th, 1860.

AN ORDINANCE

To dissolve the Union between the State of South Carolina and other States united with her under the compact entitled " The Constitution of the United States of America."

We, the People of the State of South Carolina, in Convention assembled, do declare and ordain, and it is hereby declared and ordained,

That the Ordinance adopted by us in Convention, on the twenty-third day of May, in the year of our Lord one thousand seven hundred and eighty-eight, whereby the Constitution of the United States of America was ratified, and also, all Acts and parts of Acts of the General Assembly of this State, ratifying amendments of the said Constitution, are hereby repealed; and that the union now subsisting between South Carolina and other States, under the name of "The United States of America," is hereby dissolved.

THE

UNION IS DISSOLVED!

At the first Confederate inauguration, peddlers hawked mementos, as had become traditional in Washington.

as the fulfillment of the secessionist ideal. Setting out for the state capitol on that warm, sunny day (February 18, 1861) in a specially provided coach-and-six, Davis heard the jubilant crowds cheer as the band struck up "Dixie," the northern tune that would become the Confederacy's unofficial national anthem.

The *Times* of London declared, "the inaugural ceremonies today were the grandest pageant ever witnessed in the South," and published the entire text of the new President's address, which was replete with the expectable conclusion that the "enlightened verdict of mankind" would "vindicate the rectitude" of the southern cause. William L. Yancey, one of the first leaders of the movement to secede, proclaimed of President Davis that "the man and the hour have met. We may now hope that prosperity, honor and victory await his administration."

Davis immediately commenced to apply his considerable intellectual skills to the challenge of his six-year constitutional commission. First, he sought to persuade Virginia and the rest of the upper South to join the deep-in-cotton, lower South states that had broken away from the Union in reaction to Abraham Lincoln's 1860 victory. Davis had been selected in part because he seemed the one man whose stature as a leader rose above state and personal interests. He strove to keep the loyalty of the initial states to secede by appointing their well-known, if contentious, leaders to his cabinet.

Possibly a more adept administrator might have welded

the government of the Confederacy together effectively. Davis's own wife feared that his disdain for politics and his administrative weaknesses would undo him. Illness and a certain aristocratic aloofness may also have affected his Presidential performance as the Confederacy grew to its full size, as the capital was moved to Richmond to spearhead the war effort after the attack on Fort Sumter, and as early victories turned to agonized defeats.

But perhaps the most severe personal difficulty that beset Davis was a lack of grand vision. With all his seasoned wisdom and deep devotion to the cause of independence for the South, he never articulated that inspired meaning which might have given southerners an extra boost of strength and unity on their way to nationhood. Though the President attempted to galvanize governmental power by rigorous centralization (thus alienating states-rights advocates), the focus of the effort, the nature of this thrust toward national independence, remained undefined.

★   ★   ★

If the results of the Congressional elections of 1863 can be read as a guide to the popularity of Davis's administration, his star then was in the descendant. When the Confederacy's Second Congress convened in May 1864, it was clear that Davis was in trouble for his failure to make the national destiny successfully manifest. The image of the nation ultimately seemed personified far more by General

Great Seal of the Confederacy, made in England, was intercepted by the blockade and never used by the C.S.A. It featured

a wreath of agricultural products around George Washington in an equestrian pose —an assertion of the southern heritage.

Robert E. Lee than by President Jefferson Davis. The military hero could be understood whereas the political purpose could not.

The debate will continue as to whether that failure to personify the southern cause resulted from the President's deficiencies of style or from the very nature of the nation he led. One of Davis's biographers, Clement Eaton—who does not hesitate to compare Davis to Lincoln, finding nobility and a sense of history in both—believes that whereas the former's philosophy turned backwards to the triumph of the agrarian republic during the Revolution, the latter's looked ahead to the coming decades of industrial growth. In this, Davis

should not be "blamed for the defects of his society."

★   ★   ★

We are told that, in prison, after the Confederacy's collapse, Jefferson Davis found consolation in classical writings. Upon reading Horace's comments on the fickle preference of the people for change, he wrote, "In all the affairs of life, we are reduced to choosing evils, every situation having its disadvantages."

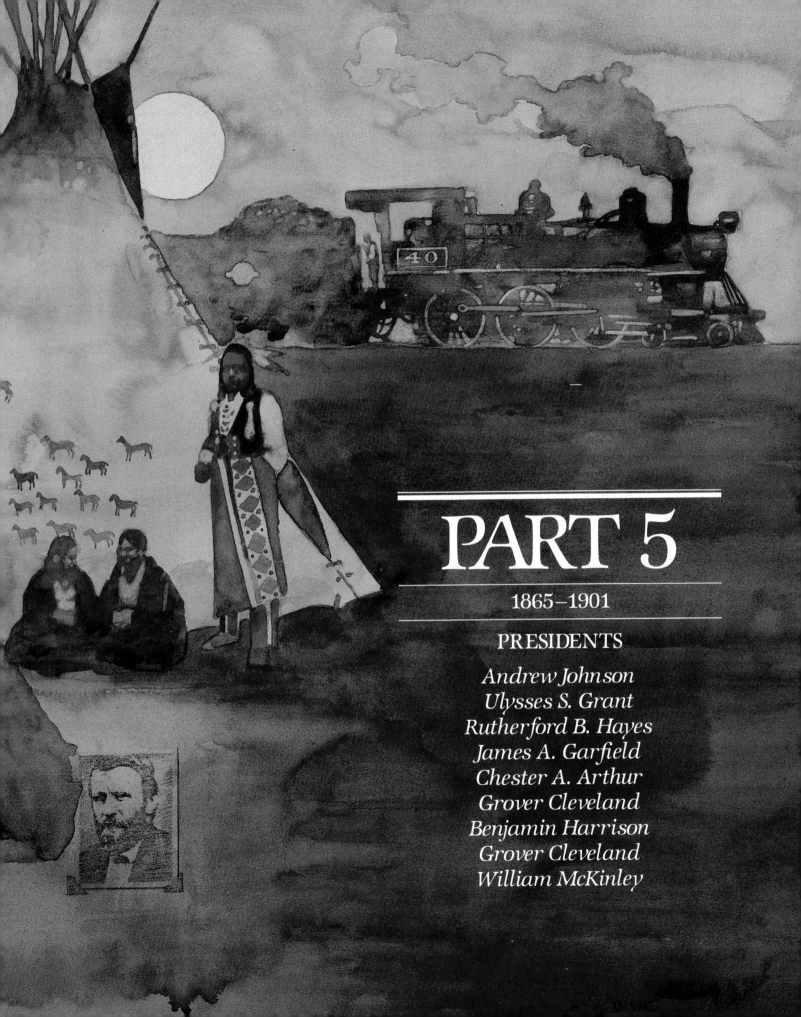

PART 5

1865–1901

PRESIDENTS

Andrew Johnson
Ulysses S. Grant
Rutherford B. Hayes
James A. Garfield
Chester A. Arthur
Grover Cleveland
Benjamin Harrison
Grover Cleveland
William McKinley

The President in the Age of the Politico

Lewis L. Gould

History's verdict on the men who served as President between Lincoln and Theodore Roosevelt has generally been negative: overt condemnation for weakness or silent contempt for failure to assert national leadership. With the exception of Grover Cleveland, remembered for his courage in the depressed 1890s, and William McKinley, Cleveland's successor and President during the Spanish-American War, they have remained, in the words of Thomas Wolfe, "The lost Americans: their gravely vacant and bewhiskered faces mixed, melt, swam together. Which had the whiskers, which the burnsides, which was which?"

Beyond their alleged mediocrity, these Presidents are usually viewed as irrelevant. Mark Twain and Charles Dudley Warner, in their 1873 novel titled *The Gilded Age*, established an image of an epoch in which national leaders were both uninspired and uninspiring. Journalists, commentators, and historians subsequently reinforced this image. The Englishman James Bryce accused American politicians of clinging to "outworn issues," and native critics such as E.L. Godkin and Henry Adams scorned contemporary affairs as squalid and tawdry. The late 19th century, wrote Vernon L. Parrington in the 1920s, was the age of the "Great Barbecue."

According to this traditional judgment, legislators debated such sterile topics as the civil service, the protective tariff, and free coinage of silver, while the real power was wielded backstage by ruthless *politicos*—senators and congressmen closely allied with party bosses and robber barons—to devise an industrial economy for their own sordid purposes. The enfeebled Presidency simply marked time until the 20th century when Theodore Roosevelt and Woodrow Wilson revived the heritage of Lincoln and Andrew Jackson.

Judging the late 19th century from this perspective distorts the nature of politics in that period and obscures important developments that led to a strengthening of the Presidency after Rutherford B. Hayes took office in 1877. So accustomed have Americans become to assertive Presidents that it is difficult to understand the prevalence of an altogether different concept of the office. Political circumstances, party ideology, and a pervasive suspicion of executive power combined to hold the Presidency in check for 36 years after Lincoln's assassination. Yet, one by one institutional and conceptual barriers fell, and the Presidency assumed much of its modern-day look by the time of William McKinley's assassination in 1901.

Elected President in 1896 with the conservative Ohio Republican machine behind him, William McKinley belied the stereotype of the passive Gilded Age Presidency and laid the foundation for expanded power of 20th-century Chief Executives.

Andrew Johnson's losing battle with Congress over Reconstruction policy between 1866 and 1868 had left the Presidency in a state of impotence. Congress asserted its power to control patronage, override vetoes, and hold the executive securely in check. The President, as Johnson's archenemy Thaddeus Stevens put it, was no more than "the servant of the people as they shall speak through Congress." Had just one more Senator voted in favor, Johnson would have been convicted of "high crimes and misdemeanors" and ousted from office.

The Presidency of Ulysses S. Grant did nothing to tip the balance away from Congressional dominance. Grant was elected in 1868 with the hope that his "prompt intelligence in unexpected and pressing emergencies" would continue to serve the nation well. But his eight years were scandal-ridden and maladroit. When informed that office-holding conspirators were pocketing money collected as federal liquor taxes, the President said, "Let no guilty man escape." After the "Whiskey Ring" probe resulted in the indictment of his private secretary, however, Grant worked to keep his old friend out of prison and forced the

Ulysses S. Grant's lack of political judgment contrasted dismally with his military prowess. His two administrations (1869–1877) were tainted by graft, fraud, and corruption.

Cabinet officer who had exposed the scandal to resign. Corruption in the War Department was an even more serious blot on the latter years of Grant's tenure. In the end, his two terms, following Johnson, left the Presidency with less power and less respect than at any other time in the 19th century.

When George Frisbie Hoar of Massachusetts took his seat in the Senate in 1877, he found that his colleagues regarded the White House as a place "to give, not receive advice." Senator John Sherman of Ohio summed up the view from Capitol Hill: "The executive department of a republic like ours should be subordinate to the legislative department." A celebrated symbol of Congressional dominance and an archetypal politico was Senator Roscoe Conkling of New York, "the curled darling of Utica," resplendent in green pants and yellow shoes. Any President trying to recapture the authority of his office would have to wrestle with what Conkling represented—the spoils system, machine politics, and Senatorial prerogatives. Political parties were just about all that mattered to Conkling, and parties were not something "built up by deportment, or by ladies' magazines, or gush."

Attitudes of the major parties lay at the heart of the issue. Republican roots in the old Whig Party, which had coalesced in opposition to the assertive Andrew Jackson, disposed them to think of the legislative branch as predominant, the executive as only executing the will of Congress (the first Republican President, Abraham Lincoln, was anomalous). As for the Democrats, when they envisioned a strong President, as Jackson had been, they thought of a *negative* force to block attempts at implementing Republican activism. In the reaction against expansion of Presidential authority during the Civil War, the office was forced back to its minimal constitutional functions.

An important political restraint on the Chief Executive was the party deadlock of the Gilded Age. Neither the Republicans nor the Democrats were able to establish a clear claim as the nation's majority party. Though the GOP won three of the five Presidential elections between 1876 and 1892 it never achieved a majority of the popular vote in any of them. Only twice between 1874 and 1894 did Republicans control the White House and both houses of Congress. The Democrats did it only once. The Republicans had an ascendancy in the Senate (which was not elected by popular vote); the Democrats were more likely to control the House. Federal and state elections outside the solidly Democratic South were closely contested, with great exertions from both sides and large voter turnouts. Strong party loyalty based on ethnocultural alle-

Rising above the cloud of popular suspicion surrounding the disputed Presidential election of 1876, Rutherford B. Hayes revitalized the executive but alienated "Old Guard" Republicans.

giances and an intense popular interest in politics distinguished the late 19th century from the late 20th.

The enduring reputation of the Gilded Age for political skullduggery has not been overshadowed even by the scandals of recent years. There were memorable episodes such as the Whiskey Ring, the Crédit Mobilier affair involving construction of the Union Pacific Railroad, and the Star Route frauds in the postal service. More important, the spoils system of political appointment, the close ties between captains of industry and politicos, and the confusion between private and public interest all constituted grave flaws in the nation's system of government. Nev-

ertheless, undue emphasis on the character and influence of the politicos, on the seamy side of American politics, obscures the constructive energies that many politicians brought to the nation's problems.

It is true that no President had the stature of Jackson and Lincoln before or Roosevelt and Wilson afterward. The size of the White House staff suggests how circumscribed the functions of the executive office were. Both Grant and Hayes had fewer than 10 clerks and secretaries. Because Congressional appropriations were small, less than $15,000 a year, Presidents sometimes had to recruit aides from other government departments. Record keeping, which had improved under Andrew Johnson, became careless in Grant's time but improved again under Hayes. Typewriters were first used by Garfield's clerks, though only with McKinley and the Spanish-American War did telephones become commonplace in the White House.

There was no elaborate security apparatus to protect Presidents. Much of the White House was open to the public, and weekly receptions for the citizenry were a Washington tradition. Residents of the capital saw Chief Executives walking alone in the evening and riding unprotected in their carriages with family and friends. Even Garfield's assassination in 1881 failed to induce greater concern with Presidential safety. As late as 1898 a British visitor said of the executive mansion: "The gates are open to pedestrians and carriages, and anyone who has business, or thinks he has, can walk up unchallenged."

The insignificance of the Presidency had roots in both Johnson's and Grant's failure of leadership. Grant's successor, Rutherford B. Hayes, began his Presidency in March 1877 under a cloud of suspicion that compounded the difficulties his office already faced. Hayes had run against Samuel J. Tilden, a New York Democrat. As the returns came in, Hayes had 166 electoral votes, Tilden 184. Victory required 185. But in Florida, Louisiana, and South Carolina, which had a total of 19 votes, Republicans and Democrats both claimed victory. Had the Reconstruction governments imposed upon those southern states by the Radical Republicans in Congress carried the day for Hayes? Or, had the Democrats carried just one of them and thereby elected Tilden? Resolution of the controversy entailed appointment of an electoral commission. Behind the scenes, interested parties weighed what the South might gain if one or the other candidate were chosen. Finally, the "Compromise of 1877" gave Hayes the disputed votes in return for Congressional acquiescence in the end of Reconstruction (meaning the resumption of white rule). Many Americans questioned

James A. Garfield takes a scythe to party "Stalwarts," political hangers-on, and corrupt sorts. Many Americans had high hopes for what was to be a tragically short administration.

Hayes's title to the Presidency, and labeled him "His Fraudulency" or "Rutherfraud" B. Hayes.

Despite this bad start, Hayes made significant headway in revitalizing the executive office. Dignified and honest, he restored much of the moral stature of the White House that had slipped away under Grant. Senators who expected to have a large voice in the selection of Hayes's Cabinet were shocked to find him making his choices without their aid. He resisted Congressional efforts to limit his power through crippling riders to appropriations bills that would have prevented enforcing federal election laws in the South. Most important, he challenged the Senate's prerogatives in allocating patronage during a prolonged battle with Conkling over the naming of a new collector of customs for the port of New York. With this Presidential victory, Hayes wrote in his diary: "My sole right to make appointments is tacitly conceded."

Hayes's exertion of federal authority in the railroad strike of 1877 set a precedent for later, more even-handed governmental intervention in labor disputes. His attempts to woo southern Democrats into the GOP failed, however, and Congress overrode his veto of the Bland-Allison Act providing for government coinage of silver. Yet his other 12 vetoes stood. By the time he prepared to return to his home in Fre-

mont, Ohio, in March 1881, Hayes could look back on a creditable record. Eight years later he remarked that if "a Napoleon ever became President, he could make the executive almost what he wished to make it."

Because of the brevity of his term, James A. Garfield of Ohio is a Presidential enigma. Some historians see him simply as an available politician who trimmed and compromised to reach the White House. Roscoe Conkling said: "He has no sand." Yet, in another light Garfield appears as a potentially important transitional figure, who, like James G. Blaine, tried to make his party aware of the sorts of policies required by an industrialized society. Like Hayes, Garfield confronted Senatorial power in the person of Roscoe Conkling. When the President nominated one of Conkling's enemies to the New York collectorship, the Senator called it "perfidy without parallel." But Garfield understood the larger issue of Presidential authority symbolized by the confrontation. "It had better be known, in the outset," he wrote, "whether the President is the head of the government, or the registering clerk of the Senate." Reviving the dormant prestige of the office, Garfield rallied public opinion. He went to the Washington railroad station on the morning of July 2, 1881, aware that he had won. There a deranged office seeker, Charles J. Guiteau, shot the President. Two and a half months later he died. Conkling left politics. "How can I speak into a grave?" he asked. "How can I battle with a shroud? Silence is a duty and a doom."

After Garfield's passing there was again a recession in Presidential power, though it was not the fault of his successor, Chester Alan Arthur. A colleague of Conkling's who ran with Garfield to balance the ticket, Arthur belied the apprehensions expressed when he took office ("Chet Arthur, President of the United States! Good God!") and proved to be an independent and competent executive. There were timely vetoes of pork-barrel measures, and Arthur added in the long run to Presidential authority when he signed the Pendleton Civil Service Act in 1883, for the growth of the federal civil service reduced the power and influence of the politicos. But a resurgence of Democratic strength in the midterm elections of 1882, continued feuding among Republicans, and Arthur's failing health all limited his achievements.

Arthur entertained more lavishly than any other President of the era, and he provided a contrast to modern attitudes toward the privacy of the executive when he told a woman who asked if he drank: "Madam, I may be President of the United States, but my private life is nobody's damned business." The verdict on Arthur's tenure was epitomized by Frank Carpenter,

"Carp," a widely read journalist of the day. "Arthur has given us a good administration," said Carp, "but it has been negatively rather than positively good."

A steady erosion in Republican strength since the end of Reconstruction in 1877 culminated in 1884 when Grover Cleveland led the Democrats to victory over James G. Blaine, the GOP nominee from Maine. Cleveland, who has generally escaped the censure that has been the lot of other Presidents of the Gilded Age, earned an enduring reputation for personal honesty and political courage. Yet his liabilities were substantial. In a dozen years of leading the Democrats, he left the party at one of the low points in its history, and left the Presidency with only shreds of its prestige. Here was an instance of a strong President seriously weakening the office he occupied.

Cleveland had enjoyed a rapid rise to political

Chester A. Arthur took office on September 19, 1881, amid fears that "Stalwarts" would become "the power behind the throne." In fact, Arthur displayed remarkable integrity and competence.

prominence. Elected mayor of Buffalo in 1881, he became governor of New York the next year. When the Democrats looked around for a Presidential candidate in 1884, here was a fresh face, a man whose laissez-faire conservatism and commitment to economy were well suited to the party's negative posture. The contest between Cleveland and Blaine was close and dirty. The Democrats attacked Blaine's honesty, raked over his personal life, and charged him with anti-Catholicism. Republicans publicized the revelation that Cleveland had accepted responsibility for an illegitimate child in Buffalo—one newspaper calling him "a coarse debauchee who might bring his harlots to the White House." Though the election was extremely close, the torrent of mud did not determine the result. Rather, the Democrats finally capitalized on the gains that had been building for several years.

Cleveland did not like politicians, nor did he have much taste for the give-and-take of politics. Regarding his Presidency as "a dreadful self-inflicted penance for the good of my country," he jealously guarded the prerogatives of the office and thereby added, incidentally, to its power. Cleveland asserted the constitutional right of the Chief Executive to remove federal officials without Congressional interference. "I shall not submit to improper dictation," he declared, and his actions perpetuated the trend toward greater executive autonomy begun by Hayes and Garfield. The quiet political scene during Cleveland's first term forestalled any general recognition, however, that his governing style was arrogant and self-righteous. "The Lord is very kind to Cleveland," one Democrat wrote. "He always tells him to do the thing he wants to do." Yet, for a nation that had not seen fit to elect a Democratic President since 1856, Cleveland's aloof posture, his legalistic vetoes of special pension bills for war veterans, and his defiance of Congress could be regarded as evidence that a Democrat was trustworthy to serve with dignity and integrity.

In 1887 Cleveland devoted his entire annual message to a plea for lowering the protective tariff—a cornerstone of Republican pro-business policy. This assault on the tariff might have provided a basis for Democratic cohesion, but Cleveland backed away from his stance in the election year of 1888, seeking to play down the tariff issue in the party platform. Selection of pro-tariff Democrats to head his campaign further quenched the enthusiasm his message had aroused. Moreover, his patronage policies were so inept that party leaders had less esteem for Cleveland than the general public did. One irate wheelhorse reflected the sentiment that "faithlessness is a passport to recognition by this mass of Presidential fat."

Nevertheless, Cleveland was the strongest candidate the Democrats could muster, and he was renominated to face the Republican choice, Benjamin Harrison of Indiana. While Cleveland accepted the long-standing tradition that incumbent Presidents did not campaign, Harrison ran a strong race, effectively addressing large crowds in speeches from his front porch. The GOP was united on the tariff issue, and most of the three million dollars it raised in campaign contributions went for pro-tariff literature. As civil service rules banned assessing office holders for campaign funds, politicians turned increasingly to the business community for money.

The 1888 campaign was replete with all the sharp tactics typical of the era. The Democrats published a letter from a Republican leader in Indiana urging election workers to "divide the floaters into blocs of five" and see that they voted many times. A California Republican posed as an Englishman and solicited the views of the British minister, Sir Lionel Sackville-West, regarding the election. An indiscreet reply favoring Cleveland was immediately made public—much to Cleveland's disadvantage, since the whole thing smacked of improper meddling by a foreigner. Republican crowds chanted, "Sack, Sack Sackville-West," and the inept diplomat was recalled. After being declared the winner, Harrison told one state boss, Matthew S. Quay of Pennsylvania, that "Providence has given us the victory." The hard-boiled Quay later remarked, "Providence hadn't a damned thing to do with it." He added that "Harrison would never learn how close a number of men were compelled to approach the gates of the penitentiary to make him president. . . ."

Benjamin Harrison, like Hayes *vis à vis* Tilden, received fewer popular votes than his opponent yet still won a majority in the Electoral College, 233 to 168. Beyond that, he had a penchant for orderly administration, instituting an improved filing system and seeing that data on the workings of the government were systematically gathered. He broadened his legislative role by holding frequent conferences with party leaders in Congress. He traveled extensively, and his felicitous remarks on these junkets anticipated the shrewd speeches of William McKinley and the "Bully Pulpit" of Theodore Roosevelt. Yet, even though Harrison was able to charm a crowd of 20,000, he was cold and forbidding in private. One politician called him "a purely intellectual being" with "no bow-

Is the hat too big? Joseph Keppler of Puck *casts doubt on Benjamin Harrison's capacity to measure up to William Henry Harrison, "Old Tippecanoe," his grandfather.*

els." Another declared that his re-election would mean "four more years in a dripping cave." Skilled at handling certain aspects of the Presidency, Harrison never mastered its human side. The White House became to Harrison a "jail," and so it was that his defeat by Cleveland in 1892 had "no sting in it."

During the "Billion Dollar" Congress that convened at the beginning of Harrison's Presidential term, the GOP enacted the Sherman Antitrust Act, the Sherman Silver Purchase Act, and the McKinley Tariff. It sought, albeit with no ultimate success, a federal elections bill that would have provided better safeguards for black voting rights. This surge of Republican legislative activism proved unpopular, as did the Republican push for Sunday closings in the Middle West, causing disastrous reverses for Harrison's party in the midterm elections of 1890. In addition, falling farm prices and a growing burden of debt fostered the People's Party in the rural South and West. The Populists called for the free and unlimited coinage of silver as an inflationary cure for shortages of hard money and credit. They also advocated taxing incomes, and government ownership of railroads. In the upheaval at the polls that accompanied Populism, the Democrats were the gainers. Harrison's administration stumbled through its final two years with only enough residual power to compel the President's renomination in 1892. Grover Cleveland returned "back home" to the White House in March 1893 after defeating him by 400,000 votes. (The Populist candidate, James B. Weaver, received more than a million votes.) The Democrats took control of both the House and Senate for the first time since before the Civil War.

Cleveland won his third nomination on the basis of his views on tariff reform and his adamant opposition to inflationary monetary schemes. He remained the only figure with an appeal to the whole loose coalition that comprised the Democratic Party. Yet, four years in private life had not tempered his disdain for politicians or made him any less imperious. He told the public not to seek any jobs or favors in Washington. He listened mostly to friends who told him he was right; as for others, he said, "If they wanted a fight he would give them one." From his unfriendly private secretary to the uniformed guards outside the White House, Cleveland made it clear that he would run the Presidency with little regard for his personal popularity—or for the impact of his conduct on Democratic fortunes. A journalist recalled that obtaining White House news was done "much after the fashion in which highwaymen rob a stage coach."

The onset of a severe depression in the spring of 1893 provided an exacting test of Cleveland's ability to lead, and he wielded the powers of his office forcefully to meet the crisis. Unfortunately he also alienated his party and embittered the electorate. Convinced that the Sherman Silver Purchase Act of 1890 had destroyed business confidence and precipitated the economic panic, Cleveland summoned Congress into special session in August 1893 to repeal the offending statute. It was a mistake to postpone tariff reform, which united the Democrats, in favor of action on the monetary question, which divided them. Mistaken too was the harsh and unyielding manner in which Cleveland used patronage and executive pressure to overcome Democratic and Populist opposition and secure repeal of the Silver Purchase Act. When Congressional leaders proposed a compromise on the matter, the President refused to see them and pounded the table vigorously as he told the Cabinet he would not

budge. By the end of 1893 Cleveland was victorious on Capitol Hill—at the cost of a split party and dwindling national confidence in his ability to govern.

Cleveland was equally stern in 1894. When a railroad strike erupted in the spring and summer, his Justice Department exerted federal power to crush Eugene V. Debs and the union that had walked out in support of workers at Pullman, Illinois. The President flexed his muscles but he lost confidence among those on whom the impact of the depression was most burdensome. In Congress the tariff reform effort culminated in the Wilson-Gorman Act, which actually raised some of the rates. An angry, factionalized party rebelled when Cleveland hurled accusations about "party perfidy and party dishonor" during this fiasco. Cleveland's clumsy exertions of authority resulted in substantial losses in the Congressional elections of 1894 and renewed criticism of his executive style. "All this idea of prerogative in the President is wholly out of place

After four-year interim, banner proclaims return to White House in March 1893 of Grover Cleveland and wife Frances, his former ward whom he had married during his first administration.

HANNALET, PRINCE OF $MARK, IN THE MODERN GRAVEYARD SCENE.

Mark Hanna, the Ohio capitalist who dominated Republican politics in the Gilded Age, is depicted as "Hannalet," contemplating labor's remains.

in our Constitution," wrote one southern editor.

By 1895 the Presidency stood about where it had been during the Grant era. Cleveland's bellicose policy toward Britain over the Venezuela boundary dispute revived his prestige, but not for long. Subsequently the administration sided with Spain on the issue of the rebellion in Cuba, a most unpopular stand with the American people. Cleveland became reclusive, his administration irrelevant in national politics. In 1896 the Democrats nominated William Jennings Bryan, a candidate whose ideology, especially on monetary policy, directly contradicted the President's.

Cleveland would fare better with historians than with his contemporaries. His conduct in office would be called a "study in courage," an object lesson in how a brave President resisted mistaken popular pressures. He would be rated among the top 10 Presidents, and by all odds the best man elected between Lincoln and Theodore Roosevelt. Yet modern scholars tend to be less certain that Cleveland's policies were as appropriate as he regarded them, and to recognize that he lacked the political insight, tolerance, and flexibility that make for truly effective leadership in a democracy.

O n this auspicious day," wrote the *San Francisco Examiner* on March 4, 1897, "the sky is blue, the birds sing and joy is unconfined. It is the last day of the Cleveland administration." Cleveland's successor was William McKinley of Ohio, a former Congressman and governor who defeated Bryan by a margin of 600,000 votes—the most decisive electoral triumph in a quarter-century. Though the Presidential contest of 1896 is famous for the amount of money the Republicans and their campaign manager, Marcus A. Hanna, spent on McKinley's behalf, the GOP victory did not rest on bought votes and coerced workers. The Republican candidate defeated the Democratic-Populist coalition that Bryan led because of Hanna's effective campaign tactics, because of McKinley's front-porch speeches that brought 750,000 people to his home in Canton, Ohio, and because of the revulsion against Cleveland that had precipitated a national Republican majority in 1894.

With McKinley, the outlines of the modern Presidency emerged between 1897 and 1901. He traveled more than any predecessor, frequently to win support for administration policies. Newspapermen were provided with rudimentary facilities inside the White House and with an explicit recognition of their professional standing in the form of travel accommodations and a system for handling news releases. There was some private access to the President. McKinley's secretary, George B. Cortelyou, who dealt with these matters, became the first true Presidential staff member. The size of that staff increased from half a dozen in 1897 to nearly 30 by 1901. The volume of White House mail also mushroomed, reaching a thousand letters a day by the turn of the century. To reach out for expert opinion, McKinley relied freely on executive commissions to gather data and shape policy.

The Spanish-American War contributed to the enhancement of McKinley's power. American interest in the Cuban rebellion against Spanish rule reflected both traditional concerns and renewed stirrings of the expansionist sentiments of the middle 1890s. Imperialistic pressures came from the proponents of an expanding overseas trade and a stronger navy and merchant marine, but, in a broader sense, they derived from a swelling national pride and a faith that the U.S.A. must take its place of world leadership.

McKinley gradually intensified diplomatic pressure to compel Spain to relinquish Cuba, along with Puerto Rico its last significant possession in the Western Hemisphere. When war came in April 1898, it was not simply because the battleship *Maine* had blown up at Havana in February, or because of the yellow press. Neither was it the result of a weak President yielding to popular hysteria. After prolonged negotiations it had become clear that Spain would not budge on the issue of Cuban independence, and that ostensible concessions were essentially attempts to buy time. McKinley determined how and when the war should be fought, and during the brief conflict itself Presidential power expanded dramatically. Telegraph and telephone lines allowed the President to keep pace with military events. A "war room" was set up on the second floor of the White House to permit monitoring the situation on both oceans where American forces were engaged. When Commodore George Dewey's squadron defeated the Spanish at Manila Bay on May 1, 1898, McKinley dispatched army units to the Philippines and secured the American foothold that would later enable annexation. As the war progressed, McKinley pressed Congress to complete the annexation of Hawaii. In negotiating an armistice with Spain in August, he obtained maximum territorial concessions.

This image of President McKinley shows him shortly before he was mortally wounded by an assassin's bullets at the Pan-American Exposition in Buffalo on September 6, 1901.

McKinley named several Senators to the American peace delegation, thus smoothing the way for ultimate ratification of the treaty. In October 1898, while the negotiations were in progress, the President toured the Middle West. He told his audiences: "We cannot shirk the obligations of the victory if we would, and we would not if we could." Here was a Chief Executive seeking to rally public opinion behind his foreign policy. When the Peace of Paris was signed in December, Spain ceding the Philippines to the United States, Senate ratification became McKinley's chief priority. He visited the South to woo pivotal Democrats, and he prodded Senators by various means. McKinley's sustained exercise of strong executive leadership resulted in ratification by a narrow margin on February 6, 1899.

McKinley subsequently dealt with the Philippine Insurrection on the basis of his constitutional war powers until Congress granted him specific authority. In 1900, without any attempt to secure prior Congressional approval, he sent 2,500 soldiers into China to rescue westerners besieged in Peking during the Boxer Rebellion. At the time of his assassination in September 1901, he was planning extensive trips outside of the continental United States, a further break with precedent. Although his style was less flamboyant and glamorous than Theodore Roosevelt's, William McKinley had laid a stable foundation for the expansion of Presidential power that followed.

The appearance of the modern Presidency was not a historical accident that depended on Roosevelt's timely accession or Woodrow Wilson's election in 1912 as the result of a Republican split. Over the last quarter of the 19th century, the natural preeminence of the office slowly reasserted itself in response to the problems of industrial growth and expanded world responsibility. Each President contributed something, either by positive action or negative example, to the renaissance of the executive branch. When Roosevelt took over from McKinley, fears were already being expressed that the Presidency was becoming too strong, that it was assuming "prerogatives which must be the envy of crowned heads." The 20th century would see Presidents become still stronger, and, too, Americans would ultimately understand the potential perils of a powerful Chief Executive. Yet, whatever the dangers of an Imperial Presidency, there would be no returning to the relative impotence and subordination from which the Gilded Age Presidents had in their turn freed the nation's highest office.

★ ★ ★ ★ ★ ★ ★ ★ ★ ★ ★ ★ ★ ★ ★

Also Rans

Frederick S. Voss

Most voters regard the great Presidential sweepstakes every four years as a race between two candidates, each backed by a major party. Yet few elections have lacked the added color of a minor-party candidate or two, and our own times yield bumper crops: Hundreds of Presidential candidates register with the Federal Election Commission for each quadrennial contest.

Although the time-honored parental boast that the newborn "will grow up to be President" may be only a remote likelihood, it is not quite so far-fetched that said pride-and-joy might run for the office. The chance of there being more than a few supporters is slim, however, for the American electorate has by and large eschewed ideological extremism in favor of gradualism. With rare exceptions third-party candidates have been irrelevant to the outcome of Presidential elections. But still they keep on running, some simply as a lark and others in dead earnest.

The initial third-party nominee for the Presidency was too serious to consider his candidacy a lark, yet too retiring to wage his campaign in earnest. William Wirt had been attorney general under James Monroe and John Quincy Adams. Though he had also served a term in the Virginia Assembly, he was fundamentally disinclined to seek elective office. When the Anti-Masonic Party

William Wirt, right, was America's first third-party candidate, nominated in 1832 by the Anti-Masonic Party. Wirt was *relieved when he ran third to Andrew Jackson and Henry Clay. At left, perennial Socialist campaigner Eugene V. Debs.*

133

tendered Wirt its Presidential nomination in 1832, his deep-seated antipathy to Andrew Jackson induced him to accept, but he never took up his own cudgels. As he frankly admitted, he did not possess any of "the captivating arts and manners" of the successful office seeker.

So throughout the campaign Wirt remained mute. When the National Republicans failed to rally to his cause, as he had hoped, and instead nominated Henry Clay, he tried unsuccessfully to withdraw from the contest. Jackson's ultimate victory was a bitter disappointment, but Wirt was nonetheless relieved that his flirtation with Presidential politics was over. "A culprit pardoned at the gallows," he told a friend, "could not have been more light hearted."

★　★　★

As the dispute over slavery escalated in the 1840s and 50s, increasingly fragmenting the major parties, antislavery factions within each began coalescing into distinct organizations. Beginning with the Liberty Party's campaign in 1840, opponents of slavery fielded White House candidates in every election.

The early antislavery candidates fared poorly. In the mid-1850s, however, armed conflict broke out between proslavery and antislavery settlers in Kansas. One result was the formation in a rural Wisconsin church of an alliance of dissident northern Whigs and Democrats. Soon this alliance became known as the Republican Party. So began the greatest success story in the history of American third parties.

Within months, the Republicans had grown into a formidable political force. By 1856 they had in fact become a major party and four years later they attained the ultimate goal of all minor parties. The Republican candidate, Abraham Lincoln, was elected President.

The abolition of slavery put to rest the issue that had mainly impelled minor-party Presidential candidacies in the antebellum decades. But, as the pace of industrialization and urbanization accelerated in the Gilded Age, and as modern corporate finance emerged, the attendant social and economic dislocations precipitated third parties in ever more variegated abundance.

★　★　★

The first Republican candidate, John C. Frémont, top, waged an emotional campaign against James Buchanan in 1856 but lost. The six-year-old party succeeded with Lincoln in 1860 and '64, however, and then kept the Presidency until 1884.

134

One of the first ideological factions to take to Presidential electioneering in the postwar years did so not as a response to new social problems but rather because it felt betrayed by the now-ascendant Republican Party. This faction was the Prohibitionists. "Cold water" converts to Republicanism had anticipated that once the horrendous blot of slavery was eradicated the party would direct its reforming impulses to the liquor question.

After the war, however, Republican strategists balked at efforts to write prohibition into the party platform. By 1869, thoroughly disabused of any hope for promoting their dry crusade within Republican ranks, some 500 delegates forgathered in Chicago's Farwell Hall to form the National Prohibitionist Party. In 1872 the party nominated its first Presidential candidate, James Black of Pennsylvania, a one-time Republican loyalist.

Attracting a mere handful of votes (5,608), Black's candidacy did not bode well. Nor did weak Prohibitionist showings in the next two Presidential contests. But in 1884, with John P. St. John as the party's standard-bearer, the Prohibitionists were filled with renewed hope. As governor of Kansas, "Lion-hearted" St. John had masterminded the victorious campaign for a statewide ban on liquor. St. John did not repeat rosy promises of national victory. Rather, he reasoned that it would not be altogether impossible to undermine the front-running candidates.

As the campaign wore on, the Prohibitionists began making inroads among voters in pivotal New York State. Fearful that St.

Prohibitionist candidate John P. St. John drew enough votes in 1884 to tip the election in favor of Grover Cleveland.

John's growing popularity was seriously damaging James G. Blaine's chances, Republican emissaries at one point went so far as to try to lure him out of the race with a bribe. As it turned out, Republican anxieties were well founded. For in the final tally the Empire State held the balance in the Electoral College, and, due in part to the 25,000 votes cast for St. John, Blaine lost the state and so the Presidency to Grover Cleveland.

★　★　★

With minor-party candidacies having become an established feature of Presidential elections, voters took the early sorties of the Prohibitionists as a matter of course. But, in an era which decreed that the woman's proper place was in the home, Victoria Woodhull's announcement in 1871 of her availability for the nation's highest office must have been somewhat unsettling.

For those acquainted with the bold Mrs. Woodhull, however, this news was no surprise. She had been shocking society regularly ever since 1868, when she and her sister Tennessee Claflin came to New York, and, with claims of spiritual powers, worked their way into the graces of multimillionaire Commodore Cornelius Vanderbilt.

Soon, Victoria and Tennie were ensconced in Wall Street as proprietors of their own brokerage house. But Woodhull's appetite for the unconventional was far from sated. Embarking with Tennie on the publication of *Woodhull & Claflin's Weekly*, she now mounted a feminist crusade that called not only for the franchise but for something considerably more radical. In late 1871, speaking in New York's Steinway Hall, she told her audience: "Yes, I am a free-lover." She further declared it her "inalienable constitutional right" to love whom she may, when she may, and "to change that love every day" if she so pleased.

By the spring of 1872, respectable society had had its fill of the "Wicked Woodhull." Yet, even as the National Woman's Suffrage Association erased her name from its rolls, she was not about to forego her Presidential campaign. In May, a motley

collection of freewheeling fanatics gathered at her invitation to offer her their nomination. They styled themselves the Equal Rights Party. Several days later she forecast a new era of Anglo-American peace—once the namesake of England's Queen Victoria was in the White House.

Woodhull's campaigning days, however, were short-lived. When attacked by Catharine Beecher and Harriet Beecher Stowe, sisters of the celebrated preacher Henry Ward Beecher, she retaliated by publishing in her *Weekly* the story (probably

Victoria Woodhull announces in her own newspaper as first woman candidate for President. Nast cartoon at right suggests characteristic sentiment toward her.

not untrue) of the good Reverend Beecher's affair with parishioner Elizabeth Tilton. As a result, election day of 1872 found Presidential candidate Victoria Woodhull sitting in New York City's Ludlow Street Jail, charged with sending pornography through the United States mail.

Though later declared innocent, Woodhull seemed to lose some of her zest for controversy. In 1877, decidedly more subdued, she left for England where she eventually found a degree of respectability as the wife of a banker. Even in her chastened state, however, she kept her eye on the White House, and in 1880 America received word that she was still available.

Compared to Victoria Woodhull, the next woman to take to the Presidential hustings seemed prim and retiring. Actually, Belva Ann Lockwood was exceptionally adept at circumventing barriers to women's rights. Refused admittance to law

The 1884 campaign of the second woman Presidential candidate, lawyer Belva Ann Lockwood (portrait, right), inspired ridicule, as seen in this engraving.

school, she went anyway as a privately tutored student. Denied her diploma on completion of the course, she complained to President Grant and got it. Barred from practicing before the Supreme Court, she lobbied Congress for a bill permitting her to do so and got that too.

Now, in the summer of 1884, Presidential nomination in hand, the determined Lockwood commenced still another campaign by embarking on a lecture tour of major cities. Though other feminists—notably Susan B. Anthony and Elizabeth Cady Stanton—dissociated themselves from Lockwood's efforts, she ultimately aroused some sympathy among the male electorate. On election day—ignoring the Republican aspirant, James G. Blaine, altogether—she quipped that she thought the real contest was between herself and Democrat Grover Cleveland. The final result, however, did not evidence a neck-and-neck race. The tally may not have been quite accurate (some Lockwood ballots are said to have found their way into a Pennsylvania wastebasket), but officially the count was: Lockwood, 4,149; Cleveland, 4,874,996.

★ ★ ★

Campaign ribbon, above, celebrates 1912 candidacy of "the Lincoln of the Wabash," Eugene V. Debs. Teddy Roosevelt, caricatured at left, faced William Howard Taft and Woodrow Wilson in 1912. The "Boy Orator of the Platte," William Jennings Bryan, opposite page, waged three losing Presidential contests.

Among the third-party Presidential candidates who came to the fore in the latter 19th century, none had a greater impact than those who carried the standard of agrarian reform. The nation's farmers increasingly saw themselves as the victims of a rapacious oligarchy of bankers and industrialists. Out of this disenchantment grew the Greenback Party and its political heir of the 1890s, the People's Party. Populism promised a drastic overhaul of the nation's economy. To the initial call for monetary inflation designed to boost farm prices were added demands for the eradication of industrial monopoly. The Populists never gained a permanent foothold in the national political arena. Yet, for a time a White House victory did not seem inconceivable at all.

Progressive Party candidate Henry A. Wallace ran against what he called "war-breeding" policies in 1948.

When the election year of 1892 rolled around and the Populist convention put forth James B. Weaver as its Presidential choice, there was good cause for optimism. Weaver, a Greenback Presidential hopeful as far back as 1880, campaigned against America's business "plutocracy" with a rare combination of fervor and dignity. In the end, with a little over a million popular votes cast for the Populist ticket, Weaver lost to Democrat Grover Cleveland. But, having captured 22 electoral votes—a feat rarely matched in the entire saga of third-party candidacies—his showing was eminently respectable. Though the Populists would never again do so well, the strength they revealed in 1892 provided the first impetus toward adoption of their program by progressive elements in the major parties. Within a single generation, most Populist reforms had become part of the nation's governmental fabric.

★   ★   ★

After the turn of the 20th century, the American political arena became ever more pluralistic and the belief that anyone might make a run at the White House took even stronger root. Among the most determined of third parties was the Socialist. Eugene V. Debs, the party's leading spirit, had his hat almost perpetually in the ring. Debs ran, and ran vigorously, even though he knew quite well that he was too radical for most voters. Nevertheless, insofar as he believed that talking about reform forcefully enough could eventually create a climate favorable to Socialist victory at some later day, he considered his five Presidential campaigns as part of a

necessary building process.

Thus, Debs set out every four years to educate the electorate. By 1908, when he embarked on his campaign train—the "Red Special"—for a rigorous whistlestop tour, the public was becoming used to his attacks on capitalism. That year 400,000 votes were cast for him—more than a fourfold increase from 1900. Four years later, with the call for reform reaching its peak within the two major parties, the Socialist tally doubled again.

Debs never did fulfill his hope of placing socialism in the mainstream of American politics. In his last campaign, however, he did succeed in adding a uniquely colorful chapter to America's election-year lore. Unalterably opposed to U.S. entry into World War I, Debs had been sentenced to prison in 1918 for making speeches undermining the national war effort. When nominated in 1920, he was still serving out his term. And so American voters faced the novel choice of casting their lot with a convict. Amazingly enough, nearly one million of them did. Shortly afterward, the victorious Republican Warren G. Harding granted him an amnesty, and America's grand old man of socialism spent the last six years of his life in quiet retirement.

★   ★   ★

When Theodore Roosevelt left the White House in 1909 after nearly eight years, the public suspected that retirement was not likely to suit him. What the public did not suspect, however, was that within four years he would be leading a third-party

challenge against his erstwhile protégé, William Howard Taft.

By 1912, Roosevelt regarded Taft as a traitor to the Republican progressive spirit. Moreover, Roosevelt's disenchantment was widely shared. And so the battle was on. While Taft quietly gathered support for renomination within closed party caucuses, Roosevelt was vocally creating a ground swell for his own GOP nomination in state primaries. Taft's strategies ultimately won out at the Republican convention, but Roosevelt was never one to take defeat easily. After delegates committed to him had stamped out of the convention hissing "thief" and "robber" at the seated Taft delegations, the hastily organized Progressive Party tendered Roosevelt the nomination denied him by the Republicans.

Predictably, in light of his enormous popularity and well-articulated call for reforms embodied in his doctrine of "The New Nationalism," Roosevelt's candidacy proved a far cry from the usual third-party effort.

Quickly dubbed the "Bull Moose" Party after TR compared his health to that robust creature, the Progressives made a good showing, outpolling Taft though not Woodrow Wilson.

A dozen years later, "Fighting Bob" LaFollette campaigned vigorously on the born-again Progressive ticket. By the election of 1928, however, with much of the country convinced that it was on the verge of a millennium devoid of want and poverty, minor-party candidates—and all their grumblings about the present order of things—appeared as little more than an eccentric echo of silenced tumult. In this most sanguine of election years, the total vote for the six minor-party hopefuls fell short of 400,000, while the Democrat Alfred Smith received 15 million and the Republican Herbert Hoover over 21 million. The days when a Socialist or Populist candidate for President could run a strong race seemed over.

The sudden collapse of euphoria after 1929 and the subsequent onset of national depression, however, brought a resurgence in the fortunes of minor parties. In 1932—even while Franklin Roosevelt pushed on to resounding victory —third, fourth, and fifth-party candidates had once again found an audience. Indeed, as FDR's New Deal reforms fell short of the expectations of some citizens, as America's involvement in global politics spawned debates over isolationism, and as the postwar decades brought the civil rights question to the fore, the tradition of minor-party candidacies revived and has waxed strong ever since.

★   ★   ★

So, with purposes almost as varied as the American people themselves, these candidates have also run. As long as the Presidency continues to be the fulcrum of power in our democratic system, they will continue to run. And, as long as the complexity of problems and issues grows as it seems to do with each advancing year, they will run in ever greater numbers—if not to win, at least to make a difference.

★ ★ ★ ★ ★ ★ ★ ★ ★ ★ ★ ★ ★ ★

Change Presidents ...and Waltz

Amy Donovan

On the evening of March 4, 1809, as Thomas Jefferson strolled into Long's Hotel on Capitol Hill to fête his successor, James Madison, the U.S. Marine Band struck up "Jefferson's March." "Am I too early?" Jefferson asked a friend. "You must tell me how to behave, for it is more than 40 years since I have been to a ball." Indeed, Mr. Jefferson was attending not only his first dance in a good while, but also the first inaugural ball staged in Washington, D.C. Some 400 others participated in the "Dancing Assembly," John Quincy Adams reporting that "the crowd was excessive—the heat oppressive, and the entertainment bad." Window panes were smashed to increase ventilation.

Washington was very much a cultural backwater in the early 19th century, and the people welcomed any appropriate occasion for a social event. The lively crush in 1809 hinted at the many inaugural jams to come. Likewise, perhaps, did President Madison's attitude anticipate that of many successors. His countenance "contrasted with the happy expression of Jefferson," and reportedly he whispered to a friend that he "would much rather be in bed." Jefferson explained, "I have got the burden off my shoulders, while he has now got it on his."

Another Washington hotel was the site of the next three inaugural balls, Madison's second and both of James Monroe's. Known variously as Davis's and as Brown's Indian Queen Hotel, this was one of the "most celebrated and important stopping places for members of Congress and other noted men who visited the capital." Monroe himself did not stay for supper at Brown's following his second inauguration on March 5, 1821 (since the fourth fell on a Sunday, the

Images of James K. Polk's Presidential predecessors embellish a silk and ivory fan carried by Polk's wife at the 1845 inaugural ball staged at Carusi's, site of inaugural festivities for every President elected between 1824 and 1844.

143

1829, though he did put in an appearance at the White House festivities that became legendary. "I never saw such a crowd before," wrote Daniel Webster from the Capitol at the end of February. "Persons have come five hundred miles to see General Jackson, and they really seem to think that the country is rescued from some dreadful danger." After the swearing-in ceremony, Old Hickory rode his horse to the White House, and "high and low, old and young, black and white, poured in one solid column into this spacious mansion." The new President soon had to escape through a back entrance.

★ ★ ★

Twenty years later, in 1849, a building was erected on Judiciary Square especially for the official inaugural ball for another war hero, Zachary Taylor. The growing size of inaugural crowds, no longer able to fit into Carusi's, necessitated the temporary "saloon" with its 8,000 feet of floor space. White cotton and draped flags covered the walls, wood stoves supplied heat, and, for the last time, candles and tapers provided light. Chandeliers rained "perpetual showers of falling tallow" on the guests. Indeed, the Grand Inaugural Ball was far from an unqualified success. One observer termed the dance floor "bad," the arrangements "chaotic," and the whole event "a crying shame." According to another contemporary account, "it was about as chaotic as Tammany with the women

Between 1849 and 1873 several inaugural balls were staged in temporary structures on Judiciary Square. At James Buchanan's in 1857, top, a 40-piece orchestra set chandeliers to swaying. Program above commemorates that inaugural ball.

nation was without a President for one day). But the Secretary of State, John Quincy Adams, attended the festivities along with his wife Louisa, recording in his diary that they arrived back home around midnight.

Beginning with John Quincy Adams's own inaugural ball in 1825, the scene shifted to the Washington Assembly Rooms, usually called Carusi's after the builder, Lewis Carusi, who had opened this dance salon at Eleventh and C streets in 1822. Much the largest structure of its kind in the city, it was here that each of the four men elected President following Adams—Andrew Jackson, Martin Van Buren, William Henry Harrison, and James K. Polk—also were fêted at the time of their inauguration.

Andrew Jackson, in mourning for his wife, stayed away from his first inaugural ball at Carusi's on March 4,

The Smithsonian has hosted inaugural balls for nearly a century. In 1973 the great pachyderm in the rotunda of the Museum of Natural History provided an apt centerpiece for a celebration staged by partisans of President Nixon.

thrown into the confusion." Among the 5,000 who attended was ex-Congressman Abraham Lincoln, who was unable to retrieve his belongings in the mob scene when the ball ended, and walked hatless back to his boarding house in the early hours of the morning.

Lincoln's own inaugural ball in 1861 was staged in a similar temporary structure on Judiciary Square, called the "White Muslin Palace of Aladdin." The dancing was spirited and some reports called the ball "a great success." Yet impending hostilities surely cast a shadow over the festivities. Southerners, who had played so substantial a role in Washington society, maintained a conspicuous absence, and soldiers guarded the building.

The second inaugural ball for Lincoln took place in the U.S. Patent Office (now the Smithsonian's National Collection of Fine Arts and National Portrait Gallery), one of the nation's finest examples of Classical Revival architecture. Women were invited to use the offices of patent examiners and Patent Commissioner David Halloway to add "the finishing touches of their toilettes." In early 1865 the times seemed more auspicious than four years before, and this ball was a greater success than Lincoln's first. The President himself led off with a stately promenade through the gallery to the east wing. Afterwards, however, there recurred the cloakroom pandemonium that had marred Zachary Taylor's ball in 1849.

But the worst confusion and loss of property occurred following Ulysses S. Grant's inaugural ball in 1869. After Congress had refused permission to use the Capitol rotunda for festivities, the

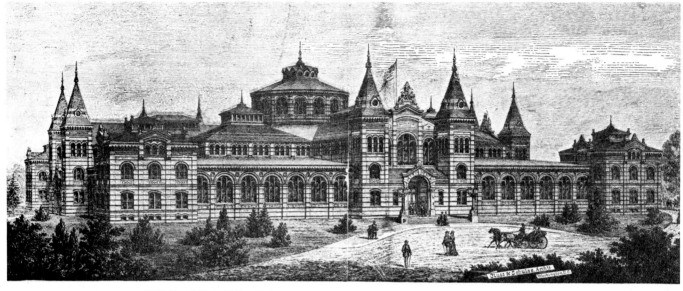

THE GRAND FETE TO GARFIELD AND ARTHUR
AT THE
NATIONAL MUSEUM BUILDING.

newly completed north wing of the Treasury Building was selected. As had been the case at the Patent Office, the space was so cut up by partitions that congestion was inevitable. So it was that Grant's second inaugural ball, on March 4, 1873, was staged in another temporary building on Judiciary Square. This was the last time for that—for, while congestion was minimized, there were other problems, even worse. Sub-zero temperatures whipped by northerly winds forced heavily wrapped guests to guzzle hot drinks and dance for sheer warmth, while caged canaries were too concerned about simply surviving to sing songs.

★　★　★

The inauguration of James A. Garfield and Chester A. Arthur coincided with the approaching completion of the Smithsonian's United States National Museum (now, its Arts and Industries Building) in 1881. Although the building was "not ready for the occupancy of the government collections," it was gaily lit up and decorated for the occasion. The ball was well attended, and when it ended the lineup of carriages "extended outside of the Smithsonian grounds and far down the street."

In 1885 the inaugural ball for Grover Cleveland in the spectacular new Pension Building—likewise still unfinished at the time—ushered in a new era. Workmen stretched a temporary roof overhead and put down a wooden dance floor. They also installed huge steam radiators throughout. The *Star* reported

that everybody felt far more comfortable than was usually the case "at the crowded private receptions for which Washington is so particularly noted."

The Pension Building—with its grand court, eight mammoth columns (75 feet high, eight feet in diameter), central fountain, and three tiers of galleries—seemed made to order for gala occasions such as inaugural balls. An unprecedented number of guests, 9,000, attended in 1885. A "perfect carnival of animation," the ball had electric lights "that almost turned night into day." The building was completed not

long afterward, and for almost a quarter-century it was the site for every Presidential inaugural ball. In 1909 some 18,000 people packed in to celebrate for William Howard Taft.

After Taft, 40 years elapsed before a President again attended an inaugural ball anywhere. A grand tradition fell victim to various personal tragedies and to stormy domestic and world affairs. In 1949, however, Harry S Truman celebrated at a ball in his honor, and then began an unprecedented multiplication of inaugural ball sites as more and more space was sought to accommodate the ever-increasing crowds. Dwight D. Eisenhower appeared at two balls in 1953 and four in 1957, while five balls fêted John F. Kennedy in 1961. In 1969 Richard M. Nixon's well-wishers celebrated at six sites, including the Smithsonian's Museum of History and Technol-ogy. And Jimmy Carter stopped in at all seven of the 1977 inaugural balls, one of which once again lighted up the grand court of the Pension Building.

★　★　★

In 1809, in a Capitol Hill hotel, 400 people tripped the light fantastic at the nation's first official inaugural ball. A century later, 18,000 attended the inaugural ball in the Pension Building. And 60 years after that, nearly twice this many celebrated at a half-dozen sites. More is not necessarily better, though—indeed, for sheer elegance it is doubtful whether anything can ever match the private celebration of George Washington's inauguration in New York City on April 30, 1789. There, the Father of His Country, displaying "grace and dignity in every movement," led out two cotillions and danced a minuet.

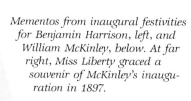

Mementos from inaugural festivities for Benjamin Harrison, left, and William McKinley, below. At far right, Miss Liberty graced a souvenir of McKinley's inauguration in 1897.

148

Harrison's inaugural ball in 1889 was the first in the fully completed Pension Building. Left, 88 years later, a reception for new V.P. Mondale.

PART 6

1901–1953

PRESIDENTS

Theodore Roosevelt
Woodrow Wilson
Warren G. Harding
Calvin Coolidge
Herbert Hoover
Franklin Delano Roosevelt
Harry S Truman

The President as Progressive

Arthur S. Link

Americans greeted the 20th century with fireworks, celebrations, and prayer. They sensed the beginning of a new era. The United States was now the richest and mightiest nation on earth. The value of manufactures it exported topped imports by more than a half-billion dollars a year. Moreover, it had acquired a colonial empire in the Caribbean and the Pacific with a total area as large as New York, Pennsylvania, and Ohio. Yet Americans faced the new century in an uncertain and anxious mood. A concomitant to the spectacular pace of industrialization had been the formation of great trusts that threatened to destroy all competition in manufacturing and transportation. The nation's immense railroad network was dominated by a scant half-dozen empire builders. Credit resources were concentrated in a handful of cities, New York above all. Powerful investment bankers such as J. Pierpont Morgan, who had contrived to consolidate industries, railroads, and utilities, largely controlled these trusts through interlocking directorates. A new phenomenon called "finance capitalism" jeopardized the very foundations of independent enterprise.

If the independent entrepreneur seemed threatened, so too did the democratic ideal of a land without extremes of poverty and wealth. The gap had been widening ever since the Civil War. The richest 1.6 percent of the population received 10.8 percent of the income and owned nearly half the national wealth in 1896, the year William McKinley was elected President. And the newly rich had a penchant for what Thorstein Veblen termed "conspicuous consumption," a style of living diametrically opposed to the traditional virtues by which most Americans still set store.

Americans were troubled, too, at the very thought of mastering alien peoples in the Philippines and Puerto Rico, acquired after the War with Spain. Had the United States abolished slavery at home only to reinstitute it abroad? An army of 70,000 men and brutal guerrilla tactics had been required to subjugate the Filipinos. How seriously were Americans to take warnings that involvement in imperialist adventures meant the end of isolation from Europe's unending turmoil and perhaps the end of democracy at home? Was such a wise observer of the American scene as James Bryce to be heeded when he called the acquisition of colonies "a complete departure from the maxims—approved by long experience—of the illustrious founders of the Republic"?

A superb leader in domestic affairs, Woodrow Wilson posed in a relaxed stance for an official photograph taken in the East Room of the White House in 1918. On reconsideration, he decided the image was too casual and had it recalled.

Whether contrary to venerable maxims or not—the Democrats made imperialism their paramount issue in the campaign of 1900—many citizens took genuine pride in the nation's new role as a world power, and agreed with President McKinley that the U.S. "could not escape the duties imposed upon it by the Ruler of Nations." Yet the American nation nevertheless seemed headed for a crisis of confidence, a crisis born of a widespread conviction that political institutions had been perverted and politicians had become mere pawns of the special interests. Consider the office of the President. From the very beginning, Americans had regarded the Presidency with utmost reverence. George Washington and Abraham Lincoln were national heroes *nonpareil*; Thomas Jefferson and Andrew Jackson were not far behind. But no President had attained anything approaching veneration since Lincoln's martyrdom in 1865. Nor, with rare exceptions, had eminent men even been considered for nomination. Indeed, in his book on *The American Commonwealth*, Bryce had titled a chapter "Why Great Men Are Not Chosen President."

Presidential candidates were nominated at national conventions dominated by state and local "machines" which in turn were controlled by "bosses," whose techniques included bribery and chicanery at the polls. Bosses wanted Presidents whom they could count on to distribute spoils generously and whom they could dominate through Congress. President Ulysses S. Grant, of course, had been the archetype. Even when strong leaders such as Grover Cleveland had managed to get elected, Congress still reigned supreme. William Jennings Bryan, one of the few candidates since Lincoln whose milieu was not the boss-ridden politics of Ohio or New York, was overwhelmed during his campaign in 1896 by the millions of dollars collected from Republican businessmen.

Even had Bryan been elected, he would have run up against a Republican high command that controlled Congress in the interests of big business. This high command included Senator Marcus A. Hanna of Ohio, President McKinley's multimillionaire mentor; and, even more powerful, Senator Nelson W. Aldrich of Rhode Island, aloof, arrogant, and the avowed spokesman of Wall Street. So set against change was Joseph G. Cannon of Illinois, who became Speaker of the House shortly after the turn of the century, that people joked at the thought of his presence at the Creation, where he would have voted against the Lord and for chaos.

Despite rumblings of discontent, especially audible in the West and South, Republican leaders felt confident as they laid plans for the election of 1900. There was no question about renominating McKinley. But in 1899 Vice President Garret A. Hobart had died, and a subsequent development deeply worried Mark Hanna, for one. Early in 1900 sentiment began building for the nomination of Theodore Roosevelt, Governor of New York and a hero during the recent war.

Normally, Hanna would simply have defied this sentiment. But Roosevelt's candidacy was being pushed specifically by Thomas C. Platt, the Republican boss of New York. Platt had permitted Roosevelt's nomination for governor because it seemed the only way to defeat a popular Democrat. Now, Roosevelt in Albany was threatening to wreck Boss Platt's whole organization. Nominate him for the Vice Presidency, Platt demanded, and get him out of New York once and for all. Hanna balked. "Don't any of you realize that there's only one life between this madman and the White House?" the Ohio Senator asked. But Platt was adamant, Hanna yielded, and in November the McKinley-Roosevelt ticket overwhelmed William Jennings Bryan and his running mate, Adlai E. Stevenson, carrying 28 of the 45 states. After the inauguration in March 1901, Roosevelt spent what was for him a quiet spring and summer. Then in September a demented anarchist mortally wounded McKinley at the Pan-American Exposition in Buffalo. He was dead within a

Uncle Sam looks on sternly as Teddy Roosevelt wrestles with the railroads—an imaginary view of a real-life battle. Roosevelt's maxim: "Don't flinch, don't foul, hit the line hard."

few days, and "that damned cowboy," as Hanna called Roosevelt, was President of the United States.

Mark Hanna's opinions notwithstanding, if ever any man had been destined for the Presidency it was Theodore Roosevelt. The scion of an old New York family, he had conquered frail health during boyhood by robust exercise. Genteel, well-off but not wealthy, he felt undisguised contempt for vulgar materialism. Freed from worldly cares, he had devoted his life to public service, first as a member of the New York Assembly, then as police commissioner of New York City, assistant secretary of the Navy, and governor. He had also done everything that boys of his generation dreamed of doing. He traveled all over. He was a rancher and cowboy, and he even caught cattle rustlers. He hunted big game, camped in the wilds, and climbed high mountains. As police commissioner, he roamed the streets of New York at night in disguise. He wrote good history books and heroic tales that boys devoured. He battled bosses and corrupt politicians. He was a brave soldier.

Roosevelt duly mourned McKinley, but in fact relished a succession to the White House even under tragic circumstances. For he knew that the country was at a critical juncture—even in 1901 it was in the throes of a popular revolt that historians now call the Progressive Movement. Progressivism was an omnibus reform campaign waged on many fronts. It had some roots in earlier programs for agrarian reform, stronger roots in the fight to overturn corrupt boss-rule in the cities. It was fueled by investigative reporters (whom Roosevelt later dubbed muckrakers) determined to probe every dark corner of American life.

Progressives were demanding measures that would permit popular control of key political processes such as Presidential nominations. They were augmenting the old Populist call for fair and equitable railroad rates with demands for regulation of all public utilities. Social reformers were seeking legislation to prohibit child labor, make factory work safer, clean up slums, and, in general, improve the quality of everyday life. Finally, a great many middle-class citizens could be counted among the ranks of progressivism insofar as they were alarmed at the unchecked concentration of financial and industrial power.

On that score, progressivism made bedfellows of small-town bankers and family farmers, retailers and consumers, independent entrepreneurs and workingmen. But it was fraught with a fundamental anomaly.

Teddy Roosevelt, left, stands with his hand-picked successor, William Howard Taft, on inauguration day, March 4, 1909. Taft's policies would drive a wedge between the two erstwhile friends.

Roosevelt himself put a finger on this after he had left office. Many people who called themselves progressives, he noted, were "really representative of a kind of rural toryism, which wishes to attempt the impossible task of returning to the economic conditions that obtained sixty years ago." "Real progressives," on the other hand, "recognize[d] the inevitableness and the necessity of combinations in business," and sought to establish effective governmental countermeasures. The problem, Roosevelt lamented, was that they were "hampered by being obliged continually to pay lip loyalty to their colleagues, who, at bottom, are not progressive at all, but retrogressive."

Some progressives, that is, wanted to assert control over business combinations, others wanted them dismantled. This is why there could be legitimate disagreement as to whether Roosevelt was properly to be termed radical or conservative. Insofar as he largely accepted the status quo, seeking to make big business "subserve the public good" but not to sweep it away, Roosevelt was a conservative. But he was a conservative who fully realized that what the country demanded was constructive leadership and progressive adaptation to the new circumstances of an urbanized and industrialized society. He, Theodore Roosevelt, would provide the requisite leadership.

As has happened so often in American history, perhaps providentially, he was the man for the hour. Temperamentally, Roosevelt had to be *the* leader. Henry Adams once called him perpetual motion personified. He was driven as by demonic forces to mastery; hence he could be ruthless when anyone stood in his way and vengeful toward his enemies. He came dangerously close to egomania. He also had deep convictions about the Presidency. Senators and Congressmen represented particular states, particular districts; party leaders usually represented special interests. The people, all the people, needed a single spokesman in whom they could place their faith. That could only be the President.

It was Woodrow Wilson who best described this concept of the Presidency, several years later in 1908:

No one else represents the people as a whole. . . . He is also the political leader of the nation, or has it in his choice to be. The nation as a whole has chosen him, and is conscious that it has no other political spokesman. His is the only national voice in affairs. Let him once win the admiration and confidence of the country, and no other single force can withstand him, no combination of forces will easily overpower him. . . . If he rightly interpret the national thought and boldly insist upon it, he is irresistible.

This was written before Wilson himself had seriously considered running for President: What he actually was describing was Roosevelt's Presidency. There had been "irresistible" Presidents before—Washington, Jackson, Lincoln—but Roosevelt inaugurated a new style of leadership. What "the President as Progressive" implies is an assertive leader who addresses basic social and economic problems and implements constructive solutions. Different leaders thought in terms of different solutions, but the *sine qua non* was a concept of the Presidency as the crucial instrumentality of change. Everything Roosevelt did was calculated to enhance Presidential power.

To achieve effective leadership, Roosevelt adopted what Arthur M. Schlesinger, Jr., has called the plebiscitary style. The plebiscitary President (there have been only three in our history—Jackson, Theodore Roosevelt, and Nixon) operates on the assumption that the people have vested their sovereignty in him. He believes that he possesses all executive power not ex-

Democratic candidate Woodrow Wilson speaks from a train platform during his vigorous whistle-stop campaign of 1912. His New Freedom program hit at monopoly and special privilege.

plicitly denied him by the Constitution. When frustrated by a hostile or uncooperative Congress, he resorts as much as possible to government by executive order. He takes the boldest initiatives in the area where he enjoys the most latitude—foreign affairs.

Roosevelt knew that his greatest resource was the affection of the American people, and he cultivated it assiduously. He spoke widely and frequently. A master showman, he moved among the crowds with an infectious gaiety, shouting "Bully!" and grinning at the people who pressed around him. His voice was high-pitched and somewhat shrill, but his listeners loved him when he snapped his large teeth, flailed his arms, and came down hard with his clenched fist.

The White House was Roosevelt's "bully pulpit," and he became something like a preacher-at-large to the American people. He thundered moralisms at them. He called for a "square deal" for capital and labor alike, and denounced "malefactors of great wealth." In an age of cheap magazines and penny newspapers, Theodore Roosevelt was a master manipulator of the press. News releases and advance texts of speeches poured from the White House. He kept in close contact with crusading reporters.

Roosevelt's relationship with Congress was characteristically a struggle. The House of Representatives, even with the arch-reactionary Uncle Joe Cannon in the chair, usually followed Roosevelt's lead. But the Senate—whose members were not elected by popular vote, and where the Republican high command had concentrated its control—fought him all the way. In 1903 he obtained passage, with little opposition, of a bill to create a Bureau of Corporations to investigate industrial combinations, and a bill forbidding railroads to offer rebates (special rates) to large shippers. The fur began to fly in 1906, however, when Roosevelt sponsored three measures aimed at controlling powerful economic interests. The most important was the Hepburn bill, landmark legislation that aimed to empower the Interstate Commerce Commission to investigate railroad rates and compel reductions if they were found exorbitant. The measure sailed through the House, but the railroads mounted an intensive lobbying campaign, and the so-called "railroad senators," led by Aldrich of Rhode Island, maneuvered to stall or emasculate the bill.

Roosevelt fought back with incredible vigor, kept the spotlight of public opinion on the Senate, and finally accepted a compromise measure. Though falling short of everything that many progressives wanted, it did—for the first time in American history—establish effective public control over the nation's largest and most important industry. The battles over the other two measures—meat inspection and pure food and drug bills—were brief but intense. Roosevelt won the day with the help of crusading novelists and journalists.

Except for the Hepburn Act, legislation during Roosevelt's Presidency scarcely began to strike at private wealth, privilege, and power. Yet he had good reason to be satisfied when he left office in 1909, for he had marshaled the vast powers inherent in the Presidency to amass an unparalleled record of personal achievement. Roosevelt struck first at the trusts. The Supreme Court had declared the Sherman Antitrust Act of 1890 inapplicable to manufacturing concerns, so he began his attack by instituting a suit in 1902 against a gigantic railroad combine engineered by J.P. Morgan. In spite of the Court, he also turned the Justice Department's guns against Standard Oil, American Tobacco, the "Beef Trust," and similar industrial monopolies. Almost single-handedly, Roosevelt had revivified the Sherman Act to put a rein on great aggregations of private wealth.

Other policies he pursued with no statutory authority at all. Asserting that a priceless national resource was being plundered for private profit, he declared that some 230 million acres of unenrolled federal lands were no longer for sale. When anthracite coal miners went on strike in 1902, he forced management to accept arbitration by threatening to send troops to seize the mines. During the Panic of 1907, he authorized U.S. Steel to absorb an important competitor with the assurance that there would be no antitrust action. He did so in order to prevent a further decline on Wall Street, and also because he believed

there were "good" trusts as well as "bad." He, and he alone, made such determinations. He, and he alone, decided what constituted "the greatest good for the greatest number," a favorite slogan.

In foreign affairs, Roosevelt took even bolder initiatives. He connived with Panamanian revolutionaries in 1903, and recognized their independence from Columbia so that the U.S. could get on with building the Panama Canal. He later boasted, "I took the Panama Canal and let Congress debate." In 1904 he announced a "corollary" to the Monroe Doctrine: Not only were European powers enjoined from intervening in the Western Hemisphere, but intervention by the U.S. was explicitly sanctioned and thus every Latin American republic became a potential protectorate. In 1905 he forced the government of the Dominican Republic to sign a treaty providing for an American receivership of its customs duties and American control of its national finances. When the Senate rejected the treaty, he kept it in force by executive order until the Senate approved a new treaty in 1907.

In dealing with Europe and the Far East, Roosevelt acted as an absolute monarch. In 1905 he mediated the Russo-Japanese War (for which he later won the Nobel Peace Prize), and he also negotiated an executive agreement stipulating noninterference with Japanese designs on Korea in return for a Japanese pledge to stay out of the Philippines. He made use of an executive agreement again in 1907 in averting a crisis with Japan and ultimately excluding Japanese immigration. In complete secrecy, he intervened in a crisis engendered by competition between France and Germany for dominance in Morocco.

Looking back, what this all adds up to is evidence that Theodore Roosevelt's was the first Imperial Presidency. Rarely did he assault the other branches of the federal government directly. But he did rule as a virtual sovereign. After Roosevelt, all Presidents would be judged, for better or worse, against his activist precepts and autonomous conduct.

Roosevelt would have been hard to follow in any event, but, as it turned out, his chosen successor, William Howard Taft of Ohio, was a disaster. Taft was kind and warm-hearted, and he wanted to carry on his mentor's policies. Indeed, he was a more vigorous trust-buster and even brought suit against two of Roosevelt's favorite good trusts, U.S. Steel and International Harvester. He secured Congressional approval of constitutional amendments providing for the direct election of Senators and a general income tax. He took few other initiatives, however, and had no talent for leadership.

Some of Taft's difficulties stemmed from his judicial temperament. He weighed all sides of great questions. He could not be vindictive. He could not hurl hyperboles such as "malefactors of great wealth," because he knew wealthy men who were not malefactors. Even more important, however, was Taft's indolence as manifested in acute obesity. Time and again he tried to reduce but failed to control his appetite, which was incredible. It is said, for example, that breakfast often consisted of a dozen eggs, a pound of bacon, and a mountain of pancakes. President Taft's weight averaged more than 300 pounds. No wonder he was slow-moving, often dozed in meetings, and put off problems until they began to overwhelm him.

Taft later said that his Presidency was an extended nightmare. At the very outset he called Congress into special session to reform the tariff, as promised in the Republican platform of 1908. The Payne bill, which put many raw materials on the free list and substantially reduced rates on manufactured goods, passed the House by a large majority. But the Senate Finance Committee, led by Rhode Island's imperious Aldrich, added 847 amendments that actually increased existing duties. Taft sat by complacently while Aldrich cynically broke party pledges. He finally roused himself to action when the bill was in conference committee and succeeded in winning some reductions. But the Taft Presidency had been mortally wounded by the Payne-Aldrich Tariff. He was, it appeared, no match for special privilege; he had lost the confidence of the American people.

By early 1912 it was a question whether Taft could win renomination without splitting his party. Roosevelt, totally disenchanted with his one-time protégé, entered the Republican preconvention campaign in February, and the ensuing battle was brutal and bruising. Roosevelt was incontestably the choice of the rank and file. But the Republican high command, which controlled the delegates from boss-dominated states, ignored the will of the voters and nominated Taft at the national convention in Chicago. Meanwhile, the Roosevelt delegates had stormed out. In August they returned to Chicago to organize the Progressive Party and nominate their hero.

The Democrats, as they had been most of the time since the Civil War, were still very much the minority party. But the rupture of the GOP made the election of the Democratic candidate, Woodrow Wilson, virtually inevitable. Wilson won only 42 percent of the popular vote but a smashing majority in the Electoral College. Democrats also seated a large majority in the House and a slim majority in the Senate.

No man in American history had such a meteoric rise to political prominence as Woodrow Wilson. He had served less than two years as Governor of New Jersey—very successfully, to be sure—and had then gone to the people and wrested control of the Democratic Party from the establishment in the same way that Jimmy Carter did in 1976. Wilson was the first truly national President since the Civil War: He had been born and reared in the South but lived all his adult life in the North. His two great American heroes were Lincoln and Lee.

In personal style, Wilson and Roosevelt were very different in some respects and much alike in others. Roosevelt adored the adulation of crowds; Wilson was embarrassed by such attention and seemed aloof. Both men were warm and intimate among family and friends. Wilson, however, took himself much less seriously than Roosevelt did. Wilson was a good conversationalist and not a monologist. Roosevelt was rash and impulsive; Wilson was deliberative, agonizing over problems. Wilson was sensitive and had a tendency toward self-righteousness, but he was less vindictive and far less an egomaniac than Roosevelt. Roosevelt was a poor speaker; Wilson was one of the greatest orators since Edmund Burke. Both men were keenly intelligent, but Wilson's mind was better disciplined. Indeed, he was unique among American Presidents in that he was a trained scholar, with a doctoral degree from Johns Hopkins University in political science, history, and economics.

Wilson and Roosevelt shared a conviction that the President should function as national spokesman and mediator among rival interests. Both believed in Presidential sovereignty in the conduct of foreign relations. Both were superb administrators. Both chose able and trustworthy Cabinets and worked well with their departmental heads. Like Roosevelt, Wilson used the press both to control the flow of information from the White House and to speak directly to the people. He instituted the first regular Presidential press conferences, granted interviews to friendly reporters, and leaked information when it suited his purposes. During the war, he created the first official propaganda agency in American history. Still, oratory was his chief instrument in influencing public opinion. Some of his passages were pure poetry. His speeches touched

Business as usual? Presidential pastimes hint at character of their administrations. Harding, left, takes time out from a round of golf to greet a child; Coolidge sharpens a scythe on Vermont farm.

hearts and minds and changed the course of history.

Wilson and Roosevelt differed most markedly in their conception of the role of Presidential leadership within the American constitutional system. Though a recalcitrant Senate forced Roosevelt to be a plebiscitary President, given his temperament he probably would have been one anyway. Wilson, since his college days, had admired the British parliamentary system, which vests executive power in a cabinet drawn from and directly responsible to the House of Commons. In his first book, *Congressional Government* (1885), Wilson had advocated adoption of the British system as a way of overcoming the chronic leadership vacuum in the executive branch. Roosevelt's revivification of the Presidency had convinced Wilson that the office embodied ample potential for effective leadership. Even so, Wilson brought to the Presidency an outlook and a method profoundly influenced by his admiration for the British system.

The President, Wilson believed, should be the leader of his party and, more specifically, the leader of his party in Congress. Thus he reinstituted the practice of addressing joint sessions. (No President since John Adams had appeared personally before the legislative branch.) It was also the President's duty, Wilson believed, to assure passage of a program that fulfilled sacred platform promises. In dealing with Congressmen and Senators, Wilson was gracious and deferential. He referred to them as "my colleagues." Nevertheless, he maintained personal control over every important piece of legislation. He went so far as to suggest that all Senate amendments to a major tariff bill be routed through him for his review. (Even the Democratic members of the Finance Committee thought that this was carrying Presidential leadership too far!) Wilson relied on patronage and the party caucus to maintain party discipline, but his chief weapon was sheer moral suasion. To a Congressman who threatened to step out of line, Wilson would simply say, "Here are our promises to the people. Here is our duty. Can we be unfaithful to the people?"

Wilson's method worked in part because the situation in Congress, prior to 1917 at least, afforded a perfect opportunity for a President who saw himself as the leader of his party in a parliamentary sense. There was no powerful Democratic counterpart to Senator Aldrich to oppose him. Moreover, the Democrats, after wandering in the wilderness for 20 years, were generally eager to cooperate for the success of their party program—to prove they were not, as Republicans often charged, "the organized incapacity of the country." Yet Wilson succeeded with Congress primarily because he himself set an example of devotion to the public good and of absolute integrity. He was thus able to wield the most effective kind of leadership possible within the American constitutional system.

He conclusively demonstrated that the President has it in his power not only to give voice to majority opinion, as Roosevelt had done, but also to fuse executive and legislative powers into an irresistible instrument of effective government.

The task that Wilson set for himself was nothing less than to build a new political economy that would operate to destroy or at least curtail special privilege, reopen channels of economic opportunity for small businessmen and farmers, and enhance the social and economic welfare of all. Wilson termed his program "The New Freedom."

He struck first at the protective tariff—a cornerstone of Republican policy for half a century and long symbolic of special privilege. Cleveland had tried to lower rates, and almost wrecked his party. Taft had promised to lower rates, and his failure to achieve this had been disastrous for *his* party. The Wilson administration's tariff, the Underwood bill, passed easily in the House. But then the representatives of special interests descended upon Washington. Wilson, at a press conference on May 26, 1913, issued a statement warning the country that an "industrious and insidious" lobby was at work to defeat tariff reform. The lobbyists went scurrying home. Wilson maintained pressure on wavering Democratic Senators. Not only did the Senate approve the Underwood bill, it actually reduced the rates set by the House. All in all, it was a victory that transformed Wilson, as a London editor put it, "from the man of promise to the man of achievement." The President was now fully up to facing his next challenge.

The most pressing of the nation's economic needs was for a monetary system to replace the one established during the Civil War, which was totally unsuited to contemporary necessities. The currency supply was tied to gold reserves and the national debt rather than to actual requirements under changing circumstances. The reserve machinery concentrated money mainly in Wall Street. Worse, control of both the money supply and credit was altogether in private hands. Wilson's remedy was the Federal Reserve Act of 1913, with its 12 regional banks, its Federal Reserve Board (Presidential appointees), and provisions for augmenting or contracting the currency supply as economic conditions changed.

Wilson kept the Justice Department busy with antitrust suits, as both his predecessors had done. But action through the courts was not, he said, sufficient; new legislation to strengthen the Sherman Act was required. Ultimately this took shape as the Clayton Act, which proscribed unfair trade practices. Congress passed that legislation in October 1914, shortly after establishment of the Federal Trade Commission, which was empowered to stop unfair competition.

By lowering the tariff, reorganizing the monetary system, and putting new teeth into the antitrust laws, Wilson had fulfilled his major campaign promises. Various other measures rounded out the New Freedom. A law passed in 1915 struck the shackles from American seamen. In 1916 came a law providing for long-term low-interest loans to farmers, a workmen's compensation law, a child labor law, and an eight-hour-day law for railroad employees engaged in interstate commerce. The Revenue Act of 1916 increased inheritance taxes and levied income taxes that grew progressively with a taxpayer's income—the first legislative redistribution of wealth in American history. Finally, the 19th Amendment, which Wilson pushed through a reluctant Senate in 1919, stipulated that "The right of citizens of the United States to vote shall not be denied or abridged by the United States or by any State on account of sex."

Wilson's achievements in domestic policy far transcended those of any previous President. In foreign affairs, he attained moral heights unparalleled before or since. He dedicated the United States to the service of mankind by advancing world peace. For a time, during 1917 and 1918, he was incontestably the world's moral leader. Then fate struck him down in his fight for the League of Nations. The forces of reaction defeated him at last. Yet his ideals and his vision remained in the hearts and minds of millions.

After Wilson, the Presidency declined in prestige and power, partly by design, partly by accident. In 1920 the two popular Republican candidates killed each other off at the national convention in Chicago, and the big industrial, oil, and financial interests were able to nominate an obscure Ohioan, Warren G. Harding. Harding and his running mate, Governor Calvin Coolidge of Massachusetts, mowed down the Democratic team of James M. Cox and Franklin D. Roosevelt in a record landslide, sixteen million votes to nine million.

The new President was handsome and amiable, and quickly dispelled from the White House the aura of gloom that had descended during Wilson's last months in office. Yet Harding was also morally lax, indolent, and slow-minded. He tried to meet popular expectations of leadership, managing rather well in fact to control a sharp recession in 1921. He was in-

A caricature by Charles Dunn of the U.S. Chamber of Commerce —one of 20,000 cartoons of himself that Herbert Hoover kept in a White House room he called his "Chamber of Horrors."

volved in summoning an international conference on naval armament. He persuaded the barons of the steel industry to institute an eight-hour day. And, in a surprisingly courageous move, he pardoned Eugene V. Debs, the Socialist leader who had been imprisoned for obstructing the war effort.

But Harding let the dynamism that the American people had come to expect from his office dissipate, and ultimately it was disclosed that his was an administration riddled by corruption unmatched since the days of Ulysses S. Grant. By the time the full extent of these scandals was exposed, however, Harding had died in the midst of a transcontinental speechmaking tour and been succeeded by Calvin Coolidge. Coolidge was dour, taciturn, and seemingly lifeless. "If you put a rose in his hand," said Gutzon Borglum of Mt. Rushmore fame, "it would wilt."

Coolidge took no initiative except to work to lower taxes for the rich, and he spent most of his time thwarting legislation to benefit farmers and consumers. Yet he was elected in 1924 by nearly as great a landslide as Harding's, even though there was a split as there had been in 1912, and the Progressive Party candidate, Senator Robert M. LaFollette of Wisconsin, garnered nearly five million votes. However lackluster compared to Roosevelt or Wilson, Coolidge retained the loyalty of the business community and considerable personal popularity. Then, to the surprise of nearly everyone, on August 3, 1927, a terse message emanated from the President's summer residence in the Black Hills of South Dakota: "I do not choose to run for President in 1928."

Calvin Coolidge, a man who rarely changed his mind about anything, was not to be dissuaded. The way was now open for the candidacy of Herbert Hoover, "The Great Engineer." Hoover had won a sterling reputation as an administrator of relief and food programs during the war, as an able and energetic Secretary of Commerce, and as the leading Republican advocate of moderate progressivism. The Democratic nominee was Alfred E. Smith, long-time governor of New York, a champion of social welfare programs, and an ardent foe of Prohibition. Smith also was the first Roman Catholic ever nominated for the Presidency. He ran well in the large cities, but his religion was a fatal handicap elsewhere and Hoover overwhelmed him by more than six million votes.

Few men have ever come to the Presidency with more popularity than Herbert Hoover. Americans revered him as a great humanitarian. He appeared as an eloquent spokesman of government in the service of the people. He entered on a wave of prosperity. But an economic recession set in only a few months after he took office, and, in 1931, it deepened into the worst depression in history. Hoover worked harder than any President before him to restore public confidence. Through the new medium of radio he continually appealed for patience and assured the people that prosperity was just around the corner. But confidence sagged and then collapsed altogether when unemployment soared and breadlines lengthened. This unprecedented crisis demanded truly bold action. Hoover was far from idle, yet he gave the impression of caring more about preventing bank failures than about feeding hungry people.

Almost instinctively, the people turned to Franklin D. Roosevelt. FDR, a year after running for Vice President in 1920, had been stricken with polio. Having overcome that handicap by sheer courage, he had served as an energetic, progressive

"President for life" Franklin Delano Roosevelt cheerfully parries questions from behind the wheel of his own car at an outdoor press conference, Warm Springs, Georgia, April 1939.

governor of New York. The very aura of greatness surrounded him. He was naturally a leader. Jaunty himself, he instilled confidence in others. He was also the most masterful politician in American history. He well remembered the administrations of Theodore Roosevelt (who was a fifth cousin) and Woodrow Wilson (whom he served as assistant secretary of the Navy, as Theodore had served McKinley), and he was determined to restore the Presidency to the position of leadership it had attained under those predecessors.

He used every one of TR's and Wilson's techniques. A fine orator, FDR could move crowds to a high pitch of excitement when he denounced "economic royalists" and "industrial dictatorship." He could inspire great effort and sacrifice when he told people they had a "rendezvous with destiny." He was a superb phrasemaker. He promised a "New Deal" to the American people. With our Latin American neighbors he would institute a "Good Neighbor" policy. America was at war with the Axis to guarantee survival of "the Four Freedoms." He reinstituted regular press conferences, often boisterous affairs, and the reporters loved him. Most important, he spoke directly to the people over the radio in a memorable series of "fireside chats." His voice radiated warmth and confidence, and he explained complex problems in simple terms that unsophisticated people could understand.

When Roosevelt was inaugurated on March 4, 1933, the private enterprise system was on the verge of collapse. He was a great experimenter. If one policy did not work, he tried another. At times, he seemed to pursue zigzag, even contradictory, courses. But he never wavered from the principle that the public interest had to prevail over private interests. He bolstered the Federal Reserve System and brought banks and securities exchanges under control. Through subsidies and limits on production, he restored prosperity to agriculture. He rectified the imbalance between capital and labor by requiring management to bargain in good faith when a majority of workers had voted to unionize. He launched a massive war on poverty with conservation programs and public works projects. He instituted unemployment insurance and a social security program. And, during the Second World War, FDR rallied the American people to the greatest concerted effort in their history.

Roosevelt was the progressive President par excellence. If necessary, he would have been a plebiscitary President; in his first inaugural he indicated that he would resort to wartime powers in order to save the country. But he always enjoyed Democratic majorities in Congress, and he worked well with Congressional leaders. There were moments of tension between the White House and Capitol Hill, particularly in 1937 when Roosevelt sought legislation to increase the number of justiceships on the Supreme Court (which had declared key New Deal measures unconstitutional)— an attempt, as ex-President Hoover first put it, to "pack" the court. But such tension did not last long, because of the mutual affection between the President and Congressional leaders.

FDR was hated by "economic royalists" and "industrial dictators" even more than they had hated TR and Wilson. Only the people loved Franklin Roosevelt. And they loved him passionately and trusted him so much that they elected him a third time and then a fourth—President for life.

A few weeks into his fourth term, on April 12, 1945, Roosevelt died suddenly. Americans grieved. They also looked with trepidation upon his successor, Harry S Truman of Missouri. "Who the hell is Harry Truman?" Admiral William Leahy, White House chief of staff, had asked Roosevelt in the summer of 1944. Millions of people asked the same question, perhaps less profanely, as the little man from Missouri took the oath of office. Truman did not inspire confidence. He had been the protégé of a notorious Kansas City machine. And he certainly did not look or speak like the patrician Roosevelt. Truman was diminutive and unpretentious. He wore thick glasses, spoke in a flat midwestern twang, and was addicted to poker. In short, he seemed the epitome of the average man from Middle America—hardly the right person to lead the nation in the great tasks of reconstruction that lay ahead. New Deal leaders feared that Truman would be a reactionary President or even attempt to dismantle the New Deal structure.

Never had appearances been so deceptive or fears so groundless. Truman's personal resources included a fundamental decency and integrity, a deep knowledge of American traditions, and a genuine compassion for the common people. At first he gave the appearance of fumbling and bumbling ("To err is Truman," people sneered). But he was merely gaining control of an administration he had inherited and setting his own course. By the early months of 1946 the American people knew who Harry Truman was: a capable, self-confident President in the progressive tradition. He was not magisterial like Wilson or patrician like FDR. Truman's style was

Lampoon of Harry S Truman and Thomas E. Dewey in 1948 recalls a famous photo of Truman with actress Lauren Bacall.

more like that of the first progressive President, Theodore Roosevelt—free-swinging and hyperbolic. In courage, he was equal to any of the three. Virtually repudiated by his party leaders, and facing what seemed certain defeat by the Republican candidate Thomas E. Dewey in 1948, Truman went straight to the people on a cross-country tour. In earthy language, he roasted the Republican-controlled 80th Congress as a "do-nothing Congress." His audiences roared back, "Give 'em hell, Harry," and—in one of the great upsets in American history—the voters returned him to the White House as President in his own right.

Truman triumphed in spite of the most formidable opposition that any President had faced since Taft in 1912 and Hoover in 1932. He managed demobilization with spectacular success; for the first time ever the nation did not suffer a depression in the aftermath of war. He won legislation that strengthened the New Deal. Most important, he mapped out a political program that would challenge the next generation: from full civil rights for blacks to national health insurance. The heart of his "Fair Deal" was a governmental guarantee of a decent standard of living for all Americans.

In foreign policy, Truman followed squarely in the progressive tradition. He instituted a program for European recovery through the Marshall Plan; he defeated Stalin's attempt to blockade Berlin; and he personally rallied the United Nations to defend South Korea against North Korean aggression in 1950. Even though he was a violent partisan in domestic politics, he drew Republicans completely into the decision-making process and established the principle of bipartisan cooperation in foreign policy.

Truman was the last progressive President, at least in the sense that he regarded his office as the crucial instrumentality for change, and then was able consistently to wield it as such. The sign on Truman's desk reading "The buck stops here" and his famous remark, "If you can't stand the heat, get out of the kitchen," epitomized the personal Presidency. He was an assertive leader with intimate ties to the people, the press, and Congress. Neither Theodore Roosevelt nor Wilson had any staff to speak of; Franklin Roosevelt and Truman had only a small group of advisers.

Dwight D. Eisenhower would bring not only a new style of leadership to the White House but also a bureaucracy. That bureaucracy would grow exponentially. It would create an isolated world of its own, a potential barrier between the President and Congress, the President and the people. This situation would destroy two Presidents, Johnson and Nixon, and it would cripple their successors.

★ ★ ★ ★ ★ ★ ★ ★ ★ ★ ★ ★ ★ ★ ★ ★ ★ ★ ★ ★

I Give You the Man Who...

Russell Bourne

By tradition, the nominating speaker withholds his nominee's actual identity until wave after wave of foaming rhetoric has washed the sweaty convention. Heroic deed upon faithful service, individual glory upon family heritage. Then, at the very end of the speech, rolls forth every syllable of the grand, entire (and entirely expected) n-a-a-a-m-e!

The place thereupon goes crazy. Trumpets blare the theme song, paraders jam the aisles, placards tangle with state standards as balloons rise into white lights' glare. Teeth, straw hats, bunting: pandemonium.

Once Will Rogers thought, during a speaker's recitation of somebody's endless virtues, that it was the Savior who was being described; ultimately he learned it was Calvin Coolidge. H. L. Mencken, observing the eruptions of another convention, concluded that the delegates were "plainly

on furlough from some home for extinct volcanoes."

Every four years the national parties stage such bizarre circuses. And without them, the political passions of the people would not be transmogrified into the majesty of The Presidential Candidate. Ever since the selection of candidates by caucus (meaning by a handful of the privileged) was done away with in Andrew Jackson's time, and the first national party convention was held in Baltimore in 1832, this peculiar, perfervid form

Ecstatic Republican delegates in the Chicago Coliseum hail the nomination of Theodore Roosevelt in 1904. Twenty years *before, Grover Cleveland had received the Democratic nomination in another Chicago building, Exposition Hall, above.*

Mirrors of the political mood, conventions range from angry to exultant. Right and below, National Guardsmen and police bear arms and show muscle at the tense 1968 Democratic convention in Chicago when the party was challenged both from left and right. Opposite, in Kansas City, President and Mrs. Ford receive an ovation. Determined to heal the nation after Vietnam and Watergate, Ford won the Republican nomination in 1976.

of democracy by pressure cooker has produced the man to head the national campaign ticket.

★ ★ ★

Conventions are held in the middle of the summer—managers appearing to have a real knack for choosing the country's hottest spot. Chicago has hosted more conventions than any other city (10 of the Presidents having been nominated there). Many TV viewers retain vivid memories of those sultry evenings during the 1968 Democratic convention when Mayor Daley's police force made life all the more torrid for demonstrators against the nominee, Hubert Humphrey.

But perhaps the most agonized of conventions was the Democrats' 14-day monster of 1924 in New York City. It took 103 ballots to get the required majority for John William Davis. That questionable accomplishment reminds one that the successful Presidential candidate who needed the greatest number of convention ballots ever was Franklin Pierce—he finally won on the 49th tally at the Democratic convention of 1852. And that suggests a conclusion about conventions: Endurance contests rarely bring forth greatness.

In fact one of the charges against conventions is that they favor mediocrity. James Bryce, in making this point, noted that brilliance tends to be mistrusted by the pragmatic American politicians who rule the conventions. Vachel Lindsay, referring to the ease with which the Republican convention of 1896 made its choice, explained that the nominee was "that respectable McKinley/The man without an angle or a tangle."

Yet sometimes superiority wins out despite all. Woodrow Wilson, who barely squeaked to a win after 46 ballots at the 1912 Democratic convention, never forgave the system. "There ought never to be another Presidential nominating convention," he declared, ". . . the nominations should be made directly by the people at the polls." This progressive idea of a nationwide primary in both parties, though still urged by some latter-day Wilsonians as a way to bring many more Americans into the selection process, is regarded as impractical by others.

★ ★ ★

Critics of conventions have insisted that, not only are they unrepresentative of the people as a whole (because of the way delegates are named by state party leaders), they have an even graver problem—control by vested interests. Warren G. Harding's manager predicted that the Republican convention of 1920 would inevitably succumb to the pressure of those interests. It would happen in the familiar pattern: "Some 15 men, bleary eyed with loss of sleep, and perspiring profusely with the excessive heat, [would] sit down in seclusion around a big table. . . ." Having made a number of interstate deals, they would agree to "put Harding over." And so they did by 2:00 a.m. in a fetid room in Chicago's Blackstone Hotel.

DRAWING BY P. BARLOW; © 1944, 1972 THE NEW YORKER MAGAZINE.

"Nobody really knows why Americans vote the way they do—and often they do not know themselves," historian Samuel Eliot Morison once remarked. But they go at Presidential politics with a passion in every home town: The reward for years of ringing doorbells and canvassing voters may be selection as a delegate to the national convention. There one gets an accreditation badge, dons the trappings and symbols of the party (opposite), and tries to concentrate despite heat and weariness (above). Not long before the issue of New Yorker at left appeared, Democratic Chairman James A. Farley commented "...there is a carnival spirit, a touch of the sawdust and the sideshow, about a national convention that makes it unique among public gatherings. ...While party conclaves may not always be successful, they are never dull."

At the colorful Democratic convention of 1976 in New York, Jimmy Carter swept the nomination on the first ballot.

Nonetheless, such political maneuvers often call for a necessary banging together of heads, the rough-house confrontation of people with people about the Presidency which (says the Constitution) we are supposed to do outside the halls of Congress or any other governmental institution. Sometimes this hurly-burly produces an unexpected but outstanding candidate. Take the Republican convention of 1860: Presenting tickets with forged signatures, Abraham Lincoln's supporters jammed the "Wigwam" in Chicago and overwhelmed the delegates for the eastern front-runner, William H. Seward; the westerners sounded like "all the hogs ever slaughtered in Cincinnati giving their death squeals together." Honest Abe won on the fourth ballot.

Loud, brassy, and expensive though they may be, conventions

are undeniably effective in the hatching of eagles. Swept along by the enthusiasm of the final moment, when all delegates hail their new leader, it's only the shrunken soul who doesn't believe that the paragon there in the lights will be "the next President of the United States!"

The platforms that conventions manufacture often seem inane, but here also the struggle to define the issues—and to grapple with them toward consensus—is essential for meaningful party opposition. The platforms, the keynote addresses, the seconding speeches . . . these might all be dismissed as an extraordinary waste of overblown language. But such speeches as William Jennings Bryan's "Cross of Gold" in 1896 and FDR's "Happy Warrior" nomination of Al Smith in 1928 have, in fact, produced a legacy of political phrases which, if not quite a literature, yields more pride than embarrassment.

As Bryan himself said, "The convention is, in a way, a photograph of the nation. All the great forces that exert a powerful influence in our country are here in person or by proxy."

★ ★ ★ ★ ★ ★ ★ ★ ★ ★ ★ ★ ★ ★ ★ ★ ★ ★

Symbols and Images

Wilcomb E. Washburn

The perception of Presidential politics as essentially a matter of symbols and images, not issues, has only recently gained currency among the intellectuals who analyze the process. Yet this has been so for more than a century and a half, and it has long been understood by the ordinary voter.

During the first 40 years of the republic, Presidents were remote, as figuratively distant from the citizenry as the framers of the Constitution thought proper. The earliest Presidents had personalities, of course, but their private lives were guarded, not projected as expressions of their public character. To penetrate that protective shield was sometimes to risk a painful rebuff, as is exemplified in the story of Gouverneur Morris's wager with Alexander Hamilton that he could get away with treating George Washington familiarly at a dinner party.

Morris clapped Washington on the back and exclaimed, "Wasn't it so, my old boy?" Frozen by Washington's icy glare, Morris later told Hamilton that though he had won the bet he

Floats symbolizing the Ship of State were created to celebrate ratification of the Constitution by state conventions. Today, *the relentless exploitation of symbolism in Presidential politics is lampooned by G. B. Trudeau's creation, Duane Delacourt.*

173

wished that he had never made it. Washington's popularity was not dependent upon qualities that permitted citizens such as Gouverneur Morris to feel close to him, but rather upon the qualities that set him apart.

Symbol he was, but a symbol of detachment from the realm of partisan politics, as befitted a man who was more a creator than a creation of the American nation. Though attacks on Jefferson and John Adams could be bitterly personal, their personalities were usually seen as illustrative of their political philosophies. Simplistic images and

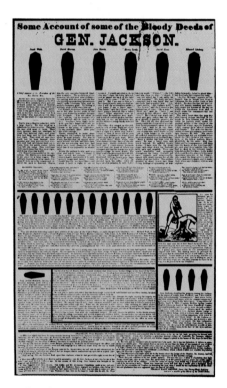

OF VETO MEMORY.

With reference to Jackson's alleged zeal to execute mutinous militiamen under his command in 1815, "Coffin Handbills" exploited a mordant symbolism. Partisans of Henry Clay in 1832 created an image of "King Andrew" simultaneously violating sound political principles and the Constitution. As Jackson's friends saw it, he wielded his power not as a despot himself but as a foe of despotism.

KING ANDREW THE FIRST.

personality-linked symbols were generally avoided in favor of rational analysis.

★   ★   ★

Which is not to say, however, that politics was entirely devoid of an emotional element. Gala parades had been staged in such cities as Boston, Baltimore, and Philadelphia to celebrate ratification of the Constitution, a document that of course included provisions for establishing the office of the President. But the deliberate exploitation of symbols associated with *personalities* began only with the candidacy of Andrew Jackson. A fundamental aspect of the symbolic "Old Hickory" was an image of military prowess. His martial exploits were not always favorably received—indeed, the so-called Coffin Handbills were a compelling weapon in the hands of his opponents—yet, pro or con, the image was one of power and determination. It was an image that remained deeply etched on the popular consciousness throughout Jackson's Presidency, especially during his fight against Nicholas Biddle and the Bank of the United States. The complex confrontation between eastern financial orthodoxy and western radicalism was increasingly personalized and cast in symbolic terms. Images of "King Andrew" on the one hand, the "Monster Bank" on the other, epitomized the emotional context of political controversies during the Jacksonian era.

The "Log Cabin and Hard Cider" campaign of 1840 combined visual symbolism with a new emphasis on music, and clearly signaled abandonment of a rational mode of political discourse for a mode dominated by personality.

Published by SAM? CARUSI Baltimore

Most important about Jackson, however, was that, unlike Washington, he was a President to whom people *could* feel akin. As one eulogist put it, "because his countrymen saw their image and spirit in Andrew Jackson, they bestowed their honor and admiration upon him."

★   ★   ★

The style of Jackson's personality-oriented Presidency was perpetuated in the race run against his hand-picked successor, Martin Van Buren, by the Whigs in 1840. The tone of the "Log Cabin and Hard Cider" campaign on behalf of General William Henry Harrison was partly fortuitous, the product of a clever response to a humorous slur printed in a Democratic

Baltimore newspaper. If the old general were given a pension and a jug of cider, so it was said, he would be content to sit quietly in his log cabin, undisturbed and undisturbing. Refutation would have been easy. Harrison was born at Berkeley on the James River, one of the great plantation houses in America, and as a territorial governor and general never fit the image of a simple rustic at all. Nevertheless, his managers seized on the image eagerly, and even embellished it to portray "Old Tippecanoe" as a paragon of humble backwoods virtues. Van Buren, in contrast, was accused of a penchant for French wines and fine fabrics.

Soon log cabins were everywhere to be seen, both in pictorial representation and in actuality, sometimes serving as local "Tippecanoe clubs," with the latch-string out and the cider barrel inviting the thirsty. Philip Hone, a wealthy New York Whig, in contrasting the shift in emphasis from abstractions to the personality of the candidate, commented that: "Now on all their banners and transparencies the temple of Liberty is transformed into a hovel of unhewn logs; the military garb of the general, into the frock and the shirt-sleeves of a labouring farmer. The American eagle has taken his flight, which is supplied by a cider-barrel, and the long-established emblem of the ship has given place to the plough. Hurrah for Tippecanoe! is heard more frequently than Hurrah for the Constitution!"

Along with a potent visual symbolism there was a new emphasis on music. Glee clubs and bands dominated by powerful brass instruments added sound and melody to the Harrison campaign.

The Democratic response to all this was to condemn "the trickery of political clap-trap," and contemporary scholars have tended to do the same. Harrison made a virtue of not speaking to the issues, asserting that "the best guarantee for the correct conduct of our Presidents is to be found in their previous lives." The resulting campaign, in the words of one historian, became "an exhibition of abuse, evasion, misrepresentation, and irrelevancies on a scale unparalleled in U.S. history up to that time."

(continued, page 181)

An Election Panorama

Although Presidential souvenirs were produced in George Washington's time, it was not until Andrew Jackson's that they became a medium for campaign symbolism. The art hit its stride following the Civil War, and enjoyed a half-century heyday from the 1880s until the 1930s. But, after World War II—aside from an occasional bit of inspiration such as canned Goldwater— the imaginative component flagged as purveyors of political symbols shifted their attention to different media.

Shown below is a display of Presidential memorabilia at the National Museum of History and Technology. This display, rearranged as a linear band, is the basis for the fold-out at right. Here, captured in slogan, symbol, and image on everything from platinum to celluloid is a history of the American Presidency. To enable keeping track of whose hat was in the ring every four years, a roster of the leading vote-getters (winner first) appears beneath the memorabilia pertaining to each quadrennial contest.

1789

George Washington
(Unopposed)

1792

George Washington
(Unopposed)

1796

John Adams
Federalist
Thomas Jefferson
Democratic-Republican
Thomas Pinckney
Aaron Burr
Samuel Adams
Oliver Ellsworth
George Clinton
John Jay
James Iredell
John Henry
Samuel Johnson
George Washington
Charles Cotesworth Pinckney

1800

Thomas Jefferson
Democratic-Republican
Aaron Burr
Democratic-Republican
John Adams
Federalist
Charles Cotesworth Pinckney
Federalist
John Jay
Federalist

1804

Thomas Jefferson
Democratic-Republican
Charles Cotesworth Pinckney
Federalist

1808

James Madison
Democratic-Republican
Charles Cotesworth Pinckney
Federalist

1812

James Madison
Democratic-Republican
De Witt Clinton
Federalist

1816

James Monroe
Democratic-Republican
Rufus King
Federalist

1820

James Monroe
Democratic-Republican
John Quincy Adams
Democratic-Republican

EXHIBIT DESIGNED BY STAPLES & CHARLES,
PHOTOGRAPHED BY ROBERT STAPLES

1880

James A. Garfield*
  Republican
Winfield S. Hancock
  Democratic
James B. Weaver
  Greenback Labor
Neal Dow
  Prohibition
John W. Phelps
  American

Garfield died September 19, 1881, and was succeeded by Vice President Chester A. Arthur.

1884

Grover Cleveland
  Democratic
James G. Blaine
  Republican
Benjamin F. Butler
  Greenback and *Anti-Monopoly*
John P. St. John
  Prohibition
Belva Ann Lockwood
  Equal Rights

1868

Ulysses S. Grant
Republican
Horatio Seymour
Democratic

1872

Ulysses S. Grant
Republican
Horace Greeley
Democratic
Charles O'Conor
Straight-Out Democrat
James Black
Prohibition
Victoria Woodhull
Equal Rights

1876

Rutherford B. Hayes
Republican
Samuel J. Tilden
Democratic
Peter Cooper
Greenback
Green Clay Smith
Prohibition
James B. Walker
American National

1824

John Quincy Adams
  Democratic-Republican
Andrew Jackson
  Democratic-Republican
William H. Crawford
  Democratic-Republican
Henry Clay
  Democratic-Republican

1828

Andrew Jackson
  Democratic
John C. Calhoun
  Democratic
John Quincy Adams
  National Republican
Richard Rush
  National Republican

1832

Andrew Jackson
  Democratic
Henry Clay
  National Republican
John Floyd
  Independent
William Wirt
  Anti-Masonic

1836

Martin Van Buren
  Democratic
William Henry Harrison
  Whig
Hugh Lawson White
  Whig
Daniel Webster
  Whig
Willie Person Mangum
  Whig

1840

William Henry Harrison*
Whig
Martin Van Buren
Democratic
James G. Birney
Liberty

*Harrison died April 4, 1841, and was
succeeded by Vice President John Tyler.*

1844

James Knox Polk
Democratic
Henry Clay
Whig
James G. Birney
Liberty

1864

Abraham Lincoln*
Republican
George B. McClellan
Democratic

*Lincoln died April 15, 1865, and was
succeeded by Vice President Andrew
Johnson.*

1852

Franklin Pierce
Democratic
Winfield Scott
Whig
John P. Hale
Free Soil

1856

James Buchanan
Democratic
John C. Frémont
Republican
Millard Fillmore
American

1860

Abraham Lincoln
Republican
Stephen A. Douglas
Democrat (Northern)
John C. Breckinridge
Democrat (Southern)
John Bell
Constitutional Union

1848

Zachary Taylor*
Whig
Lewis Cass
Democratic
Martin Van Buren
Free Soil (Democrat)
John P. Hale
*Free Soil (Barnburners-
Liberty)*
Gerrit Smith
National Liberty

**Taylor died July 9, 1850, and was
succeeded by Vice President Millard
Fillmore.*

1964

Lyndon B. Johnson
Democratic
Barry M. Goldwater
Republican
Eric Hass
Socialist Labor
Earle H. Munn
Prohibition
Clifton De Berry
Socialist Workers
John Kasper
National States Rights

1968

Richard M. Nixon
Republican
Hubert H. Humphrey
Democratic
George C. Wallace
American Independent
Eldridge Cleaver
Peace and Freedom
Henning A. Blomen
Socialist Labor
Fred Wolf Holstead
Socialist Workers
Earle H. Munn, Sr.
Prohibition

1972

Richard M. Nixon*
Republican
George S. McGovern
Democratic
John G. Schmitz
American Independent
Linda Jenness
Socialist Workers
Louis Fisher
Socialist Labor
Gus Hall
Communist
Earle H. Munn, Sr.
Prohibition
John Hospers
Libertarian

*Nixon resigned August 9, 1974, and
was succeeded by Vice President Gerald
R. Ford.

1976

Jimmy Carter
Democratic
Gerald R. Ford
Republican
Eugene J. McCarthy
No party affiliation
Roger McBride
Libertarian
Lester G. Maddox
American Independent
Thomas Anderson
American
Peter Camejo
Socialist Workers
Gus Hall
Communist
Margaret Wright
People's
Lyndon H. LaRouche
U.S. Labor
Benjamin C. Bubar
Prohibition
Jules Levin
Socialist Labor
Frank P. Zeidler
Socialist

1888

Benjamin Harrison
  Republican
Grover Cleveland
  Democratic
Clinton B. Fisk
  Prohibition
Alson J. Streeter
  Union Labor
Robert H. Cowdrey
  United Labor
James L. Curtis
  American
Belva Ann Lockwood
  Equal Rights

1892

Grover Cleveland
  Democratic
Benjamin Harrison
  Republican
James B. Weaver
  People's
John Bidwell
  Prohibition
Simon Wing
  Socialist Labor

1896

William McKinley
  Republican
William Jennings Bryan
  Democratic
John McAuley Palmer
  National Democratic
Joshua Levering
  Prohibition
Charles H. Matchett
  Socialist Labor
Charles E. Bentley
  National

1900

William McKinley*
  Republican
William Jennings Bryan
  Democratic
John G. Woolley
  Prohibition
Eugene V. Debs
  Social-Democratic
Wharton Barker
  People's
Joseph F. Malloney
  Socialist Labor
Seth H. Ellis
  Union Reform
Jonah Fitz Randolph Leonard
  United Christian

*McKinley died September 14, 1901, and
was succeeded by Vice President
Theodore Roosevelt*

1952

Dwight D. Eisenhower
Republican
Adlai E. Stevenson
Democratic
Vincent W. Hallinan
Progressive
Stuart Hamblen
Prohibition
Eric Hass
Socialist Labor
Darlington Hoopes
Socialist
Farrell Dobbs
Socialist Workers

1956

Dwight D. Eisenhower
Republican
Adlai E. Stevenson
Democratic
Thomas C. Andrews
States Rights
Enoch A. Holtwick
Prohibition
Eric Hass
Socialist Labor
William E. Jenner
Texas Constitution
Farrell Dobbs
Socialist Workers
Henry Krajewski
American Third
Darlington Hoopes
Socialist

1960

John F. Kennedy*
Democratic
Richard M. Nixon
Republican
Orval E. Faubus
National States Rights
Eric Hass
Socialist Labor
Rutherford L. Decker
Prohibition
Farrell Dobbs
Socialist Workers
J. Bracken Lee
*Conservative Party of
New Jersey*
C. Benton Coiner
*Conservative Party
of Virginia*

*Kennedy died November 22, 1963, and
was succeeded by Vice President Lyndon
B. Johnson.*

1932

Franklin Delano Roosevelt
Democratic
Herbert Hoover
Republican
Norman M. Thomas
Socialist
William Z. Foster
Communist
William D. Upshaw
Prohibition
William Hope Harvey
Liberty
Verne L. Reynolds
Socialist Labor
Jacob Coxey
Farmer Labor
Poster C. Roberts
Recovery
Laven Keshibian
Phoenix

1936

Franklin Delano Roosevelt
Democratic
Alfred M. Landon
Republican
William Lemke
Union
Norman M. Thomas
Socialist
Earl Browder
Communist
David L. Colvin
Prohibition
John W. Aiken
Socialist Labor

1940

Franklin Delano Roosevelt
Democratic
Wendell L. Willkie
Republican
Norman M. Thomas
Socialist
Roger W. Babson
Prohibition
Earl Browder
Communist
John W. Aiken
Socialist Labor

1944

Franklin Delano Roosevelt*
Democratic
Thomas E. Dewey
Republican
Norman M. Thomas
Socialist
Claude A. Watson
Prohibition
Edward A. Teichert
Socialist Labor

1948

Harry S Truman
Democratic
Thomas E. Dewey
Republican
James Strom Thurmond
*States Rights Democratic
("Dixiecrat")*
Henry A. Wallace
Progressive
Norman M. Thomas
Socialist
Claude A. Watson
Prohibition
Edward A. Teichert
Socialist Labor
Farrell Dobbs
Socialist Workers

*Roosevelt died April 12, 1945, and was
succeeded by Vice President Harry S
Truman.*

1904

Theodore Roosevelt
Republican

Alton Parker
Democratic

Eugene V. Debs
Socialist

Silas Comfort Swallow
Prohibition

Thomas E. Watson
People's

Charles H. Corregan
Socialist Labor

Austin Holcomb
Continental

1908

William Howard Taft
Republican
William Jennings Bryan
Democratic
Eugene V. Debs
Socialist
Eugene W. Chafin
Prohibition
Thomas L. Hisgen
Independence
Thomas E. Watson
People's
August Gillhaus
Socialist Labor
Daniel B. Turney
United Christian

1912

Woodrow Wilson
Democratic
Theodore Roosevelt
Progressive
William Howard Taft
Republican
Eugene V. Debs
Socialist
Eugene W. Chafin
Prohibition
Arthur E. Reimer
Socialist Labor
Blauford F. Ziggfeld
Reparation

1916

Woodrow Wilson
Democratic
Charles Evans Hughes
Republican
Allan L. Benson
Socialist
James F. Hanley
Prohibition
Hollister Purdue
State Designation
Arthur E. Reimer
Socialist Labor

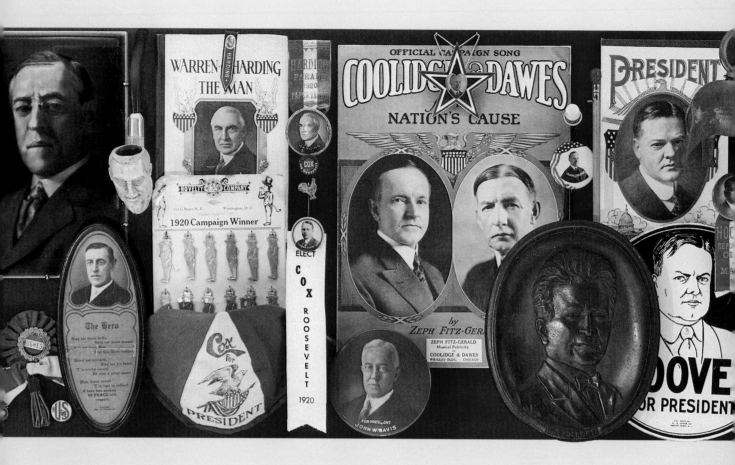

1920

Warren G. Harding*
  Republican
James M. Cox
  Democratic
Eugene V. Debs
  Socialist
Parley Parker Christensen
  Farmer Labor
Aaron S. Watkins
  Prohibition
William W. Cox
  Socialist Labor
Robert C. Macauley
  Single Tax

**Harding died August 2, 1923, and was
succeeded by Vice President Calvin
Coolidge.*

1924

Calvin Coolidge
  Republican
John W. Davis
  Democratic
Robert M. LaFollette
  Progressive
Herman P. Farris
  Prohibition
Frank T. Johns
  Socialist Labor
William Z. Foster
  Workers (Communist)
Gilbert Owen Nations
  American
Beason A. Cropp
  Anti-Red
William J. Wallace
  Commonwealth Land

1928

Herbert Hoover
  Republican
Alfred E. Smith
  Democratic
Norman M. Thomas
  Socialist
William Z. Foster
  Workers (Communist)
Verne L. Reynolds
  Socialist Labor
William F. Varney
  Prohibition
Frank E. Webb
  Farmer Labor
Wilcox Rondo
  Proportional Rule

(continued from page 176)
Another has characterized the Whig log cabin as "a nostalgic prop, a publicity gimmick without focused moral content."

I would assert, on the contrary, that the log cabin *was* a symbol of focused moral content, designed as such, and received as such. Its modern-day equivalent would be the 30-second television spot commercial, which ignores issues, ignores party label, and concentrates on some aspect of the candidate's personality, usually one that links him closely with the ordinary voter. Not without effect did Jimmy Carter, after officially changing his name from James Earl, carry his own luggage and engage in other unpretentious activities which were like those of the average citizen.

While the television spot is a more appropriate contemporary equivalent to the 19th-century transparency or banner, gimmicks similar to those provided New Year's Eve merrymakers continue to be produced for political campaigns (look, for example, at the end of the foldout, left). But the parallel is superficial, since contemporary campaign ephemera—for all its campy flavor—lacks the compelling power of the earlier images. Of course, this is because the technology of communicating the most powerful symbolism has now shifted to a different medium.

★　★　★

The increasing importance of providing a candidate with a "personality"—even if he was known to be strongly committed to "issues"—was demonstrated in the campaign of 1860. Abraham Lincoln had acquired something of a reputation, as the Albany *Atlas and Argus* put it, as "the ugliest man in the Union." His gift for expression and his personal magnetism might have gone for naught if such an impression had ultimately prevailed with the voters. For this reason the presentation of a new Lincoln image was necessary, and a major component of that image was supplied by Mathew Brady's photograph taken on the occasion of Lincoln's address at the Cooper Institute in New York City on February 27, 1860.

The address itself was significant (showing a small but sophisticated New York audience that Lincoln was no hayseed), but the photograph—in its distribution throughout the country—provided a perfect antidote to hostile caricatures and jokes. Here was all the intelligence, compassion, and grace that the whole world would later know to have been at the heart of Lincoln's character. The Cooper Institute photograph can be considered as the first significant visual image of a candidate that was not just casually illustrative of his character but directly demonstrative of it.

The campaign of 1860 did not focus solely on the features of the candidate. It also employed a symbol reminiscent of the Harrison log cabin, in this case a rail presumably split by Lincoln during his youth on the Illinois frontier. Whether or not the introduction of this rail into the Republican Convention of 1860 was a calculated ploy, the "railsplitter" image was born, to appear on countless campaign

The "railsplitter," a key symbol in the 1860 Republican campaign, suggested a combination of power and probity.

banners to exemplify the noble qualities of the frontiersman.

★　★　★

The muster of American Presidents who have been generals, a long one, suggests the popular sense of a close relationship between military and political leadership. (Leadership of land forces, that is, for the nature of naval leadership is quite different.) While George Washington may serve as a tutelary deity in this regard, the basic symbolic virtue derives from the character

181

As the photographic art improved, the quality of a candidate's appearance became all the more crucial to success. In February 1860, Lincoln went east to visit his son Robert at school and to address an audience at the Cooper Institute. He also had a photograph taken by Mathew Brady, and copies of that image, right, soon far outnumbered less flattering images formerly prevalent, above. Looking back, Lincoln felt that his New York speech and Brady photograph probably made him President.

of a special sort of general, the sort known to have been tough and uncompromising but also ready and willing to share the hardships of combat. Jackson was cast in this mold, and the emotional bond he achieved with his troops proved to be transferable to the electorate as a whole. Harrison and Zachary Taylor also capitalized on a "strict but fair" image. Although his opponents ridiculed Franklin Pierce's army record—even publishing a book on his "military accomplishments" that was blank—he did rise from private to brigadier general during the Mexican War, and the nickname "Young Hickory of the Granite Hills" did achieve some currency among Democrats.

The Civil War produced a crop of military men who entered the political arena afterward—the first being Ulysses S. Grant, who, like Taylor before him, combined a rumpled, common appearance and simple habits with uncommon determination and accomplishment. Rutherford B. Hayes, James A. Garfield, and Benjamin Harrison all were able to capture the Presidency partly on the basis of creditable records during the Civil War.

But the image of generalship did not prove to be a permanent key to the White House, for an even more attractive image began to emerge in the late 19th century —the image of the President as moralist and preacher, and the White House as a pulpit. This style echoed that of William Gladstone in England, and may be said to have come into American Presidential politics with Grover Cleveland, a preacher's son.

Though Cleveland was the only President elected in the period from Grant to McKinley who had not commanded troops during the Civil War, his image was definitely the harbinger of a new style that depended on the voter's perception of the candidate as first and foremost a man of strong moral fiber. The mere denunciation of evil (personalized as corrupt politicos and robber barons) sometimes served in lieu of action, but Cleveland, for one, clearly had the courage of his convictions. So indelible was his image of rectitude that he was able to weather the charge that he had sired an illegitimate child in his youth, an allusion recorded in the opposition chant:

Ma, ma, where's my pa?
Going to the White House,
ha, ha, ha.

When the charge was first aired, Cleveland faced it openly. While the effect of the revelation on the campaign of 1884 is uncertain, Cleveland did emerge the victor, and it is probable that he gained

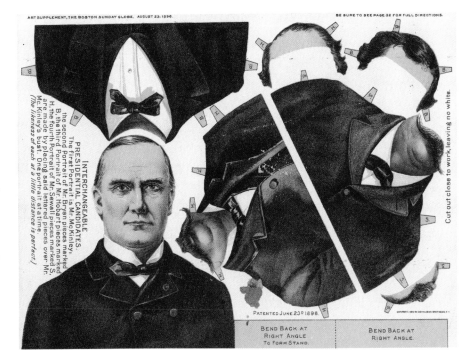

Cut-outs, top, satirize candidates whose personalities and politics seem interchangeable. One clearly defined aspect of Grover Cleveland's personality was his paternity of a child out of wedlock. Had women voted, he would have been defeated. Right, William Jennings Bryan championed inflationary policy based on "free and unlimited coinage of silver at the ratio of 16 to 1." "Gold bug" symbolized his "sound money" foes.

183

as much for his honesty (from an entirely male electorate) as he lost as a result of his indiscretion.

★ ★ ★

Warrior and preacher images proved irresistible when embodied simultaneously in the person of Teddy Roosevelt, the hero of San Juan Hill and apostle of the strenuous life. The Roosevelt quotation selected as the motto for the title page of Theodore Hagedorn's *Boy's Life of Theodore Roosevelt* is suggestive of this style: "Aggressive fighting for the right is the noblest sport the world affords." Roosevelt's rhetoric, which epitomized the values of the new moralistic imagery in politics, smacked of nothing so much as

evangelism: "We fight in honorable fashion for the good of mankind . . . we stand at Armageddon, and we battle for the Lord."

Woodrow Wilson, like Cleveland a preacher's son, would also stake his run for the Presidency on the force of his moral character and, once there, use the office as a pulpit from which to preach a moral crusade against evildoers at home and abroad. Some would even say that Franklin D. Roosevelt—until the Second World War presented him with the opportunity to play Commander-in-Chief—cast himself as a cleanser of the temple. Whatever the case, FDR's most indelible qualities were not matters of politics but of personality, for here was a President who, like TR, like Lincoln, possessed that most elusive quality, charisma.

★ ★ ★

Personality factors, while increasingly recognized for their voter impact, have been treated by most political scientists as aberrations that tend to distort such basic patterns in two-party politics as the "equilibrium cycle." Charisma (from the Greek word meaning a spiritual gift or talent divinely granted as a token of favor) has even been called a "latent *disease* in the body politic" by one scholar. Yet, references to charisma are nothing more than a way of attempting to incorporate the indefinable into a practical definition of politics. Charisma is something that links the voter emotionally to the character of the candidate rather than rationally to his beliefs. Symbolic log cabins and split rails aimed at the same thing.

While all candidates have personalities that can be defined or redefined by employing symbols and projecting images, only a rare few possess charisma, and often neither they nor their managers know how best to exploit it. Hindsight may suggest that Jimmy Carter had it on that inauguration day in 1977 when he walked along Pennsylvania Avenue, but seldom afterward. If scholars and campaign managers fully understood what caused voters to act as they do, we would see many more wealthy campaign consultants. But nobody can do much more than grope for an answer.

Campaign tactics, to be sure, have changed radically. The long discourse on political issues has

been superseded by the 30-second spot on the six o'clock news. In essence the contemporary unit of political communication is a capsule message capable of conveying some significant aspect of the candidate's image into the living room. It is *not* concerned with the issues he may have to face.

★　★　★

While parties continue to construct campaign "platforms" from diverse "planks," as well as to perform many other functions that are of concern primarily to special-interest groups (if they have any vestigial significance at all), the real campaign is staged in a world of impressions conveyed pictorially and visually rather than through the written word. The techniques of impressing the electorate have changed, from the banner or transparency held aloft, to the electronic picture. But what remains crucial, as it has been since Andrew Jackson's time, is to capture or enhance personal qualities and to project them effectively. Some observers have grasped this fact; many have not. Political success still favors individuals who, by accident or by design, fit currently favorable images while eluding the grasp of those who have misconceived the nature of the process by which Americans choose their President.

In an apparently spontaneous break with tradition, Jimmy Carter put himself on an equal footing with the people by walking up Pennsylvania Avenue toward the White House following his 1977 inauguration. A ready intimacy with nature remains an important component of positive Presidential imagery: Carter ran western white water in 1979.

THE WHITE HOUSE
WASHINGTON

August 9, 1974

Dear Mr. Secretary:

I hereby resign the Office of President of the
United States.

Sincerely

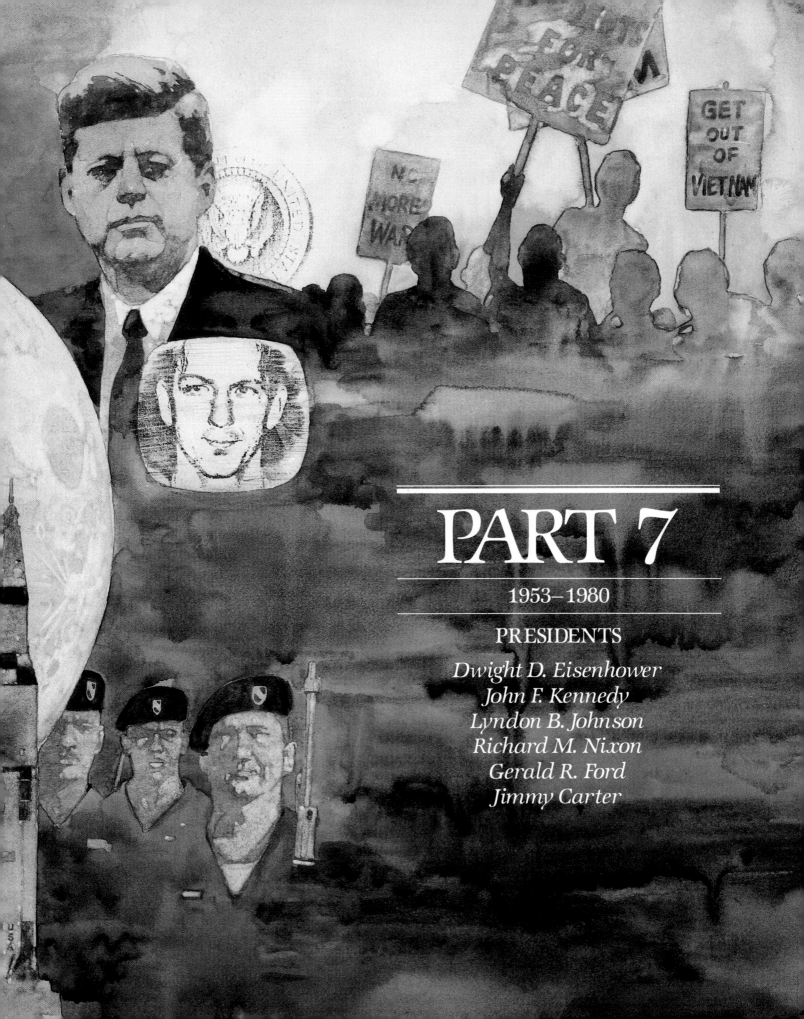

PART 7

1953–1980

PRESIDENTS

Dwight D. Eisenhower
John F. Kennedy
Lyndon B. Johnson
Richard M. Nixon
Gerald R. Ford
Jimmy Carter

The President in the Age of PR

Hugh Sidey

George Washington had a media problem and recognized it as such. Too often when we are confronted with the communications dilemmas of today we assume that they are a new species—the creation of television that is superficial, magazine journalism that is too slick, and daily newspapers that are too fast. In his own time, Washington was somewhat more limited, having to depend on word of mouth and the papers to spread his gospel and convince the populace (a modest four million) of his wisdom and foresight. Naturally, even then the advantage of the printing press over the coffee house was apparent. It is reported that Washington, having pondered, conceived, and put to paper a Presidential message which he thought important (has there ever been another kind?), sat back and worried that it was too long for newspaper publication. So even at the dawn of the republic cranky editors with their cold eyes for excess verbiage had become powers to consider in the conduct of the public's business.

When we condemn modern packaging of the Presidency it is easy to lose sight of the fact that in earlier times the problem seemed just the opposite. The men who were seeking to manage a shrinking and dangerous world at the beginning of this century yearned for ways to talk to the people. Woodrow Wilson noted, "one of the serious difficulties of politics in the country . . . is provincialism—the general absence of national information and national opinion." He took his campaign for the League of Nations to the country by railroad, traveling something like 8,000 miles and giving 37 speeches. The effort helped break his spirit and his health. The League failed, but not before he had tried something else that no other politician had tried—he gave a speech over radio. Regrettably, the reception was so poor that listeners could only catch a few words. Yet the start had been made.

Warren G. Harding had as many flaws as any President in our history, but as a newspaper publisher himself he did have a sense of the approaching world of mass communication. Though radio was still more of a curiosity than a political tool, he gave it a try and the results were gratifying. "We heard you as plainly as if you had been in our living room," one startled citizen wired the White House. By 1923 Harding was a regular broadcaster, using radio to help with his appeal for a World Court and carrying a transmitter on the Presidential train. Something called "a Presidential

Media meets master: Just as the communications industry reached technical maturity, John F. Kennedy appeared on the stage, skillfully using the press to his advantage. Here the Democratic nominee delivers his acceptance speech in the Los Angeles Coliseum.

network" of radio stations sprang up in this cause.

Calvin Coolidge, who is best remembered today for not talking much, nevertheless was an important link in media development. Stepping into office after the death of Harding, Silent Cal's inaugural address was carried on 21 radio stations to some 15 million Americans. In his first year in office Coolidge spoke an average of 9,000 words per month over radio, and his talks reached more people than ever before in history. The medium was on the way.

Franklin D. Roosevelt, the handicapped President, understood perfectly. His voice was his power. Through the airwaves he could reach across the land,

and he understood that when he was before those microphones he was not just speaking words but was the central actor in the world's most fascinating drama. Roosevelt sculpted his lines as if he were Shakespeare, weighing and balancing every verb for its impact. He called in a Navy corpsman before every fireside chat to spray his throat and tend to his sinuses so that the Presidential timbre would register all the nuances he felt in his heart. And when he broadcast to those audiences—sometimes as many as 60 million— he soared and swooped over the country through his marvelous baritone. John Dos Passos described Roosevelt's voice as "the patroon voice, the headmaster's

Roosevelt, like Kennedy, intuitive about the power of the media, enhanced his popularity by reaching the public through radio. His intimate fireside chats were a strong weapon against the

often hostile press. Although Roosevelt gave only 27 fireside chats in six years, their impact was so great that many people remember them as weekly broadcasts.

admonishing voice, the bedside doctor's voice that spoke to each man and to all of us."

Our age of total communication was rushing in on us and we hardly understood. As a boy in the dismal latitudes of depression and drought in Iowa, I can recall the nights of the fireside chats. Windows and doors on my street were open for maximum ventilation. The old cathedral radios of every house were tuned to hear the President. I wandered as a five-year-old from porch to porch, pondering this strange phenomenon that had stilled traffic in my village. Every adult had been drawn off the sidewalks and out of the porch rockers. Our appetite to know and to know now was established. When Roosevelt asked for mail the sleepy office for Presidential letters was inundated. Half a million letters piled up in a few days. At the end of the famous Hundred Days of Roosevelt's ascendency it was literally true that FDR had only to suggest to Congress that if he did not get his way he would take to the air, and legislative roadblocks would magically disappear.

Nonetheless, the U.S. still was a nation informed primarily by the printed word. Roosevelt was astute enough to understand that what was down in print often soaked deeper into the national spirit than the ephemeral broadcasts. Thus, he established almost daily meetings in his office with the press. He did not allow direct quotation except when specified, and he adroitly steered the subjects. He loved the afternoon joust, sometimes manipulating the print journalists with skill that rivaled his radio dramatics.

Then came television. The first telecast from the White House was made by President Harry S Truman, launching the Food Conservation Program. From then on, as the new industry rushed to fill the world with live pictures, almost every major Presidential address was telecast. Truman was the first President to hire a media adviser to help with the broadcast preparations and to coach him with his delivery. His announcement of the outbreak of war in Korea in the summer of 1950 was a landmark in TV. The *New York Times*'s video critic wrote:

> For the first time in a period of national emergency, the person at home not only heard the fateful call for sacrifices to preserve his freedom, but also saw the grave expressions of the President as he explained to the country what it would mean.

The purists may date the age of the Presidential package as 1952. It was the year of Ike, the last of the great world heroes, maybe the last of the warrior Presidents. The marriage of this national idol to the burgeon-

ing communications industry was so natural that hardly anybody had second thoughts. He had been the center of world attention as he coordinated the diverse and difficult personalities that carried the Allies to victory in World War II. Warm and mellow, with an underlying stratum of determination, Ike was irresistible.

By 1952 the boys in the back rooms figured that TV was going to dominate their future and they had best make plans for it in their campaigns. They calculated that there were 19 million sets and some 58 million viewers in the nation. The networks carried both party conventions live. Despite the new format and the clumsy cameras, the show was a stunner for most Americans. They saw Ike triumph over the stuffy Robert Taft in Chicago. They watched Adlai Stevenson respond to the draft. Eisenhower and Stevenson then waged what could be described as the first mass media campaign. When Ike took office his savvy press secretary James Hagerty announced to the world:

> We are in a day of a new medium—television. I would like to work out with television representatives . . . a system whereby the President could give talks to the people of the country— possibly press conferences—on television. . . about once a month.

A few weeks earlier, when the campaign was still young, something else had happened that foreshadowed modern politics even more accurately. It was the "Checkers" speech by Vice-Presidential candidate Richard M. Nixon. Though television was again the principal technology, there was more to the Checkers affair. This was a total media assault.

The issue was the propriety of Nixon's accepting an $18,235 political expense fund from 76 California supporters when he had been a Senator. Ike ("clean as a hound's tooth") found the fund dubious when he first heard of it and privately uttered dark thoughts about throwing Nixon off the ticket. Nixon moved fast. Already plugged into the Southern California world of show business, and a man always sensitive to new political gimmicks, he immediately made plans for a TV spectacular to "explain fully" about the fund. He hired an advertising agency to stage the show. The agency flew in Hollywood soap-opera directors, and rounded up the best make-up artists and prop men available. Some 25 million Americans, nearly half the total number of potential viewers at that time, tuned in. The Mutual network estimated that nine out of 10 radio homes were listening.

Nixon, with his wife seated behind him, took 30 minutes to explain the necessity of the fund and his own innocence in using it. He talked of his mortgaged home, his wife's cloth coat, and even his dog Checkers which had been given to the family. He was not going to give Checkers back no matter what. He ended by asking those in sympathy to phone or wire the Republican National Committee. An avalanche of wires, letters, and phone calls followed. Nixon flew to Wheeling, West Virginia, to see the one man who mattered above all the rest—Ike. Like everybody else in the political campaign, the general had watched the speech and was awed by the virtuosity of Richard Nixon. All was forgiven. When Nixon stumbled into Ike's arms, the Presidential candidate shaped history for the next 25 years by saying, "You're my boy." In one deft stroke of media wizardry, Nixon had surmounted one of his famed six crises and had demonstrated the power not only of electronics in politics but the added dimension of expert staging and production.

Throughout the Eisenhower years television enlarged its beachhead at the White House. The first television news conference was filmed on January 19, 1955. But none of Ike's news conferences was ever broadcast live because his strategists feared that he would garble his sentences and say something damaging to his leadership. While more and more formally set speeches were broadcast live, the networks worried about the demands for time that were cutting into their lush take. Toward the end of his second term, Eisenhower asked for air time to give an address about the tension developing over Quemoy and Matsu. The TV executives, in their collective concern, balked about granting the President the choicest hour. Ike had to wait until past prime time before he could alert the nation.

If the instruments of media could carry White House imagery beyond anything ever dreamed before, then there was another side that was not always considered. Those same marvels of optics and electronics, those same reporters and commentators who helped a President spread his message, could also turn and look into the White House, demand access to heretofore secret rituals and private moments. Before long the growing group of journalists was demanding a virtual role in White House operation.

James Hagerty, former *New York Times* correspondent and aide to Governor Thomas Dewey, was a shrewd press secretary. He understood the revolution in progress. A man invested with the power of the President of the United States was far more than just an executive. He was a symbol, an example, an inspirer—most of all an actor on this huge stage

the media had created. Nothing about him was off limits. Persistent reporters tried through guile or intimidation to wedge their way through the security barriers. Hagerty met the new age head on.

TV cameras were allowed into Cabinet meetings—but under the strictest supervision. Cabinet members were given lines and cues to memorize. There followed a televised "dialogue" between the President and Secretary of State John Foster Dulles, Ike looking interested while the peripatetic Dulles reported on his latest globetrotting.

There was very little illusion about what was happening. The world of modern merchandising was a fact of American life. The Eisenhower administration was filled with its enthusiastic practitioners. "We suddenly realized we were busy manufacturing a product down here, but nobody was selling," admitted one high official to the *Wall Street Journal*.

Perhaps even more important than these efforts at staging events for television programming was Hagerty's intuitive understanding that the daily flow of news had to be constant to satisfy growing consumer appetites. When Ike had his heart attack in 1955, Hagerty unerringly calculated that both for the good of the nation and his boss all the facts of the illness needed to be made public—and by men of authority and knowledge. Never before had the story of Presidential pulse beat and bowel movement been spread across America's page one and detailed in the broadcast news. But, as Hagerty had figured, it calmed an apprehensive world and gave Ike and his White House new plaudits for candor.

There was something else. The overwhelming power to educate vast numbers of people was clearly illustrated. Almost overnight inordinate fears of heart attack were reduced. The physical facts of the illness were learned, as well as new ideas about treatment. And, most important, the knowledge that victims could recover and live useful lives replaced the folklore that a heart attack ended a person's useful existence.

When Ike was struck with ileitis later, *Life* magazine enlivened its pages with a color diagram of the President's lower colon, the facts eagerly supplied by the White House. The rule being formulated in those critical years of media development was, first, to establish the facts of any given episode, then get them to the public fast, and bring them into the best possible light by continued and expert testimony. When a story about Ike painting by numbers appeared, there was no denial. A far more serious moment occurred when it became known that a U-2 spy plane had been shot down over the Soviet Union. The initial response

Five months after his heart attack, Eisenhower announced for a second term, left. A few months later, Ike went into surgery after an attack of ileitis, and press secretary Hagerty, backed by doctors, above, assured the public that Ike would still be able to run for President.

of the Eisenhower government was that such secret operations had to be protected. In the first hours of the unfolding crisis, the State Department denied the stories. But the new realities soon overwhelmed everybody. Once again James Hagerty's counsel was heeded and the U-2 missions were admitted, explained, and even used to promote a muted pride in the nation's ability to produce such technology and to spy on the Soviet Union.

When John F. Kennedy walked onto the political stage it was as if the times and the man were made for each other. It should be stated here forcefully that for all the power of media to burnish any person's image, at least in the short run, an individual still must possess an extraordinary range of personal skills to establish any enduring presence in the national mind. There is as yet no instance in the upper echelons of politics where a mountebank or empty pretty boy could sustain his hold on an electorate by means of modern media techniques. John Kennedy was a man of substance. In addition, he possessed a striking profile, a rare eloquence, a sense of history, a commanding stage presence, and an understanding of how the media world was evolving.

From his first encounters with the media it was plain that Kennedy would prosper. As 1960 approached, Kennedy had a full grasp of the new age. He was a Pulitzer Prize-winning author, a former reporter for Hearst, and at one time had wanted to be a writer for *Fortune*. His friends were journalists and scholars, TV commentators and show business personalities. He

probed them for ideas, watched their shows, and read their articles. He knew their editors and their deadlines and even developed an uncanny ability to spot the sources of news leaks. He was as plugged into the media as any politician could be.

The Kennedy family, with its rich story of struggle and success, was a marvelous ingredient for the media planners. Kennedy's war heroics were trotted out on cue. The rousing weekends of touch football, sailing, and political argument at Hyannisport furnished an inexhaustible source for Sunday features along with the inevitable footage for television. Senator Kennedy rationed access with skill. The media was allowed tantalizing glimpses of the family at work and play, but never brought fully into the most intimate circles. The controversial father, Joseph P. Kennedy, whose fortune was estimated at 400 million dollars, was left deliberately in the background as the campaign moved along.

It was a total effort beyond anything yet seen. Let us call it media-pak. It ranged from serious authors like James MacGregor Burns writing serious books, through interviews with TV personalities like Walter Cronkite, to campaign songs by Frank Sinatra, to the lowly bumper sticker and campaign button. Kennedy was the impresario. No detail was too small. He made the advance man a vastly more important part of politics, realizing that the TV cameras would be on every speech and in every meeting. The best of them all, Jerry Bruno, who later wrote a book titled *The Advance Man*, learned the basic trade from Kennedy. Why had the crowd been so small? Why had not Bruno checked to find out there was a football game at the same time? What about the band, the loudspeakers? Kennedy cut his hair for television. When his voice began to give out he hired a speech therapist who taught him to use his diaphragm properly for voice projection like an opera singer.

As he approached the debates with Richard Nixon, Kennedy knew that his appearance on television would be crucial. He slowed his campaign before the first encounter and insisted on a two-hour nap just before air time. Nixon, still suffering from an infected knee, never slackened his pace. He entered the studio near exhaustion and looked it. Television viewers awarded the debate victory to Kennedy and many, including Nixon, believe that this decided the election. Radio listeners, who could not see Nixon's shadows, either gave the edge to Nixon or at least called the debate a tie. But most Americans made their judgment from television.

All of this experience and the apparatus was transferred to the Presidency after Kennedy arrived at the White House. There had been, despite Kennedy's great popularity with working reporters, considerable editorial opposition to him in major publications. Kennedy rightly calculated that it would continue. The most important media calculation he made as President was to enlarge the role of TV, reach over the heads of columnists and editorial writers whenever he could, and talk directly to the people. "Kennedy's character could be felt in every word," Ted Sorensen would write later. Press Secretary Pierre Salinger, reading his boss's mind, proposed that JFK be the first to open his press conferences to live TV coverage. Old-time reporters were appalled at the idea. Diplomats quaked at the prospect of careless Presidential words flying around the world and upsetting their tidy games. But Salinger knew his man and Kennedy knew his medium. Kennedy made it work. Those television press conferences, totally dominated by the President, became known as the best show in Washington.

John Kennedy planned his overseas ventures, such as the summit meeting with Nikita Khrushchev in Vienna in 1961, with the same precision as he had planned his campaign. Proper locations were selected for major speeches. Advance men not only made the necessary security preparations but educated their foreign hosts in the arts of crowd manipulation and camera location. Film was daily flown back to the United States in time for the evening news shows.

Electronics boldly advanced into the private doings of the White House. Cameras were allowed in when Kennedy and his brother, Attorney General Robert Kennedy, planned their moves in the Alabama integration confrontations. Informal conversations with television correspondents in the Oval Office were carried live. Suddenly, it was apparent that Kennedy had become more than a public official. He was a media star, an entertainer of broad appeal and impact. Historian Arthur Schlesinger, Jr., not the least alarmed by this development since he was Kennedy's house intellect, found the press conferences to be "superb" shows, "always gay, often exciting, relished by the reporters, and by the television audience." Some of the newsmen worried about it. They had become props on this new stage. They gathered, sometimes 400 strong, and, with cameras focused on them, lights blazing, they asked their questions. They felt self-conscious and, because of the setting, often did not insist on hard follow-up questions. The President could shut off a tough question with a simple "no comment" and then wheel to another side of the auditorium and point to one of the horde always clamoring for his attention. The cameras would instantly leave the other questioner, the action would shift to another subject, the audience would be swept along.

It is one of the ironies of Kennedy's time that the greatest single media extravaganza occurred following his death. Not before, or since, had so many people watched, heard, and read of such sorrow and pageantry. The world stopped. The media took over. The Kennedy legend was born.

The Kennedy assassination shoved American politics back a generation. Lyndon B. Johnson, who was a disciple of Franklin Roosevelt and a youth of the Great Depression, was fully aware of the media but he remained deeply suspicious. He had lost to Kennedy at the 1960 convention, he believed, at least in part because he was viewed as a "cornpone" politician with a funny accent. Yet he knew the routines of media management. He had practiced such control when he was Senate majority leader. Writers were awed by the hulking Johnson, who let it be known to one and all covering the Senate that they were housed, given credentials of access, and let into his presence for occasional questions in direct proportion to their friendliness. "I figure that most people believe about 90 percent of what they read," Johnson once told aide Bill Moyers. "If I can get the papers to print what I want, most of the people will believe it."

As the man who could take up the Presidency and gather together the diverse elements of government authority within minutes of Kennedy's death, Johnson was superb. No other politician could have equaled that performance. And no other man on the national

During the 1960 campaign Senator John F. Kennedy and Vice President Richard M. Nixon faced each other in four televised debates watched by 101 million Americans. Moderator Howard

K. Smith sits between the candidates, as commentators in foreground analyze the discourse. Kennedy's performance gained him votes, and he won the election by an extremely narrow margin.

scene could have capitalized so completely on sympathy for the slain Kennedy and guided hundreds of pieces of major legislation, creating the Great Society. As in much that he did, Johnson overdid legislation. Nevertheless, it was a majestic performance.

In the White House, Johnson's approach to the media was little changed from his Senate days. He expected understanding, sympathy, and even affection. He did not expect the harsh criticism that is inherent in the Presidency. Johnson thought he could manage the media. Flying down to his ranch with a group of reporters, he laid out his philosophy about Presidential reporting. When the journalists wanted to know

the facts of any controversy, they were to come straight to him. He would tell them the truth. Thus, with the story from the horse's mouth, they would not need to print rumors and lies from his enemies. And, he added while lounging over a seat on Air Force One, if he happened to do some things that were naughty, well, he said to his thunderstruck audience, they were expected to forget about it.

Johnson talked to reporters more than any other modern President. Arthur Schlesinger, who remained at the White House a few months after Kennedy's death, marveled at how LBJ found any time to do Presidential work. He spent hours with journalists, walking the back lawn with them, swimming in the White House pool with them, talking with them over dinner. During Johnson's first year he appeared on TV more than Kennedy had in nearly three years.

But Johnson still wore the chip on his shoulder. He sensed that he was not getting across as John Kennedy had done. He blamed the media. He approached his media encounters with stealth and suspicion. He often refused to disclose the subjects of his broadcasts beforehand. He treated the networks as personal property, expecting them to accommodate his demands at any time. In 1964 Johnson orchestrated a settlement of a railroad strike so that he could rush up to the CBS studio during Walter Cronkite's broadcast and break in with a personally delivered statement. Johnson considered the media just another part of his administration.

But Johnson was violating cardinal rules. He did not always tell the truth. At first there were small fibs about the size of the budget and his intentions in Vietnam. He sometimes put out incomplete details or played coy to mislead reporters. Then his attempts to deceive the media about the war grew more blatant. Trust, the very cement of government power, began to erode, and no media wizardry would replace it.

Johnson tried. He opened up his walks with his dogs to TV. He let cameras come down and explore his ranch. He tried contact lenses for his press conferences, face makeup, an electronic teleprompter. Any device which promised an improvement in his broadcast image was given a riffle. None did the job.

As his time in office drew to an end, the American public had become thoroughly suspicious of Johnson. He had misled them too often. He also had failed to calculate that the media is basically a conduit, and messages can flow both ways. While Lyndon Johnson was telling the country how he was directing the war in Vietnam, the realities were coming back into American living rooms and onto the front pages. No matter how much the President raved against network camera crews who photographed the hideous battles, and against correspondents who predicted defeat, the story of that war flooded back to the United States until it engulfed Johnson. If John Kennedy was the President who ushered in media-pak, Lyndon Johnson was its first victim.

Next on the great stage was Richard Nixon, perhaps the most experienced of the Presidential politicians in the new media. He had, after all, starred in the first political soap opera,

"Checkers," and saved his career. He had also been defeated by the wan image he projected in the first Presidential debate. He approached the 1968 election with total calculation. He would not be surprised by camera lenses. He would not open himself to hostile pencil reporters. He collected more money for his onslaught than any President before him. He hired the best ad agencies and put his packaging in their hands. His advance men were younger, more eager, and more numerous than any previous crew. Nixon's media strategy called for control. He devised his own citizens' press conferences in which selected panels asked him selected questions. The Democratic candidate, Hubert Humphrey, might have scored needed campaign points in a series of debates but that was ruled out by the equal-time provision of the Federal Communications Act, much to the relief of the Nixon forces.

After the Nixon campaign a small book appeared, *The Selling of the President*. Its author, Joe McGinniss, had watched the Nixon media planners closely and best summed up their approach this way: "It was as if they were building not a President but an Astrodome, where the wind would never blow, the temperature never rise or fall, and the ball never bounce erratically on the artificial grass."

Once in the White House, Nixon continued his efforts to control the media. He increased the use of prime TV time, and set up an Office of Communications for the executive branch, responsible for maintaining the administration's image. Since televised Presidential press conferences were unruly, Nixon cut down on them. He used a live conversation format with network reporters that gave him more control. And Nixon used the air for major policy pronouncements on everything from Vietnam to economics.

The approach was total. The Office of Communications saw to it that Cabinet officers jetted around the country to explain their programs and to cast a warm glow over the administration's achievements. Press releases about Nixon's successes flooded out to local newspapers and TV stations. The Office of Management and Budget estimated that in fiscal year 1971 the executive branch of the federal government spent 164 million dollars for public relations of all kinds.

Nixon's success in maintaining respect, if not affection, during his first term encouraged him to put more distance between himself and the public. Thus, his efforts to limit access and to package tidy dramas increased with each year in power. Church services were staged in the East Room. Nixon picked the preacher and the audience. Interviews with writers were a rarity and, when they were granted, they entailed strict

Nixon's trip to China in 1972 surpassed all previous media events. Three cargo planes airlifted television gear to ensure instant coverage. Nixon walks on the Great Wall, left. But his triumph was short-lived. On August 9, 1974, Nixon, daughter Tricia at his side, bade a tearful farewell after his resignation.

understandings on how the material was to be used and when. He insisted on assurances that he would be on the cover of *Time* magazine, for instance, before he would consent to talk on the record about his first trip to Europe in 1969.

Nothing in the exotic world of media quite rivaled the 1972 journey of Richard Nixon to China, the communist land that he had deplored for a quarter of a century. The visit was made for TV. Writers were granted passage on the mission but in limited numbers. The television networks were allowed to ship their crews in weeks ahead of time. They set up so that live broadcasts of ceremonies could be beamed back by satellite. Three huge cargo planes carried a portable transmitting station and 50 tons of additional equipment to China. Itineraries and points of interest were mapped for the network luminaries like Barbara Walters and Walter Cronkite who would come with Nixon. Standing on the Great Wall, Nixon reached his high water mark. In the first days of his odyssey the networks carried hours of continuous live coverage. An estimated 100 million viewers lapped it up.

Then came Watergate. Once again the double-edged sword was felt. If all those Nixonian triumphs could be sent out by air and print to the American people, the evidence of wrongdoing could be gathered and focused with equal force. Nixon fought a delaying battle. He erected even higher barriers around the Oval Office. It was not enough. Ironically, one of the very devices he had cooked up as the ultimate guardian of the Nixonian image did him in. To assure a total and accurate record of conversations he had with anybody who came to his office, Nixon installed secret recorders that activated on the sound of a voice. Those tapes held the evidence of the President's wrongdoing that drove him from office.

The wonder of Jerry Ford's time is not that he was defeated after finishing the last two years of Richard Nixon's term, but that he almost won. He was saddled with more political burdens than any candidate of this century. There was Water-

Technicians wire President Gerald Ford and ABC's Harry Reasoner with microphones for a talk at Camp David. During the Nixon years, the grounds had been off limits for newsmen.

gate and the Nixon legacy, not to mention the disgrace of Vice President Spiro Agnew. The country was in recession when Ford took office and the Vietnam war was in its final convulsions, revealing what a dismal failure the expenditure of 55,000 American lives and 160 billion dollars had been. Ford had at his disposal the vast apparatus of Republican image-making but it was dispirited and in disarray. Further, while the media was larger than ever, basking in having helped defrock Nixon, the public skepticism about what they were reading and watching was growing. With bizarre fascination, Americans read book after book, article after article, watched hour after hour of television on the great White House debacle. In that environment media-pak would not work well. Something new had to be devised. In Georgia there were some young men who had something new.

They began with a quiet and good man, a born-again Christian who had been successful in business and in state politics. Governor Jimmy Carter had the time and the money to run for President. He had the health and the desire. He was a man of blue jeans and simple tastes, a kindly but firm advocate of the poor and underprivileged. He was a pied piper for the laid-back generation, those who had seen too much of the Imperial Presidency, who were suspicious of men who relished pomp and power. Carter's message was love and goodness. It seemed straightforward and refreshing.

The outlines of the Carter approach were written in a 1972 memo by Gerald Rafshoon, the Atlanta adman and media adviser:

> He is still the man who [as governor] said the time for racial discrimination is over. He still has a Kennedy smile. . . . What he does not have is depth to his image. . . . It will take more than the hand-shaking and the projection of "I understand the problems of the average man" image to put Carter over. This is still his greatest asset and it must be projected but he will also have to convince press, public, and politicians that he knows how to run government. . . .

Rafshoon then outlined a precise timetable for image

development. That memo was supplemented by another, this one written by Hamilton Jordan, Carter's young political strategist. Jordan broadened the package. It outlined strategy for the primaries, counseled Carter to learn about foreign policy, and to see foreign lands. The Jordan memo also suggested that Carter write a book and pointed out how important it was to woo the "eastern liberal news establishment."

Carter followed this road map with great devotion. He traveled abroad. He wrote a book. He wooed reporters and he carefully selected his primary campaign efforts. Traveling behind that Kennedy smile he invaded the farm homes of Iowa, the church basements of New Hampshire. The message was primarily Jimmy Carter, a man of grace and warmth and decency. It won him the nomination.

But laid-back mediapak with the blue-jeaned Carter talking about bringing truth and love to the swamps of Washington was not as effective in a national campaign as it had been in the primaries. When Carter's electronic audiences grew from a few thousand to several million the low key did not sound so good. He lost 30 points in the national polls against an accidental President with a penchant for falling down ramps and hitting his head on airplane doors. Carter won, but barely.

Questions nagged at the new President-elect. What did he stand for? What should he do besides bring grace to high office? He talked of many things and, indeed, in his first months had his Cabinet and staff devise programs aimed at alleviating or achieving solutions for dozens of national problems. Meantime, he sent off his diplomats to seek more disarmament agreements with the Soviet Union and a comprehensive peace in the Middle East.

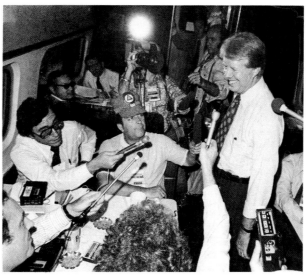

During a whistle-stop campaign trip, a relaxed Jimmy Carter answers reporters' questions. His organization mounted one of the most media-intensive campaigns ever.

To convince a hesitant population and nudge a reluctant Congress his way, Carter continued his image campaign. He stripped the White House of ceremony, banishing "Hail to the Chief" from most occasions. He held town meetings and a Saturday afternoon call-in with Walter Cronkite as his master of ceremonies. He carried his suit bag when he traveled and eschewed fancy restaurants and clubs. Sometimes he stayed with plain people out in the country. He was photographed around the White House in bare feet. Jimmy Carter was going to lead by following, to be President by building his image on the ground floor.

It did not always work. His peace prospects were delayed and frustrated. His legislation bogged down. Inflation worsened and American influence around the world continued to decline. Carter won some notable victories such as the new Panama Canal treaty, civil service reform, a new trade act. He normalized relations with China and finally hammered out both a strategic arms limitation accord and a Middle East peace treaty between Israel and Egypt. But, strangely, the sum of his achievements seemed to add up to less than the total of the parts.

Fundamental questions remained. Had Carter finally discredited media-pak politics by overexpenditure? Was the American electorate so educated and aware now of the techniques of instant education and manipulation that imagery with too little substance was readily discerned? The huge media industry was not going to turn away just because Jimmy Carter's standing in a confused and difficult political world did not respond to the conventional programming. But certainly in the campaigns of the 1980s there would be a reappraisal of how to package and present a President of the United States.

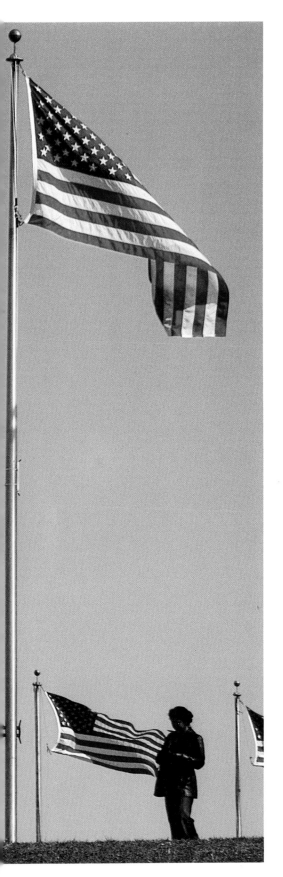

★ ★ ★ ★ ★ ★ ★ ★ ★ ★ ★ ★ ★ ★ ★

Taking the Presidency Home

Russell Bourne

"Want some Lincoln incense?" asked the smiling woman at a vendor's table outside the house where Lincoln died. She held out a dubious looking packet with an image rather distantly related to that of the martyred President.

"Oh, no. Kennedy's the only one who really sells," another vendor told me. He operated out of a van parked on Independence Avenue not far from the Smithsonian's National Air and Space Museum. The van's open side was hung with T-shirts and banners, gaudy souvenirs of a trip to the capital. Discouraged when I showed little interest in the Kennedy paperweight, he cried, "Just wait, mister!" and dashed down the sidewalk to confer in Korean with a buddy who ran the next stall. Then back to me with a triumphant grin. "I can get you Washington for the same price—$1.50!"

It was quite depressing. I had hoped to find some clue to the remembrances of the Presidency that visitors to Washington preferred to take home as talismans. Something like a statue for a niche or a framed portrait

Visitors to Washington, D.C., find Presidents commemorated in monuments, statuary, and in ephemeral sorts of souvenirs. Left, *youngsters romp at the base of the Washington Monument; above, street vendors hawk geegaws and postcards.*

to hang alongside the Constitution had been what I assumed patriotic visitors would want to purchase. I'd even settle for a lamp with a scene of Jackson's victory at New Orleans. But possibly I was looking in the wrong places . . . or possibly my views of the proper objects for veneration were ridiculously outdated.

Even along the Avenue of the Presidents, Pennsylvania Avenue, where I continued my quest, the shops hawked Presidential remembrances of only the tawdriest sort. A wind-up Carter ("Jimmy the Walking Peanut"); a salad plate with all the Presidents mashed together; a leering postcard of Nixon. It was obvious not only that the tourists who thronged the avenues with me were looking for souvenirs of other kinds (ankle bracelets with the "Key to Washington" being particularly popular) but also that the Presidency had no particular claim on their attention.

Yet, continuing my hagiological journey westward to the White House, I found myself one morning in line with others waiting for admission at the East Wing entrance. An English collegian shivering in the wind beside me quipped to his friend that "the place seems to have recovered nicely from when we burned it in 1814."

Indeed it had; it looked glorious. And, after an unhurried tour of the rooms on the main floor, we filed out beneath the handsome portico with a glowing feeling that we'd been to the best open house of the year. The wife of a cowboy-hatted gentleman

The White House is surrounded by a modest wrought-iron fence that permits an unimpeded view from either side.

exclaimed, "Why, we got to see everything!" But a Frenchman, perhaps more used to castles than to mansions for the people, remarked, "C'est tout?"

A group of school girls waved up at the second-floor windows. "Amy might really be watching us, you know." Another school girl, when asked if she'd like to live there, replied: "No, because all those nice things really belong to someone else. But, on the other hand, wouldn't it be fun to say to some boys, 'Hey, come on over . . . we live at the White House!'"

So thoughts were turning here to the actual Presidency, the responsibility of being a part of that family, the personal reality of exercising that power.

The Washington Monument, to which I walked next, makes no promise to introduce you to the man. (The man, in fact, has succeeded in ignoring most attempts at introduction.) But how powerfully it symbolizes his primacy! I stood at the base of the knoll, watching the tip of the

What is a visit to the nation's capital without taking home pictures? And what picture is truly complete without the photographer in it? A visitor sets up a family shot before the Lincoln Memorial, then rushes to get in the frame.

Around the Washington Monument runs an indelible scar 152 feet above the ground, exact evidence of where construction stopped in troubled antebellum times. The monument stands one-third of the distance between the Lincoln Memorial and the Capitol. Smithsonian Castle and Library of Congress are to the right.

Designed by sculptor Daniel Chester French to show the President in wartime, the figure of Lincoln and its surrounding temple, top, nonetheless conveys a feeling of peace. The completed figure's right hand taps a forefinger, above; the other hand, left, is clenched (note curiously large thumb that fascinated French).

555-foot obelisk cleave the clouds; it seemed to move majestically across the sky. Thank heaven Robert Mills's entire 1836 design, which called for a columned, circular base, was too expensive to build. An exclamation point, someone called it. Or, as a kid at the top said, "Number One!" He would take that home.

Another boy, this one encountered at the Lincoln Memorial, was taking home something else: a pair of jeans worn at the seat from sliding down the grand balustrade beside the 41 steps leading up to the temple's main floor. He waved as he zoomed to the bottom. His parents could attend the lecture by the National Park Service guide, who was pondering the meaning of the raised forefinger on the right hand of Daniel Chester French's 19-foot statue of "the brooding Lincoln." That raised finger signifies a decision in formation. The left hand clenches in determination, the left foot tenses to spring the figure forward—charging all the way from its seat to drive a point home at the Capitol at the other end of the Mall. Meanwhile the finger taps off the seconds of considering this way or that.

★ ★ ★

Crossing the Mall at right angles, a sight line runs from the oval office of the White House to the leveled gaze of Thomas Jefferson, standing in his memorial near the Potomac. Again, it's something of a confrontation or a continuing challenge. But, strangely, Jefferson is smiling.

At his feet a woman was asking the guide about the curious columns that hold up the thrice-life-sized statue from the back. Corinthian, with tobacco and corn motifs on the capitals, they recall Jefferson's own designs for Virginia's State House. "Without 'em," the guide explained, "all the weight would be on Tom's ankles and they'd crack."

It's the chamber itself, of course, that wins you over to regard this as the most perfect expression of the Presidency's vital, enduring relevance. The mighty words from the Declaration of Independence on the walls; the openness to the light and the mind; the feminine rounding of the dome, whether seen from outside with its subtle shadings (best at dawn or twilight) or from inside with its sweeping shadows (best on a hot summer's day).

So I asked the woman who had been talking to the guide, "But what about the smile? For such a commanding figure—a smile?"

"He was thinking of something bright to say," she answered . . .

And that's what I took home.

Mirrored in the Tidal Basin, the Jefferson Memorial, right, reflects both the architectural precepts and the democratic beliefs of the third President: ". . . institutions must advance to keep pace with the times," reads the inscription.

208

Cartooning the Presidency

Caren W. Keshishian

In November 1884 Grover Cleveland defeated the GOP's James G. Blaine by one of the smallest margins in history. Four days before the election, Joseph Pulitzer's *New York World* had run a cartoon by Walt McDougall depicting a palatial dinner in Blaine's honor at Delmonico's. It was captioned "The Royal Feast of Belshazzar," an allusion to the Biblical tale in which handwriting appeared on the wall to foretell the fall of Babylonia. The imagery was superb, and the Democrats rushed the cartoon up on billboards all over the city. Had Blaine carried New York, he would have won the election. He lost the state by a mere 1100 votes. Though John P. St. John of the Prohibitionists had played a part too (see page 135), Walt McDougall's role in putting Cleveland in the White House had been very substantial indeed.

★ ★ ★

The political cartoon is a paradoxical kind of commentary, at once pungently direct and artfully oblique. It has been with us since the beginning of the republic—indeed, even earlier, for Ben Franklin is considered our first indigenous cartoonist. There was nothing humorous about "Join, or Die" (humor, let it be noted, is not obligatory for cartoonery), but it was an effective incitement to action. And it was widely distributed, a concomitant of cartoonery that *is* essential. The strength of the art is a strength in numbers.

Congress and Treasury busy at his bid, "Trust Giant" John D. Rockefeller eyes the White House in 1900. First cartoon in an American newspaper (1754) was drawn by Ben Franklin promoting his plan to unite colonies under a president general.

LOOK ON THIS PICTURE,   AND ON THIS,

ORDER
LAW
RELIGION

HERE IS___

THIS WAS___

Jefferson's "radicalism" was a favorite Federalist target. Here, his underpinnings are contrasted to Washington's—religion, law, and order. Below, in 1800, Jefferson is shown trying to burn the Constitution on the "Altar to Gallic Despotism."

THE PROVIDENTIAL DETECTION

During the nation's first 40 years the vitality of cartoonery remained constricted. Some constraints were purely technical. More important, however, was a "figuratively distant" Presidency, as Wilcomb Washburn puts it. That distance disappeared when Andrew Jackson came along.

Old Hickory appreciated the power of symbolism. He personalized political issues, he achieved an emotional bond with the common man, and he wielded power in ways that no President before him had. All this was conducive to an efflorescence in the art of cartoonery. The strong man was strongly challenged; his challengers were in turn strongly challenged. Politics became the province of everyman.

Yet, more often than not, we find the antebellum cartoon baffling. King Andrew treading on

the Constitution (page 174) is a timeless sort of image. Far more typical, however, is the cartoon full of obscure symbols and full of characters discoursing in tiny words we can scarcely read, and wouldn't understand even if we made the effort.

Not until the Civil War did a style emerge that is readily comprehensible from our latter-day perspective. A single name stands out above all others: Nast. Nast began his career at 15 as a draftsman for Frank Leslie. During the war, he switched from basic illustration to abstract political commentary, training his biggest guns on northerners who were less than totally dedicated to conquering the South. Lincoln said, "Thomas Nast has been our best recruiting sargent."

But Nast hit his true stride when he found his ultimate nemesis: "Boss" Tweed, who came to epitomize everything evil about the Democratic Party. Tweed is said to have cried out, "Stop them damn pictures . . . I don't care so much what the papers write about me. My constituents can't read. But, damn it, they can see pictures."

Joseph Keppler, as pro-Democratic as Nast was pro-Republican, was clearly Nast's spiritual successor. On the pages of his big, colorful weekly, *Puck*, Keppler established a fundamental convention of the political cartoon—the omnipresent motif which becomes part of a visual vernacular. In the case of Benjamin Harrison, for example, this motif was a disparity between

THE MODERN BALAAM AND HIS ASS.

Typical of cartoonery of the Jacksonian era, "The Modern Balaam and His Ass" hit Jackson for a monetary manifesto called the Specie Circular. Left, in 1857 the Dred Scott decision and repeal of the Missouri Compromise fractured the parties so badly that in 1860 there were four major contenders for the Presidency.

LINCOLN'S TWO DIFFICULTIES.

Lin. "WHAT? NO MONEY! NO MEN!"

Before it was evident in England that the Union would win, John Tenniel of Punch *depicted Lincoln beset with difficulties. Although the ultimate evolution of Uncle Sam was still a half-century off, his visage is emerging here and would be further defined both by Nast and Keppler.*

his size and the size of Old Tippecanoe's old hat (page 128). A small man literally, too small for the job.

★   ★   ★

In the late 19th century the weeklies began to lose their edge and were finally upset on their own turf by another journalistic medium. Cartoons went to dailies such as Pulitzer's *World* and Hearst's *Journal.* There they sacrificed deliberation and polish but gained in vigor and economy. Everything was ready for Teddy Roosevelt to come back from San Juan Hill.

Roosevelt was a cartoonist's dream, being a walking caricature in life—larger than life, enormous teeth, squinty eyes behind steel-rimmed glasses, bushy moustache. His policies were emblematic. Even when flaying him, cartoonists seemed to love him. Cartoonists focused also on Bryan, who made a better caricature than the man who succeeded him as leader of the Democrats. Woodrow Wilson's style of evangelism somehow didn't work for the cartoonists.

During World War I, and again during the early years of the Great Depression, cartoonery became strained, often flat. One senses an almost palpable relief when FDR springs onto the editorial pages, cigarette holder, broad grin, head cocked confidently. As with TR, the cartoonists loved to hate him.

Out of the Depression, into another war, and again the cartoons seem flat. But in the 1950s one name truly stood out from an otherwise Ozzie-and-Harriet background. Herblock was the backyard kid peering in the

As seen by Puck in early 1880, Boss Conkling is in a dilemma: He wants Grant back in the White House, but his enemy Blaine has the nomination locked up. The cartoon missed on two counts: Tilden did not even run for the Democrats, and the actual GOP nominee Garfield was missing from the puzzle altogether.

In 1902, after suffering the indignity of caricature as a parrot, a Pennsylvania politico had a bill drafted barring the "depicting of men . . . as birds or animals." Walt McDougall responded by making him a beet, Boss Matt Quay a "dying oak."

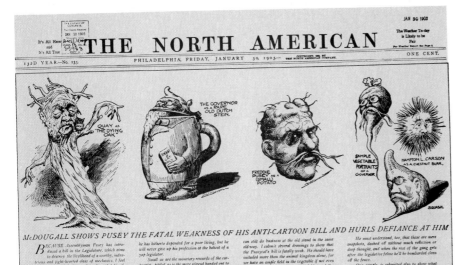

THE NORTH AMERICAN

PHILADELPHIA, FRIDAY, JANUARY 30, 1903 — THE NORTH AMERICAN COMPANY.

132D YEAR—No. 133.

ONE CENT.

The Weather To-day is Likely to be Fair

It's All Here and It's All True

McDOUGALL SHOWS PUSEY THE FATAL WEAKNESS OF HIS ANTI-CARTOON BILL AND HURLS DEFIANCE AT HIM

BECAUSE Assemblyman Pusey has introduced a bill in the Legislature, which aims to destroy the livelihood of a worthy, industrious and light-hearted class of mechanics, I feel called upon to defy him and to show that his efforts, by no matter whom they were originated, will avail him nothing. The bill forbids the use of "unhuman" animal forms in caricaturing human beings in this Commonwealth. So little appreciated are the diverse resources of a caricaturist and so restricted the scope of his genius is supposed to be by the legislator with the two-inch forehead and the six-inch moustache area that he imagines he can shake off the gifted artist by closing the animal world to him. The cartoonist may be compelled to sport with his zoo of trained performing parrots, owls, lions, bears, skunks and bats upon which he has hitherto depended for a poor living, but he will never give up his profession at the behest of a yap legislator.

Small are the monetary rewards of the cartoonist, pitiful as is the mere stipend handed out to him every week, he still has a vast pride in his Art, and when one considers that it is perhaps, apart from officeholding, the only profession requiring no real toil and the only one in which brains are absolutely unnecessary, it will be easily seen why the cartoonist clings to his job.

Mr. Pusey's threat does not cause us to quail. After the bill is passed even that word quail will be prohibited, I suppose, but that is en passant, as we say in Atlantic City. No action has yet been taken by the Cartoonists' Union in opposing this bill, not because we are afraid to go to Harrisburg and face the Legislature, but because even if it passes we can still do business at the old stand in the same old way. I submit several drawings to show that the Pusey cat's bill is fatally weak. He should have included more than the animal kingdom alone, for we have an ample field in the vegetable if not even the mineral kingdom. An untried field, too, fuller perhaps of possibilities than the old biological branch.

Every cartoonist has a Noah's Ark full of worn, broken and decrepit animals, bugs and such, but the fresh vegetable field is untouched. What chances of caricature lie in the tomato, the string bean, the cucumber, the onion and the leek cannot be guessed. I have made a few studies showing the possibilities of the carrot, squash, potato and chestnut, just to show what a journeyman cartoonist can do when pushed to the wall. Mr. Scat can take warning by these.

He must understand, too, that these are mere snapshots, dashed off without much reflection or deep thought, and when the rest of the gang gets after the legislative feline he'll be bombarded clean off the fence.

One sample is submitted also to show what can be done with purely inanimate objects. There are many such beside the old Dutch stein which I have used that will adapt themselves to the purpose, but this will suffice to show Mr. Pusey what we can and will do if his silly bill passes. I oppose, however, that when he reads this Assemblyman Kitty will add the word "vegetables" to the bill and try to squelch us in that manner. But I still have several other deadly weapons in reserve, and I defy him to do his very bitterest.

WALT McDOUGALL.

213

America's affection for Teddy Roosevelt was captured by Jay "Ding" Darling just after the old Rough Rider died in 1919.

windows of the powerful in Washington. His cartoons weren't funny, they hurt. They grappled effectively with the politics of the Cold War era, when nothing was what it seemed to be.

Then came Vietnam and Watergate. Cartoonists thrived— somehow the murk brought out the sublime in the likes of David Levine and Edward Sorel, whose caricatures are classics. The Levines and Sorels played brilliant games for the elite, but Garry Trudeau rode forward from a newly franchised youth population, and repositioned perceptions of politics back into the living room, that entrepôt of the human comedy. Trudeau did unnervingly accurate portraits of all the henchmen of Watergate but never portrayed a President, perhaps the most telling assessment of all. And the most hopeful too, for the President was represented by the White House itself. The traditions continue even if the man falls.

★   ★   ★

The art thrives—the best work is a keystone of any Op/Ed page. While varnished oil portraits preserve Presidents like flies in amber, the real classics of the visual record may be the cartoons, which capture the Presidents as people in motion, presented with the off-center heraldry of the events of the day. This is who they were as public figures.

The surgical scar ebulliently displayed by Lyndon Johnson became a map of Vietnam in this David Levine cartoon.

A popular view of Congress, and sometimes a President's view too. Both during Ike's Presidency and Truman's, Congress was controlled by the opposition party.

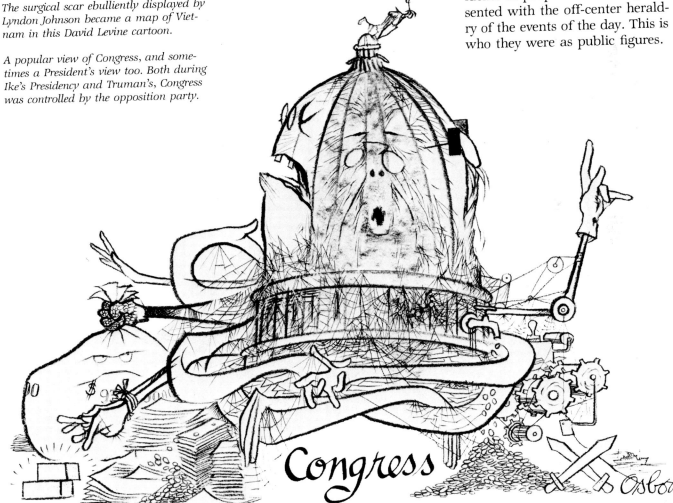

Congress

★ ★ ★ ★ ★ ★ ★ ★ ★ ★ ★

The Once and Future Presidency

Stephen Hess

The way that American citizens regard their Chief Executive has changed remarkably since the first President was chosen unanimously by the electors in 1789. While only George Washington was awarded this office without opposition, throughout most of the nation's history the American people would have agreed with the British statesman who said of the Presidency in 1861: "To my mind there is nothing more worthy of reverence and obedience. . . ." After World War II, however, something strange happened: Every President except one—Dwight D. Eisenhower—steadily lost favor in the opinion polls the longer he remained in office. Of late, Americans clearly have not felt much "reverence" for their Presidents.

Various explanations have been suggested for this turn of events. Some say that the only problem with the Presidency is that inferior people have been elected. "The country is filled with individuals with the potential of a Washington, Jefferson, Lincoln, Wilson, or FDR," declared the eminent historian Henry Steele Commager in a recent interview. "But where do these people go? Perhaps into science or the arts, certainly not into national politics." Recent Presidents may have been less capable than their predecessors. Yet it is always tempting to romanticize the past, and we ought not forget that for every Washington there was a Zachary Taylor; for every Lincoln, at least one James Buchanan; a Warren Harding as well as a Woodrow Wilson.

Still, it is probably true that the way our system of nominating major-party candidates has evolved does put a premium on those who are best able to raise huge sums of money and run helter-skelter through 35 state primary elections—abilities that are not necessarily the ones most essential to performing the duties of Chief Executive. As a corrective, partial public financing of the Presidential contest was tried for the first time in 1976, and proposals have been aired for instituting regional primaries or even a national primary. It is worth recalling, on the other hand, that a "bad" system—characterized by political bosses making deals in smoke-filled back rooms—produced the Lincolns and the Franklin D. Roosevelts. Then there remains only to consider the validity of what the English social scientist Walter Bagehot said of Lincoln's election: "Success in a lottery is no excuse for lotteries."

Another explanation for the chronic slippage in popular esteem that has bedeviled recent Presidents is based on the proposition that great leaders are produced in response to great crises. There are several apparent instances of this in American history, but most often cited is Lincoln's leadership during the Civil War and FDR's in the Great Depression. Leadership may thus be a product of the times, rather than of the availability and election of sterling candidates. Though evidence of this can be read in the records of the past, it is also true that in times of crisis the American people have generally rallied 'round the President, offering a form of popular support that may actually be a requisite for effective leadership. Furthermore, while the theory that great troubles somehow generate great leaders seems to have the ring of truth, it is little comfort to a nation whose present problems may not be cataclysmic as in 1861 or 1933, yet are certainly serious enough to demand a very high order of leadership.

But then there is yet another idea to consider, an idea epitomized in the words of Professor Commager:

The President is increasingly a creature of society—a creature of its psychology, its standards, its expectations, a creature of its advertising. . . . We get the kind of men who are not bold, who are not innovative, who are not resourceful—or, even if they could be, they still won't risk it.

What this amounts to saying is that, yes, the Presidency is in a sorry state, but the fault lies in ourselves, not the White House. How does one respond? Certainly one may marshal evidence counter to the proposition that our "modes of thought" are awry. We are a people, for example, who voluntarily contribute more to charities and non-profit organizations than any other society in history. If our failures are evident in our leaders, then so too are our strengths. Each must assess for himself our strengths and weaknesses.

My own view of what has been happening to the Presidency—without meaning to imply that the problems are subject to only one interpretation, and certainly not to impugn the wisdom of Professor Commager—is that it has become harder to run a democratic country. Not just the United States. The so-called failure in leadership can be seen in other parts of the world, and is reflected in a greater rate of government turnovers wherever free elections are held, including Canada, Great Britain, Sweden, Australia, New Zealand, Portugal, India, Israel, and Japan. In our country, there is now a wide gap between popular expectations of what a President should do and the realities of what a President can do. It would be incorrect to claim that the Presidency is no longer a powerful office; a President is far from being a hapless giant. Nevertheless, there are greater constraints on his ability to exercise national leadership.

While Presidents are elected as Democrats or Republicans, they serve a nation that increasingly considers political parties to be irrelevant. Government has taken over most of the social services that used to be provided by the parties. (Whatever else one may say about "machines" and machine politicians, they often provided citizens with a broad range of tangible benefits, asking nothing in return but their votes.) Television enables candidates to make themselves known directly to the voters without the aid of party apparatus. Moreover, many people cannot detect sufficient ideological differences between the parties to warrant identifying with either one. A President once could expect a degree of loyalty simply because he was the leader of a party, but a society in which parties have little impact denies the Chief Executive this base of support.

Then, too, American political parties have ordinarily represented so many divergent interests that each component group has had to compromise in order to remain within the party. In Jefferson's day, in Jackson's, Teddy Roosevelt's, FDR's, even Eisenhower's,

those compromises were made. As the parties have declined, however, many Americans have begun to organize themselves around specific causes, such as pro-abortion or anti-abortion, pro-busing or anti-busing. The parties have traditionally tended to mute the intensity of any given issue; but not only are issues such as abortion and integration not to be muted, they also do not divide voters in ways coincident with established party alignments. When it comes to energy policy, taxes, the environment, government regulation, there does not seem to be a position clearly identifiable with one party or the other.

Since the end of World War II there have been 16 years when the White House was controlled by one party and the Congress by the other, a state of affairs to which some observers have attributed the difficulties of the Presidency. But the experience of Jimmy Carter—a Democrat serving with a Democratic Congress—should make it evident that no President can any longer expect much comfort from members of Congress merely because they share the same party label. What is true of a President is equally true of U. S. Senators and Representatives: Their election is the result of their own efforts to achieve a personal following, not the efforts of a party machine. Rarely do they "owe" the President anything by virtue of his being the party head. Furthermore, since it seems inevitable that the President is going to lose popularity as his time in office lengthens, it is to the interest of legislators belonging to the same party to disassociate themselves from him (and, of course, to attack him if they are of the opposition party).

Thus an American President is on his own. This puts tremendous demands on his ability to persuade. Presidents, of course, have virtually unlimited access to the means of communication. It is inconceivable that a President should call a news conference and no reporters show up, or that a President should want to make a major address and the television networks refuse to give him air time. Yet, while different Presidents may have different rhetorical skills, they all face a common problem that was once described by Franklin D. Roosevelt in this way: "Individual psychology cannot be attuned for long periods of time to a constant repetition of the highest note in the scale." In other words, there are limits to how much public persuasion even the most artful speaker can accomplish before he loses his audience. The paradox is that while modern Presidents must often seek support directly from the people, the more they appeal directly, the less effective their appeals are apt to be. There is no way to repeal the law of diminishing returns.

At the same time, Presidents are also having greater difficulties in the area of "private" persuasion, such as bargaining for the support of legislators. The reason is simply that Presidents have fewer rewards to offer than they once had. Out of a federal civilian work force of over two million, only about 2,000 are Presidential appointees. Government contracts are supposed to be awarded on the basis of competitive bidding. The famous adage of 19th-century American politics was, "To the victor belongs the spoils." Today, some state governors have more patronage to distribute than does the man in the White House. Instead of economic rewards (jobs and contracts), Presidents have been forced to rely more on symbolic rewards, such as invitations to White House dinners. However much coveted, such rewards simply do not embody as much power to swing a legislator into line as does a job or a contract for one of his constituents.

Other realities of the modern Presidency relate to the size and complexity of government. Obviously it was a lot easier for a President to govern when he could gather in one room all of the people to whom he had delegated responsibilities. In our own age of Big Government, many executives must act in the name of the President without ever talking with him—and, in some cases, without ever having met him. Yet it is not just that government has become so much bigger—hence more bureaucratic, and less responsive. In addition, the President is the head of a government that is now expected to perform many tasks it was not formerly concerned with at all. These involve challenges that would be incredibly difficult to meet under any circumstances, such as cleaning up environmental pollution. In an increasing number of instances, the government has either assumed or inherited problems that *nobody* has been able to cope with. Do educators really know why some children can't read? Do economists really know how to deal with unemployment and inflation at the same time? Can anyone make an intelligent cost-benefit analysis of any new welfare program? Yet we turn for answers to the government, and specifically to the Chief Executive. As Columbia University Professor Henry F. Graff puts it, "The White House has become the dumping ground of last resort for society's unsolved and unsolvable technological, social and economic issues."

These are forces that work against all Presidents. In addition, peculiar or unique forces may affect any particular President. Franklin D. Roosevelt was in office on December 7, 1941, when Pearl Harbor was attacked; Jimmy Carter was President when OPEC raised the price of oil in June 1979. Presidents are increasingly buffeted by events that are not of their own creation. They are held most closely responsible for the state of the domestic economy and for the state of international relations—the two areas in which there are the largest number of forces unresponsive to whatever controls a President might try to exercise.

Since times change, so too do the exigencies of effective leadership. Dwight Eisenhower, for example, felt that his role was to establish a sense of calm after what he viewed as the divisiveness engendered by Harry S Truman. Gerald Ford sought to make his mark through a candid and open mode of conduct after the behind-closed-doors Presidency of Richard Nixon. Jimmy Carter, like Ford, had to preside over a country racked in a single decade by the Vietnam war and by Watergate. In practical terms, this has meant having to contend with a variety of Congressional enactments designed to prevent future Vietnams and repeat Watergates by placing constraints on Presidential autonomy.

The American constitutional system of checks and balances often produces shifts that resemble a child's seesaw: When the President is up, the Congress is down; when the Congress is up, the Presidency is down. How this has worked in specific periods of American history has been reviewed by the authors of the seven main essays in this book. Although there are advantages and disadvantages to Congressional supremacy, just as is so when the Presidency is ascendant, the teeter-totter principle is for better or worse the way American government seeks a golden mean. The real puzzle is how to put together an effective collaborative leadership combining the best that a specific Congress and a particular President have to offer. It has happened from time to time in our history, but not often.

In the wake of twin national disasters, Vietnam and Watergate, Congress assumed an assertive posture. This became President Carter's inheritance, and —without regard to his personal skills—probably no Chief Executive has ever been so hemmed in by Congressionally imposed restrictions. Congressional assertiveness is especially evident in foreign affairs, the realm wherein Presidents have traditionally had the greatest leeway to act in the name of the nation. Whether in treaty-making, or the stance taken on specific disputes, or broad-gauge policy matters, Congress has made it clear that it no longer intends to be a President's rubber stamp. In some instances, members of Congress are merely responding to constituent groups, just as they do on domestic issues. For example, regarding the dispute over Cyprus, there is now for the first time considerable organized pressure on Congress from Greek-Americans. But Congressional involvement in foreign affairs may also reflect the emergence of a new-style legislator: younger, better educated, with more interest in issues beyond the borders of his or her own district.

Vietnam and Watergate of course affected the American people as well as their representatives in Washington. These events—and undoubtedly such persistent problems as inflation and the energy crisis—have shaken confidence in those who run governments, whatever their specific role. A Harris Poll in late 1978 showed that during a nine-month period "high confidence" in the Presidency had dropped from 23 to 14 percent. Yet it had also dropped regarding Congress from 15 to 10 percent, regarding state governments from 19 to 15 percent, and regarding local governments from 21 to 19 percent. The rates of declining confidence may be different, but the evidence is clear that people who govern at all levels have been targeted for public disfavor. The problem is not one of the Presidency alone.

This attitude is partly fed by the news media, which, by definition in a free society, looks for and reports on all malefactions of the public trust. Things that are "right" about the government are sometimes "news," though not often; but all the things that are "wrong" are sure to be reported if they can be uncovered. Presidents since George Washington have had their problems with the press, as both Richard Morris and Hugh Sidey have noted in this book. But leaders now must learn to live with the very highest degree of scrutiny from the media. In an earlier age, it is probable that trust in the President was the norm—that is, a President had to earn popular distrust by some specific iniquity. Now the reverse may be true.

Possibly the most frequently suggested reform for what ails the Presidency is a constitutional amendment creating a single, six-year term. The main idea is that, since the President would not have to be running for a second term throughout his first, he could risk being "bold, innovative, and resourceful." At least, the risk need not involve political suicide. Former Senator Mike Mansfield stated this rationale thus:

A President under a single, six-year term would not be removed entirely from politics, but the amount of time he would have to allot to politics would be decreased considerably and by the same token the amount of time he would be able to

spend on looking after the national interest, both domestically and in the field of foreign policy, would be increased.

The notion of "depoliticizing" the Presidency, whatever its virtues, is not universally applauded. What we are dealing with, says political science professor Thomas E. Cronin:

. . . is a highly political office and it cannot be otherwise; its political character is for the most part desirable. Efforts to remove it from politics are naive and politically harmful. An apolitical presidency, uninterested in re-election, and aloof from concerns of the great political parties, would probably be a highly irresponsible presidency.

On a less theoretical level, the problem with the proposal is that if a good President were elected, the nation would have him in the White House for two years less than under the present system; if a bad President were elected, the American people would be stuck with the consequences for two years more than under the present system.

In addition to schemes for changing the rules regarding the President's term of office, a great deal of attention has been devoted to potential means of freeing him from what Professor Commager calls "the endless demands on his time and thought, endless demands . . . which distract him from the main task of leadership." Ideas for improving this situation include a suggestion from Dwight Eisenhower's younger brother Milton to create two executive Vice Presidents—one to supervise domestic agencies, the other for international relations—with the President relieved of day-to-day management responsibilities. Representative Henry S. Reuss of Wisconsin thinks that in addition to the President there should be "an elected Chief of State [who] would free the President from many of the draining ceremonial functions which now occupy much of his time." Such schemes, of course, are based on the premise that the job has become too much for one person to handle. Many scholars doubt that the constitutional duties of the Presidency are divisible without causing friction and stalemate; there can be only one leader of the executive branch at a time.

Those who would tinker with the form of the Presidency—or even propose switching to a parliamentary mode of governing—may be overlooking the considerable capacity for self-correction built into the present system. Some of the factors that now are working to the disadvantage of the President are reversible. Today the Congress is "up," but the whole of American history suggests that there will come a time when the seesaw tilts back, and the President will be "up" again. This will happen when the Congress stumbles badly, as badly as Presidents did in Vietnam and Watergate. Most likely the stumbling block will involve foreign affairs, where there is little evidence to indicate that Congress is in a better position to make effective policy than the President. Also there will come a time—probably when there is a sharp upturn in the economy—when the American people will have a far more sanguine attitude about political leaders in general, and Presidents will gain more latitude to act.

By recounting the new realities that make it more difficult to do a good job of being President, I do not mean to imply that it makes no difference who is in the White House, or that the burdens are now such as to sink any occupant. George Washington, Andrew Jackson, and Abraham Lincoln were not great Presidents simply because they lived in earlier times. There are obvious qualities of wisdom, imagination, even daring that distinguish one President from another, and that have not died out in contemporary civilization. There are skills of language, judgment, and negotiation that leaders either learn or are born with. Furthermore, we are finding out a great deal about personality type *vis à vis* the Presidential office. There are people who are more fit psychologically to be President than others, and who can make a special creative endeavor out of exercising power in a democratic framework. A fortunate advantage of the American system is that the Constitution places very few restrictions on who can be President. The parliamentary system requires that the prime minister come from the legislature, but Americans can cast their net almost as wide as they can imagine. Any native-born citizen over the age of 35 is eligible to be President.

Presidents *are* restricted in their actions, and that is by fundamental design. James Madison noted that the founders of the American republic were primarily worried about "the overgrown and all-grasping prerogative of an hereditary magistrate." So the basic question, then and always, is how much power the people should entrust to a leader. The powers of the President are considerable, even if the constraints are also considerable. The powers and constraints, however, are fluid, in flux. They change in reaction to past events and in relation to present circumstances. They change, too, as Presidents display different degrees of skill and fortitude in leading the nation.

The Authors

Noble E. Cunningham, Jr., is Professor of History at the University of Missouri, Columbia. His most recent books are *The Process of Government Under Jefferson* and a three-volume edition of *Circular Letters of Congressmen to Their Constituents, 1789–1829*.

Robert J. Donovan, formerly Washington Bureau Chief for the *New York Herald Tribune* and the *Los Angeles Times*, is Senior Fellow at the Woodrow Wilson School of Public and International Affairs, Princeton University. He is completing his second volume on the Presidency of Harry S Truman.

Lewis L. Gould is Professor of History at the University of Texas. His books include *Progressives and Prohibitionists, Reform and Regulation: American Politics, 1900–1916*, and *The Presidency of William McKinley*.

Stephen Hess is Senior Fellow in Governmental Studies at the Brookings Institution, and Fellow of the Faculty of Government, John F. Kennedy School of Government, Harvard University. He is co-author of *The Ungentlemanly Art: A History of American Political Cartoons* and author of *Organizing the Presidency*.

Margaret Brown Klapthor, Curator of Political History in the National Museum of History and Technology, is author of numerous publications about the Presidents, the First Ladies, the White House, and the objects of material culture relating to the Presidency.

Michael L. Lawson, who received his doctorate from the University of New Mexico, is Research Historian in the National Portrait Gallery, Smithsonian Institution. He has helped organize several recent exhibitions, including "The Great Crash."

Arthur S. Link is Professor of History and Director of The Wilson Papers, Princeton University. In addition to editing the 32 volumes of Woodrow Wilson's papers now in print, Professor Link is author of more than two dozen books, the most recent being *Woodrow Wilson: Revolution, War, and Peace*.

Richard B. Morris is Gouverneur Morris Professor of History Emeritus at Columbia University. He is co-editor of the *New American Nation* series, editor of the papers of John Jay, and author of numerous books in-cluding *The Peacemakers*, *Great Presidential Decisions*, and *Encyclopedia of American History*.

Mark E. Neely, Jr., Director of the Louis A. Warren Lincoln Library and Museum, Fort Wayne, Indiana, received his doctorate from Yale University. He is editor of *Lincoln Lore* and author of the forthcoming *Lincoln Encyclopedia*.

Edwards Park, born in New England, grew up with a strong sense of history which shows in *Smithsonian* magazine, for which he writes a monthly column and serves on the Board of Editors. He has written several chapters in previous Smithsonian Exposition Books.

Robert C. Post, who served as editor for *Every Four Years*, is now coordinator of the exhibition program in the National Museum of History and Technology.

Marvin Sadik is Director of the National Portrait Gallery, Smithsonian Institution. He has organized many exhibitions of American historical portraits, and is author of numerous museum catalogues and other publications on a wide range of subjects.

Hugh Sidey is Washington Contributing Editor for *Time*, and formerly its Washington Bureau Chief. He has written a regular column on the Presidency for 15 years, and is author or co-author of four books on Presidents Kennedy, Johnson, and Ford. He appears regularly with "Agronsky & Company" on PBS.

Frederick S. Voss is a historian in the National Portrait Gallery, Smithsonian Institution, where he has been involved in the conception of numerous special exhibitions including "We Have Made a Nation."

Wilcomb E. Washburn has been at the Smithsonian Institution for 22 years. A former Curator of Political History, National Museum of History and Technology, he is currently Director of the Smithsonian's Office of American Studies and serves as President of the American Studies Association.

Note: Contributors to *Every Four Years* not listed above are staff members of Smithsonian Exposition Books.

Suggestions For Further Reading

American Heritage, *The American Heritage Pictorial History of the Presidents of the United States* (New York, 2 vols. 1968)

Bailey, Thomas A., *Presidential Greatness: The Image of the Man from George Washington to the Present* (New York, 1966)

Binkley, Wilfred E., *President and Congress* (New York, 2d ed. 1962)

Brogan, D. W., *Politics in America* (New York, 1954)

Brown, Stuart Gerry, *The American Presidency: Leadership, Partisanship and Popularity* (New York, 1966)

Brown, William B., *The People's Choice* (Baton Rouge, 1960)

Burns, James MacGregor, *Presidential Government: The Crucible of Leadership* (Boston, 1966)

Corwin, Edwin S., *The President: Office and Powers, 1789–1957* (New York, 4th ed. 1957)

Cunliffe, Marcus, *American Presidents and the Presidency* (New York, 1976)

David, Paul T., *et al.*, *The Politics of National Party Conventions* (Washington, 1964)

Finer, Herman, *The Presidency: Crisis and Regeneration* (Chicago, 1960)

Fisher, Louis, *President and Congress* (New York, 1972)

Hamilton, Holman, *White House Images and Realities* (Gainesville, 1958)

Hatch, Louis C., *A History of the Vice-Presidency of the United States* (New York, 1934)

Hofstadter, Richard, *The American Political Tradition* (New York, 1948)

Hyman, Sidney, *The American Presidency* (New York, 1954)

Jensen, Amy LaFollette, *The White House and Its Thirty-Five Families* (New York, 1970)

Kallenback, Joseph E., *The American Chief Executive* (New York, 1966)

Kane, Joseph N., *Facts About the Presidents* (New York, 3d ed. 1974)

Klapthor, Margaret B., *The First Ladies* (Washington, 1979)

Koenig, Louis W., *The Chief Executive* (New York, 1975)

Laski, Harold, *The American Presidency, An Interpretation* (New York, 1940)

Lorant, Stefan, *The Glorious Burden: The American Presidency* (New York, 1968)

McConnell, Grant, *The Modern Presidency* (New York, 2d ed. 1976)

Means, Marianne, *The Woman in the White House: The Lives, Times and Influence of Twelve Notable First Ladies* (New York, 1963)

National Portrait Gallery, *'If Elected . . .' Unsuccessful Candidates for the Presidency, 1796–1968* (Washington, 1972)

Neustadt, Richard E., *Presidential Power* (New York, 1960)

Pollard, James E., *The Presidents and the Press* (New York, 1947)

Rienow, Robert, and Leona Train, *The Lonely Quest: The Evolution of Presidential Leadership* (Chicago, 1966)

Roche, John P., and Leonard W. Levy, eds., *The Presidency* (New York, 1964)

Roseboom, Eugene H., *A History of Presidential Elections* (New York, 1964)

Rossiter, Clinton, *The American Presidency* (New York, 2d ed. 1963)

Schlesinger, Arthur M., Jr., *The Imperial Presidency* (Boston, 1973)

Tourtellot, Arthur B., *The Presidents on the Presidency* (New York, 1964)

Tugwell, Rexford G., *The Enlargement of the Presidency* (Garden City, 1960)

Tugwell, Rexford G., *How They Become President* (New York, 1964)

Warren, Sidney, *The Battle for the Presidency* (Philadelphia, 1968)

Warren, Sidney, *The President as World Leader* (Philadelphia, 1964)

Washburn, Wilcomb E., "The Great Autumnal Madness: Political Symbolism in Mid-Nineteenth-Century America," *The Quarterly Journal of Speech* XLIX (December 1963): 417–431

Wildavsky, Aaron, ed., *The Presidency* (Boston, 1969)

Index

Illustrations and caption
references appear in *italics*

Picture Credits

Special Note:

Every Four Years was photocomposed in Zapf International Light, a typeface designed by Hermann Zapf (born 1918). Having created such contemporary classics as Palatino and Optima, he is considered one of the greatest contemporary type designers.